MILTON STUDIES
XXX

MILTON STUDIES

XXX * *Edited by*

Albert C. Labriola

UNIVERSITY OF PITTSBURGH PRESS
Pittsburgh and London

MILTON STUDIES

is published annually by the University of Pittsburgh Press as a forum for Milton scholarship and criticism. Articles submitted for publication may be biographical; they may interpret some aspect of Milton's writings; or they may define literary, intellectual, or historical contexts—by studying the work of his contemporaries, the traditions which affected his thought and art, contemporary political and religious movements, his influence on other writers, or the history of critical response to his work.

Manuscripts should be upwards of 3,000 words in length and should conform to the old *MLA Style Sheet*. Manuscripts and editorial correspondence should be addressed to Albert C. Labriola, Department of English, Duquesne University, Pittsburgh, Pa., 15282–1703. Manuscripts should be accompanied by a self-addressed envelope and sufficient unattached postage.

Milton Studies does not review books.

Within the United States, *Milton Studies* may be ordered from the University of Pittsburgh Press, Pittsburgh, Pa. 15260.

Library of Congress Catalog Card Number 69–12335

ISBN 0-8229-3772-7

A CIP catalogue record for this book is available from the British Library

US ISSN 0076-8820

Published by the University of Pittsburgh Press, Pittsburgh, Pa. 15260

Manufactured in the United States of America

Printed on acid-free paper

Eurospan, London

CONTENTS

MILTON STUDIES
XXX

MILTON'S DIATRIBAL VOICE:
THE INTEGRATION AND
TRANSFORMATION OF A GENERIC
PARADIGM IN *ANIMADVERSIONS*

Maureen Thum

The failure to recognize that a work belongs to a particular literary
genre causes universal difficulties to critics; at its worst it causes us to
attack pear trees for not producing apples.
—*F. Anne Payne,* Chaucer and Menippean Satire[1]

THROUGHOUT HIS OEUVRE, Milton demonstrates a remark-
able ability to adopt and to transform a variety of generic paradigms.[2]
His polemical tract *Animadversions upon the Remonstrants Defence
against Smectymnuus* (1641),[3] written to counter Joseph Hall's *A Defence
of the Humble Remonstrance,*[4] is a case in point.

I wish to show that *Animadversions* is far more controlled and distanced than previous critical analyses have suggested. The tract is not, as
numerous critics have contended, the expression of an often spontaneous
and indecorous spilling over of anger and spite directed personally at
Joseph Hall, Milton's "adversary" in the dispute.[5] Nor, despite certain
correspondences, is it modeled primarily on contemporary polemical pam-
phleteering techniques.[6] And, while the pamphlet does appear on the
surface to present a dialogue with Joseph Hall, Milton's rhetorical stance
cannot be traced back to the far more "venerable" model provided by
Socrates in the Platonic dialogues, with his careful attention to dialectic
and his astute dismantling of received ideas.[7] Instead, *Animadversions*
represents Milton's conscious use of a popular and literary generic paradigm which has escaped the attention of previous critics: that of the
Cynic-Stoic diatribe.[8]

Recent discussions of literary genre suggest that the reader's knowledge of and assumptions about a particular generic code play an important
role in shaping reader expectations, and thus in determining the reader's
approach to a given text. As Heather Dubrow comments, "Genre . . .

3

functions much like a code of behavior established between the author and his reader."[9] Alastair Fowler advances much the same argument. Generic cues or markers have, according to Fowler, "a strategic role in guiding the reader. They help to establish . . . an appropriate mental 'set' that allows the work's generic codes to be read."[10]

As a corollary to the above statements, I wish to argue that the decoding of generic cues can be essential to an accurate critical assessment of a text. If a reader, for whatever reason, has no access to or fails to recognize a particular generic code and its concomitant signals, then reading and interpretation may be limited or even impeded. If generic markers pass unnoticed or remain unrecognized, the reading can be considerably skewed.

Animadversions provides an exemplary case. The failure to take into account the generic pattern which served as the model and point of departure for Milton's tract has resulted in incomplete or even faulty readings of the text. Critics have puzzled over various apparent anomalies, contradictions, and disjunctions which appear to suggest not only Milton's vengefulness, but his inconsistency, his lack of control, his occasional penchant to "impassioned apocalyptic outburst,"[11] and his failure to sustain a carefully controlled argument.[12] Some critics have even interpreted the apparent absence of a generic precedent in a positive light, as a sign of Milton's originality, of his refusal to be straitjacketed by an adherence to previous polemical models.[13]

A reexamination of *Animadversions* in its relationship to the diatribal paradigm suggests a very different reading of the tract. Contrary to previous critical assessments, *Animadversions* is not a spontaneous and vengeful personal attack, characterized by inconsistency and lack of control. Nor is it a work to be understood solely within the relatively restricted context of contemporary polemical pamphlets. The tract is a carefully and consciously articulated literary work operating within a long tradition of polemical discourse. This tradition, which includes Greek, Latin, biblical, and patristic precedents, may be traced from antiquity through to the Reformation and the Renaissance.

The Diatribe as Generic Paradigm

Before discussing Milton's transformation of this literary model, I wish to define the term *diatribe* as precisely as possible by focusing briefly on its generic form and function. I will not attempt to present a fixed classification, but instead, a view of a kind of countergenre in process, a countergenre which often shares shifting and overlapping boundaries with its well-known counterpart, the philosophic dialogue. I also wish to offer some explanation as to how the diatribe could operate as a generic model without official recognition by critics and theorists.[14]

In her discussion of Renaissance genre-systems, Rosalie Colie makes a telling observation about the use of generic paradigms in literary texts: "from 'real' literature as opposed to criticism and theory . . . we recover what is far more important, the unwritten poetics by which writers worked and which they themselves created."[15] The diatribal paradigm is representative for precisely this sort of "unwritten poetics." The generic pattern of the diatribe has functioned as a working (i.e., living) generic paradigm for literary works from about 300 B.C. to the English Renaissance and beyond. Nevertheless, it has, with few exceptions, been neglected almost completely in literary criticism and theory. As far as critical and theoretical literature in the English language is concerned, it has been, quite literally, a lost genre.[16]

Although the diatribe functioned as an unwritten poetics, informing numerous polemical works in Greek, Latin, and the vernacular, the term never gained official critical recognition corresponding to its actual widespread usage as a generic paradigm in polemical writing.[17] Not until the late nineteenth century was the diatribe officially recognized in critical commentary. Several German classical scholars working in the 1880s and '90s—including U. Wilamowitz, E. Weber, and P. Wendland—were among the first to describe the characteristic literary strategies and functions of the diatribe.[18] The fact that prose genres in general were neglected or disregarded in various treatises on poetics until the late eighteenth and early nineteenth centuries—that is, during the period when the diatribe flourished as a polemical model—may help to account for its late discovery by critics and theorists.[19]

In the early decades of the twentieth century, R. Bultmann and A. Oltramare examined the use of the diatribe both by the Apostle Paul and by early Christian writers. Wilhelm Capelle and Henri Irénée Marrou further consolidated and extended this knowledge in the late 1940s and '50s. Although Cappelle and Marrou mapped out wide, as yet unexplored areas of possible research, very little subsequent scholarship has followed their lead.[20] Given the relatively isolated and sporadic attempts to deal with the diatribe as a literary genre, it is scarcely surprising that this generic form has been overlooked in discussions of Milton and the tradition of Reformation and Renaissance polemical prose.

The diatribe can perhaps best be defined by contrasting it with its more familiar counterpart, the scientific and philosophic dialogue, particularly as represented by Plato. Both the diatribe and the Platonic dialogue

derive from a far earlier, long-standing tradition of oral and written dialogue.[21] A comparison with Plato's dialogues is particularly pertinent in
this context since *Animadversions*, on the surface at least, resembles a
dialogue, with its clearly marked division of the words attributed to the
Remonstrant (Hall) and to the Answerer (Milton). The resemblance is
deceptive, however, as a closer look at both the dialogue and the diatribe
will demonstrate.

Clear points of correspondence certainly exist between the dialogue
and the diatribe; indeed, as already suggested, the diatribe may be seen
as a countergenre to the dialogue. While the forms diverge, they may also
intersect and overlap from time to time. In Plato's dialogues, as in the
diatribe, for instance, a salient characteristic is the use of the fictive
interlocutor or interlocutors. But, despite the superficial resemblance,
the fictive interlocutor functions quite differently in the dialogue as opposed to the diatribe.

The various fictive voices in the Platonic dialogue frequently serve as
a means to illustrate the dialectic process which allows Socrates to unmask
faulty thinking and to find and examine unspoken assumptions. In Plato's
dialogues, the questioner may involve a fictive character in a dialogue
which reveals the naive or foolish nature of his views (*Meno*). The speaker
may unmask ironically the inadequacy of an intelligent opponent
(*Protagoras*), and prove the absurdity of a particular line of argument
(*Protagoras, Lysis*). In some cases the dialogues are a burlesque used to
lampoon frivolous or specious argumentation (*Euthydemus*).

The polyphonic form of the Platonic dialogue corresponds to its function as a tool to put into question and to dismantle fixed assumptions. In
Plato's dialogues, clearly delineated, relatively autonomous speakers are
frequently assigned distinct roles and correspondingly individual voices in
a dialectical exchange. The dynamic nature of the exchange derives at
least in part from the fact that Socrates, often the primary speaker,
teacher, philosopher, and protagonist, does not simply expound a set of
preconceived notions which he expects his various interlocutors to accept
without question.

Instead, the purpose of these fictive dialogues is, as Irwin Edman has
commented, "not to expound a 'Platonic' system, but rather to be renditions of that joint co-operative thinking of younger spirits awakened by a
great teacher to a spirit of independent personal thinking and search. The
archetype of such a teacher . . . is Socrates" who becomes, Edman continues, "a symbol of the examined philosophical life."[22] Concerning the Socratic method, Edman explains:

Throughout the dialogues, the true mark of a philosopher for Socrates is ability in dialectics. That involves, among other things, for him, a talent for tracing any idea back to a postulate which it involves or upon which it is based, for detecting . . . the common element in an apparent diversity of ideas, and for following the implied consequences of the assertion or denial of a proposition.[23]

Socrates draws his interlocutors into active participation in the argument, thus demonstrating how a dialogic exchange can become a critical tool for putting into question received notions, and for examining unspoken assumptions and premises.

The interlocutors themselves are *not* simply automatons or puppets in a pseudodialogue intended to inculcate an unassailable doctrine or system of beliefs. Instead they are allowed, for the most part, to speak in their own voices. In some cases, it is true, the interlocutor simply answers pro forma, providing little more than a foil for and impetus to Socrates' line of argument. Or the speaker, whether Socrates, or another primary speaker, addresses a fictive audience which all but disappears, except as an attentive and approving (or, in the case of the *Apology*, disapproving) backdrop. In these cases, the dialogue and the diatribe may be seen to overlap. But, for the most part, particularly in the earlier dialogues, the reader is presented with dialogic exchange and/or with autonomous interlocutors. In the *Symposium,* and in later dialogues attributed to individual speakers, a single line of argumentation may appear to be validated, only to be countered implicitly by its juxtaposition to diverging points of view, whether in the same, or in a different dialogue. By presenting a multiplicity of perspectives which are never resolved completely into an inflexible monologic discourse, Plato affirms, at least implicitly, the validity of a polyphonic approach to philosophical inquiry. At the same time, he undercuts both explicitly and implicitly any attempt to present a systematically expounded philosophic dogma.[24]

The diatribe differs often markedly from the dialogue both in its function and in its form. Scholars conjecture that the diatribe derived originally from the oral homiletic tradition of the wandering Cynic and Stoic "preachers" who used this form as an effective means to harangue and to convert groups of people at a popular level. Thus, from the beginning, the diatribe functioned as a means to persuade, to convince, and to indoctrinate. The emphasis is not, as in the dialogue, on a careful examination of propositions and assumptions; the view of the speaker is for the most part set and even inflexible.

Unlike the Platonic dialogue, the diatribe does not present a reasoned and often ironic dismantling of fixed assumptions. Nor does it juxtapose a multiplicity of diverging points of view. Despite individual differences among Cynic and Stoic philosophers, both the method and the moral/philosophical messages of the diatribe are almost stereotypical. Ideas, concepts, and assumptions are not dissected critically, but, as in the case of Musonius Rufus and Epictetus, they are frequently reduced to their simplest terms and declaimed as unassailable, revealed truths. The diatribe often presents a call, in Wilhelm Capelle's words, to "inner rebirth," to a striving toward "greater and greater perfection in a life of virtue," and to peace of mind.[25] All of these virtues are to be acquired through the renunciation of this world, and particularly through the denial of the passions that otherwise determine a human being's actions and hamper freedom of will.[26] As the characteristic message suggests, the diatribe is not an invitation to explore a set of beliefs from a variety of perspectives. Nor is it the demonstration in dialogic form of how one questions received notions. Instead, the purpose of the diatribal speaker is the conversion of the listener or the reader to a particular way of thinking, to a specific set of beliefs about the human condition, and to a corresponding "philosophic" way of life which entails an often radical rejection of this world and its deceptions.

In keeping with its homiletic function, the diatribe, unlike the polyphonically conceived Platonic dialogue, is an essentially monologic discourse, firmly controlled by the voice of the primary speaker. The essential paradox—a paradox disregarded in previous critical studies of this generic form—is that the diatribe only *appears* to contain autonomous dialogues and a multiplicity of autonomous speakers.[27] The primary speaker in the diatribe—the equivalent of Socrates in many of Plato's dialogues—may be compared to a playwright who functions simultaneously as the stage director. Not only does he compose the dialogic exchange but he also directs movements of the actors, the fictive interlocutors, whom he presents before his audience on a hypothetical stage. His control is complete, since he also assumes the actor's roles, speaking for them, ostensibly in their voices, much as does a ventriloquist, who adopts different voices in order to establish a pseudodialogue with a hand-held puppet. The well-done performance, as in the case of the ventriloquist, is rivetting at least in part because of the sheer technical virtuosity required to carry it off. At its best, it is the rhetorical device of *dialogismos*—speaking in the voice of another—extended, modified, and sustained to produce a sophisticated, interrelated series of fictive interlocutors, whose seeming objections and counterarguments are used as a means to reaffirm the validity of the speaker's univocal stance.[28]

For the most part, Plato effaces himself. He disappears behind the scenes, allowing his fictive characters to speak for themselves. He focuses as much on the dialectical and polyphonic method of approach as on the philosophical message. By contrast, the diatribal speaker appears both as writer and director, who controls and manipulates the fictive voices of his pseudoprotagonists. In his rapid shifting of stances, his quick turns from his fictive interlocutors to his "real" audience, the speaker allows no time for deliberate, careful reasoning and carefully thought-out lines of argument. There is, for the most part, no true dialogue. All the rhetorical and structural devices are designed not to promote intellectual exchange, but to silence, to overwhelm, to denigrate, or to dismiss any possible opposition to the fixed view of the speaker. The fictive interlocutors, having no voices of their own, are often simply the mouthpieces for a generally held opinion, which the primary speaker rudely, unceremoniously, and sometimes obscenely, contradicts or dismisses. Thus, the speaker makes use of intimidating and denigrating devices: invective, lists of vices, scurrility, and the like. He does not argue with his interlocutor, or present a logically reasoned case. Instead, he berates, admonishes, and castigates his fictive interlocutor.

One of the most frequently used rhetorical strategies of the diatribe is the series of rhetorical questions which follow one another with almost bewildering speed. Epictetus and Teles, for instance, may ask from five to ten questions in rapid succession. The asking of a question would appear to indicate the initiation of dialogue. In this case, however, dialogue is aborted both by the sheer number and by the nature of the questions. They function not only—indeed, not even primarily—as questions, but also as indirectly worded objections, responses, admonishments, and accusations formulated as if they were questions. That is, they are for the most part "loaded" questions, which contain implicitly their own expected response. Such concatenations of questions form a closed rhetorical chain, designed not to initiate, but to prevent any real critical inquiry.[29]

In keeping with the oral derivation of the diatribe, the sentences are short, the tone conversational. The discourse is often colloquial, with striking analogies and metaphors from everyday life. The analogies are designed not so much to elucidate, as to diminish and to dismiss the opposition, and to condemn "wrong" ways of thinking, not by argument, but by association with negative and deprecatory images. Although less so in the case of Epictetus, the discourse is at times, particularly in the Bion fragments, vulgar and may even be scurrilous and obscene.[30]

Parody, satire, irony, invective, puns, vulgar jokes, lists of vices are used to single out, to attack and to diminish the fictive opponent. Authorities are invoked—poets and philosophers, including Socrates himself—and cited frequently. They are summoned not in order to elucidate the argument, but instead to lend the weight of their authority to the fixed notions being inculcated, and thus to silence any opposition. The fictive interlocutor is seldom given more than a proforma chance to voice objections.

Not reason, but rhetorical weaponry is of prime importance in this form of indoctrination and—in extreme cases—mental warfare. The weapons include the entire arsenal of classical rhetorical devices. (Since such devices were used almost universally by those with classical training, the presence of several such devices alone is not enough to allow the form to be designated as diatribal.)

The use of the diatribal paradigm was by no means limited to the recorded contributions of a few Stoic and Cynic philosophers. Writings informed by the diatribal model may be found in patristic, and biblical sources, and with great frequency among the Reformers. The diatribal tradition of the Stoic and Cynic philosophers was integrated almost immediately into Christian polemical and apologetic writings, at least in part, scholars have suggested, because of the startling similarity of themes. (For instance, the call to conversion, and the requirement of adherents and disciples to renounce this world and its deceptions, are key aspects both of the Cynic-Stoic and of the Christian message.) Educated Christian writers, particularly after Clement of Alexandria and his contemporaries in the second century A.D., often adopted the diatribes of Musonius Rufus, Epictetus, and others almost word for word.[31] Stanley Stowers has demonstrated clearly that the letters of the Apostle Paul may be seen as exemplars of the diatribal model. Even a brief glance at the vernacular writings of the Reformers from the time of William Tyndale, indicates that the diatribe was a widespread generic paradigm for their polemical prose.[32]

As the above discussion of possible models suggests, in exploring the historical and literary context for Milton's use of the diatribe, I am not attempting to establish a single, specific source or text. What I wish to argue here is *not* the specific influence of one particular writer on Milton's *Animadversions*, whether it be the Apostle Paul, Epictetus, St. Augustine, William Tyndale, or one of the many other representative writers who used this generic model. Instead, by pointing to a multiplicity of possible sources and texts, I wish to establish the prevalence and the characteristics of a literary paradigm that Milton clearly adopted and modified, whatever the specific source, as an unwritten poetics for *Animadversions*.

THE UNWRITTEN POETICS OF *ANIMADVERSIONS*

Even a cursory reading of Milton's *Animadversions* in light of the diatribal model reveals clear points of correspondence. A more detailed look at key features of the diatribal patterns in the tract reveals that the resemblance is more than just superficial. There is, for example, a strong thematic and functional similarity. As in the diatribe, the positions are already established at least in part by earlier precedent; the question of episcopacy had been the subject of previous debates, so that the arguments and counterarguments were not new.[33] As in the diatribe, Milton argues according to revealed premises. He neither presents a logically structured refutation of the stand taken by his opponent, nor does he demonstrate the logical consistency of his own stance, as one would expect in a philosophic dialogue. Unlike Socrates in his dialectical engagement of an opponent, Milton does not—nor does he propose to—argue according to logically conceived propositions which are themselves explored critically and dismantled.

But the absence of a dialectical approach does not mean that this tract is a "joke"—even if a serious one—or an exercise in self-cancellation as Stanley Fish has concluded in his evaluation of a similar disregard for logical argumentation in *The Reason of Church Government*.[34] Milton's purpose in *Animadversions* is not that of the dialectician, but that of the proponent of a system of beliefs. His intent is to convince, to convert, and, if necessary, to overwhelm his audience with a marvelous rhetorical display that will capture the attention, dazzle with its brilliance, and lend his "argument" an almost visionary intensity. By the same token, he does not wish to refute his opponent in a dialectical sense. Instead, he wishes to unmask Hall's stance as worldly, hypocritical, and absurd—also a recurring theme of the diatribe—and thus to put into question the validity of a status quo for which Hall was the spokesman.

The rhetorical strategies of *Animadversions,* like those of the diatribe, are consistently shaped by the monologic nature of a discourse controlled firmly by the voice and the—in Milton's case, dissenting and nonconformist—message of a single speaker. As in the diatribe, Milton uses an array of rhetorical devices not as a means to communicate, or to initiate a dialectical exchange, but instead as weapons to assault and to discredit his opponent's position. Lists of vices, invective, satire, irony, parody, hyperbole, grotesque metaphors, puns, and numerous other forms of rhetorical weaponry are used individually or—in Milton's transformation of this paradigm—conjointly in a series of brilliant strategic maneuvers. Taken together, they have a strong cumulative effect which is close to the rhetorical equivalent of sensory overload.

Such a conflation of multiple rhetorical devices is exemplified in Milton's acerbic characterization of the Church of England's clergy. Within the Church hierarchy, so Milton suggests, ordinary, upright, and intelligent men are not considered to be capable of interpreting or preaching the word of God. Instead, the only men considered capable are those trained by the established Church, who "spend their youth in loitering, bezzling and harlotting, their studies in unprofitable questions, and barbarous sophistry, their middle age in ambition, and idleness, their old age in avarice, dotage and diseases" (*Animadversions*, p. 677). Using the well-known analogy of the three ages of man as his point of departure, Milton targets an entire array of vices and abuses which he perceives as rampant among the clergy in the established Church. He combines a series of strategies: caricature, analogy, parallel structure, sarcasm, invective, the reversal of expectations as the decorous are treated indecorously. The resulting sharply delineated caricature of the clergy is then contrasted ironically with an equally cryptic characterization of the "sober, considerable men" (dissenters like Milton), who despite their probity are deemed incapable of preaching and disseminating the word of God because they are not members of the established clergy. Milton frequently uses such kaleidoscopic displays of rhetorical weaponry in *Animadversions* as part of an entire strategy of disclosing his opponent's position as inherently reprehensible, since it supports a corrupt establishment.

Milton also transforms and further intensifies the characteristically earthy and memorable comparison so frequently employed in the diatribe as a polemical tool. Whereas the earthy metaphor of Epictetus, with its reference to body parts and bodily functions, intentionally offends against the expected decorum of philosophic discourse, and thus jars the listener or reader into a state of attention, Milton's metaphors approach the grotesque and the surreal. His metaphorical characterization of the Church of England liturgy, for instance, presents an incongruous picture that allows him to attack his opponents simultaneously on several different fronts: "And indeed our *Liturgie* hath run up and downe the world like an English galloping Nun, proferring her selfe, but wee heare of none yet that bids money for her" (*Animadversions*, p. 680). The intentional juxtaposition of incongruous terms denies the dignity of the official liturgy of the Church of England by associating it on the one hand with the traditional Catholic (i.e., "evil") symbol of virginity and purity—the nun—and on the other with prostitution and even bestiality. The conflation of such images as that of the nun and the galloping horse produces a creature part beast, part human being, further underlining the absence of true dignity Milton discerns in the traditional liturgy. Such metaphors function as satirical means to diminish and redefine the argument of his opponent— the collectivity represented by Hall and the Church of England—in negative terms, producing, in effect, a vividly rendered caricature.[35]

In addition to the above, relatively brief metaphorical forms of castigation and redefinition, Milton frequently uses extended, grotesque analogies which serve to redefine the opponent's position and to suggest its intellectual and moral bankruptcy. He portrays, for instance, the gargantuan image of the "*Colossus,*" Antiquity, "that like a carved Gyant terribly menacing to children, and weaklings lifts up his club, but strikes not, and is subject to the muting of every Sparrow" (*Animadversions,* p. 699). The initial fantasy, drawn from English and Celtic folklore, is widened as the poet presents image after image from widely diverse sources (everyday life, popular lore, the Bible, the ancients, the history of the early Church), all of which suggest idolatry, hubris, and senseless vaunting of power. These images appear in cacophonous juxtaposition as a means to expose, to reduce, and to ridicule his target, which is not Antiquity itself, but Antiquity as it is used by Milton's opponent, Hall. We have, in effect, a many-facetted, caricature of custom and usage, a grotesque portrayal in images of the argument Hall has advanced to buttress his position in favor of a liturgy hallowed by tradition:

If you let him rest upon his *Basis,* hee may perhaps delight the eyes of some with his huge and mountainous Bulk, and the quaint workmanship of his massie limbs; but if yee goe about to take him in pieces, yee marre him; and if you think like *Pigmees* to turne and wind him whole as hee is, besides your vain toile and sweat, he may chance to fall upon your owne heads. Goe therefore, and use all your Art, apply your sledges, your levers, and your iron crows to heave and hale your mighty *Polyphem* of Antiquity to the delusion of Novices and unexperienc't Christians. (*Animadversions,* pp. 699–700)

With the weapons of scripture and truth, Milton continues, he and his fellow dissenters

shall not doubt to batter, and throw down your *Nebuchadnezzars* Image and crumble it like the chaffe of the Summer threshing floores, as well the gold of those Apostolick Successors . . . together with the iron, the brasse, and the clay of those muddy and strawy ages that follow. (*Animadversions,* pp. 700–01)

This analogical means to define the argument—here portrayed as the activity of a despised collectivity—moves far beyond the expected scope of the usual diatribal metaphor in both extension and function. Milton achieves an almost surrealistic and expressionistic effect in such highly elaborated analogies. We do not find the expected "dignified" and "decorous" Milton in these conscious grotesqueries; but we do find a Milton who is certainly no less powerful, expressive, and impassioned in his images of the grotesque, and even the absurd. If, as Rosalie Colie suggests, the "breaking of decorum . . . has to do with social as well as aesthetic premises," then Milton's intentional breach of the decorous and the dignified may be seen as both an aesthetic and an ideological expression of his dissent.[36] He is attempting to reveal the actual indecorousness of a stance which parades itself, with hypocritical insistence, as decorum, order, and tradition.[37]

In addition to his use and combination of various rhetorical devices, Milton cites, in typical diatribal fashion, various authorities—classical, biblical, and vernacular—throughout the pamphlet in order to provide further intensification of the overwhelming flood of images, analogies, and other rhetorical devices intended to drown out the voice of his opposition. Included is an extended quotation from the May Eclogue of Spenser's *Shepheard's Calendar* (*Animadversions*, p. 723). There is even an appeal to divine authority in a prayer which is clearly directed as much against his opponents as it is toward his ostensible audience, God.

As in the diatribe, Milton adopts here a far more conversational style than in any of his other polemical tracts. The sentence structure itself frequently evinces the nervous intensity of the diatribe: the questions and answers are often very brief, particularly if one compares them to Milton's famous and lengthy Ciceronian periods which make extensive use of subordination and careful hypotactic ordering of thought within a single sentence edifice. In *Animadversions*, Milton does not, however, remain solely in conversational mode. Instead, he uses the longer, more discursive, carefully structured sentences as a foil for the colloquial, and for the brief conversational flash. His conversational mode is characterized by pithy comments in the form of sentence fragments, and punctuated by frequent rhetorical questions, apostrophes, and exclamations. "Ha, ha, ha" is his response to one of Hall's contentions (*Animadversions*, p. 726).

Like the grotesque metaphors and analogies, as well as the other rhetorical devices already discussed, these syntactical strategies serve to redefine members of his opposition in ironic and unflattering terms. Milton uses a series of denigrating apostrophes followed by a rhetorical question, for example, to unmask the spirituality of the established clergy as a pretense, and to reveal the real motivating factors in their lives to be purely materialistic concerns: love of dainty foods and pretentious houses:

O stale-growne piety! O Gospell rated as cheap as thy Master, at thirty pence, and not worth the study, unlesse thou canst buy those that will sell thee! O race of Capernaitans, senslesse of divine doctrine, and capable onely of loaves and belly-cheere! . . . I would faine aske these men at whose hands they seeke inferior things, as wealth, honour, their dainty fare, their lofty houses? (*Animadversions*, p. 719)

The final question is typical of the diatribe, in that it appears on the surface to suggest the interrogative mode, and thus to be a means to initiate dialogue. But the seeming question is actually an accusation in disguise, a means to prevent dialogue.

As I have indicated throughout my discussion, all of the above rhetorical strategies operate within, or function complementarily to one of the key strategies of the diatribal paradigm: the ventriloqual verbal exchange, or pseudodialogue. Despite its often intense surface dialogization, the diatribe is both rhetorically and thematically a form of monologic discourse. The pseudodialogization operates conjointly with the rhetorical devices already discussed as a means to overwhelm the opposition, and to prevent the kind of intentionally unresolved jostling and juxtaposition of very different points of view so strongly characteristic of the early Platonic/Socratic dialogues, and of menippean satire in general. The diatribe gives no sense of an intellectual and philosophical relativism which not only permits, but also points up, the validity of often highly divergent points of view. Instead, it adopts a nonrelative polemical stance. The answers it offers are final, and are not subject to the scrutiny or dismantling one would expect in the dialectic of Socrates.

As with other elements of the diatribal pattern, Milton uses the pseudodialogue with full knowledge and control of its paradoxical and even contradictory nature. Indeed, in *Animadversions,* the conflict between seemingly dialogic and essentially monologic strategies is intensified to an unusual degree even for the diatribe. Thus, Milton adopts what *appears* to be the form of an actual dialogue, even going so far as to assign separate roles to each of the ostensible partners in the exchange. But the apparent dialogic form of *Animadversions* is deceptive. Despite the fact that there are ostensibly two different speakers—Milton and Hall, the Answerer and the Remonstrant, both of whom are actual personages in the debate—and despite the fact that Milton does not misquote Hall's actual words, no real exchange takes place.[38] Instead, in diatribal style, the opponent is redefined and thus fictionalized. He is, as in the diatribe, not the real individual Hall. He is rather an imaginary interlocutor, whose individuality is subsumed in his role as representative for the officially promulgated status quo.

In his fictionalized form, Hall appears not only as the single voice which he assumes in his own tract, but through a careful series of associations, Milton alters the persona presented in Hall's *Defence,* transforming Hall's projection of himself as a lone individual into the representative for a wide variety of opponents. Milton insistently, and from the beginning, multiplies his single opponent into countless adversaries across a wide spectrum of opinion. In the preface to *Animadversions*, Milton redefines Hall both as an individual writer of a tract, and as the self-proclaimed representative of an institutional and ideological collectivity: Hall is not merely one man expressing an individual point of view; he is an "enimie to truth and his Countries peace" who represents an entire body of opinion, since he "stands up for all the rest to justifie a long usurpation and convicted Pseudepiscopy of Prelates" (*Animadversions*, p. 662). Hall, as Milton recognizes, is no mean opponent. He is a skilled rhetorician who understands well how to sway his audience to sympathy and to discredit his opponents through rhetorical means. Thus, in his defence of a "traditionall corruption," Hall "uses no common Arts, but . . . a wily Stratagem" (*Animadversions*, p. 663). But, as Milton objects, the resulting rhetorical stance is a "grand imposture" (p. 663), and Hall as spokesman for the status quo is a "false Prophet," a "cheat of soules," and the very embodiment of "Sophistry" (p. 664). Again and again in the first few pages of the pamphlet, Milton insists on Hall's identification with a wider collectivity as he speaks scornfully of "your whole faction" (p. 666), of "you, and the Prelaticall troop" (p. 667). Throughout the tract, he uses many other similar collective forms of address as a repeated reminder of Hall's identification with a despised establishment.

By so doing, Milton is pointing up a contradiction—or as Milton sees it, a sleight of hand—in Hall's own tract. Hall assumes the role of injured innocence in his dedication of *A Defence*. He presents himself as a man "modestly asserting the true right of Liturgie and Episcopacie" who has been slandered and attacked. He evinces seeming surprise and grief that "so meek and gall-lesse a Discourse could have irritated any the least opposition" (*Defence*, p. i), and he claims to be baffled at the unexpected "scandalous Libels" (p. i) which have been "insolently managed by many unknowne hands" (p. ii).[39] By alleging the attack to be directed solely and gratuitously at himself as an individual, Hall attempts to dismiss his opponent's actual motives, religious dissent, and to redefine their actions as deriving from a very different source: from petty, absurd, and groundless injuriousness. His self-projection as a lone, suffering, insulted individual set upon by an uncouth rabble is clearly contradicted in his dedicatory remarks to his tract, where he presents himself not as a mere individual, but instead as a representative of king and status quo. Hall's dedication— "To the King's most Sacred Majestie" and "Most dread Soveraigne" (*Defence*, p. i) by his "Majesties zealously-loyall Subject" (p. iii)—is telling. As his words indicate, despite his assumed modesty, Hall feels the weight of established order, indeed, of monarchy itself, behind his words:

As one therefore that hates to betray the truth by an unfaithfull silence, I doe cheerfully enter these lists; rejoycing to hope that your Majesties Eye may be the Judge and Witness of my successe. Neither shall it be displeasing to Your Majestie, that your most honourable Peeres, and most faithfull Commons, now assembled, shall see the injustice, and ungroundednesse of that bold Appeale, which was made to them, by my daring Answerers. (*Defence*, pp. ii–iii)

Thus, while protesting that he is the "humble remonstrant," viciously attacked for personal reasons, Hall simultaneously assumes the role of public spokesman for the king. This is the underlying contradiction, and the concomitant rhetorically established fiction which Milton is at pains to expose throughout *Animadversions*.

The dispute is more than a question of individual personalities, or even of individual personae as Milton makes very clear.[40] What concerns Milton are the principles Hall is defending as spokesman for a collectivity. This is much the same collectivity that appears in various guises throughout Milton's polemical pamphlets of this period. D. M. Rosenberg has commented succinctly on Milton's social and political stance in the polemical tracts on political liberty in which Milton "vigorously opposed royal absolutism, and expressed contempt for the institutions of the ruling elite, their titles, privilege of birthright, and landed property."[41] By aligning himself emphatically with the king and with a religious institution which supported the king and a ruling elite, Hall became for Milton the representative of an entire establishment. It was an establishment that Milton abhorred, since it embodied social, political, and religious convictions in diametrical opposition to many of the nonconformist views Milton held and passionately defended.

Throughout *Animadversions*, Milton explores and widens the dialogic possibilities of the diatribe. Responding to his collectively perceived opponent, Milton himself speaks collectively, adopting the voice of an entire community of the like-minded, transforming the personal duel into a wider argument concerning political, social, and religious principles. In an ideological battle against an entrenched establishment, he assumes the role of representative for the "underdogs"—the countercollectivity not only of the Smectymnuans but of all those who, like them, harbored similar nonconformist religious and political convictions.

As a "collectivity," rather than as an autonomous and clearly defined persona, Milton adopts a number of distinct voices: he speaks as the intentionally injurious polemicist, as the parodist and satirist, as the just and pious man, and as the prophet praying to God for the eradication of those who are identified not simply as Milton's foes, but as the enemies of God himself.

Milton not only assumes a multiplicity of roles as primary speaker. He also speaks in the voices of various fictive interlocutors in an extended form of *dialogismos*—speaking in the voice of another—which is characteristic of the diatribal paradigm. As the primary speaker, he stages the debate for the reader, adopting both the voices of those with whom he aligns himself, and the voices of various adversaries. This is true not only of his carefully orchestrated exchange with a rhetorically redefined Hall, but also of fictive exchanges with various explicitly and implicitly portrayed interlocutors. In typical diatribal fashion, he moves, often with startling rapidity from one voice to another in an interplay punctuated by sudden turns as he addresses the implied reader, and comments on the staged debate.

I will cite a short exchange between Remonstrant and Answerer to give a brief glimpse of the sophisticated elaboration of *dialogismos* which characterizes *Animadversions*. In the following passage, as is characteristic of the diatribe, dialogization operates in conjunction with a number of other typically diatribal devices. Thus, we have exemplified the rapid movement of dialogue, the plays on words, the hyperbole used to discredit the opponent's stance, the use of questions which block rather than initiate dialogue, the adoption of different voices, and the quick shift from one fictive—or in the case of Hall, redefined or "fictionalized"—speaker and/or audience to the other.

In the passage, Hall, the Remonstrant, has been allowed to voice an objection. Milton begins his answer using *we*, thus identifying himself with those whose point of view he defends in opposition to the collectively used *you*, which refers to his opponents: "Wee know where the shoo [*sic*] wrings you, you fret, and are gall'd at the quick" (*Animadversions*, p. 668). After castigating his opponents in the voice of a dissenter, he then switches, a few sentences later, abruptly to the stance of one standing outside the fray. He no longer uses *we*, but instead refers to those whose cause he is defending as *they*, using the third plural, as if he were no longer among them:

Who could be angry therefore but those that are guilty, with these free-spoken, and plaine harted men that are the eyes of their Country, and the prospective glasses of their Prince? (*Animadversions*, p. 670)

In the stance of an objective outsider, he here defends the "plaine harted men" (among them himself!) whose purpose is to present an unvarnished version of reality both to their fellow citizens and to the ruling elite. The shift in stance of the primary speaker has also brought about a shift in implied reader or listener. Previously, he had addressed his opponent as his primary audience. But the above rhetorical question indicates that

Milton's implied audience has changed abruptly, since the question is directed at least in part toward a potentially sympathetic audience, also watching from outside the fray as the staged debate between the dissenters and the defenders of the status quo continues.

In the next sentence, the speaker has again abruptly shifted his viewpoint. He now speaks ironically in the voice of his opposition, presenting accusations directed against the "plaine harted men" of the previous sentence: "But these are the nettlers, these are the blabbing Bookes that tell, though not halfe your fellows feats" (*Animadversions*, p. 670). Although the words "these are the nettlers," and "these are the blabbing Bookes" are clearly the words of Milton's opponents, hurling accusations at the dissenters, we have an abrupt and ironic shift in speakers occurring midsentence. With the word *your* the reader is brought to a sudden halt. "Your feats" refers to the deeds of Milton's opponents, which have been exposed by these very "blabbing Bookes." The Answerer has reversed his point of view, and is again speaking as a representative for those maligned, demonstrating that the initial words were meant as a parody of his foes' voices. With its ironic double view, this sentence has the almost uncanny effect of a photographic double exposure.

As Answerer, Milton now allows Hall, the Remonstrant, once more to voice a proforma objection, quoted directly from Hall's own pamphlet. The objection is followed by the speaker's response, ridiculing the remonstrant's rhetoric with a grotesque metaphor:

Remon. I beseech you brethren spend your Logick upon your own workes.
Ans. The peremptory Analysis that you call it, I beleeve will be so hardy as once more to unpinne your spruce fastidious oratory, to rumple her laces, her frizzles, and her bobins though she wince, and fling, never so Peevishly. (*Animadversions*, pp. 670–01)

The metaphor portrays the Answerer in the act of dismantling Hall's pretentious rhetoric, an act which is likened to the unpinning of elaborate apparel of an aristocratic woman. Significantly, it is portrayed as a violent, physical assault on decorum and image. In this metaphor, despite the apparently personal reference to Hall's prose, the connection is maintained between Hall and the collectivity he represents; that is, between Hall's apparently individual style of rhetoric and the vain and pretentious trappings—the rhetorical finery—of a ruling elite.

Immediately following this metaphorical threat *cum* definition, the Answerer allows the Remonstrant a further objection, only to ridicule the objection, by demonstrating that Hall's mixed metaphor is faulty, since it suggests an occurrence contrary to physical laws:

Remon. Those verbal exceptions are but light froth, and will sink alone.
Ans. O rare suttlety, beyond all that *Cardan* ever dream't of, when I beseech you, will light things sink? when will light froth sink alone. Here in your phrase, the same day that heavy plummets will swimme alone. (*Animadversions*, p. 671)

The Answerer now turns in sudden apostrophe to the implied reader, an apostrophe which serves doubly as a call to the reader to judge the case, and as an indirect indictment of the Answerer's opponent:

Trust this man, Readers if you please, whose divinity would reconcile *England* with *Rome*, and his philosophy make friends nature with the *Chaos, sine pondere habentia pondus*. (P. 671)

The Latin quotation, drawn from Ovid's *Metamorphosis*, is an intentional parody of Hall's parading of scholarly erudition as a means to discredit and to insult the intelligence of his "untaught" opposition.[42]

The Answerer's turning from one implied audience to another is characteristic of the diatribe. Frequently the shifts are rapid and intentionally unsettling, so that the reader is momentarily uncertain who is being addressed, and is thus constantly drawn into the argument, required to distinguish among parties, and to take sides in a kind of staged debate in which the reader is both audience and participant.

If one reads *Animadversions* in light of the diatribal paradigm, Milton's rhetorical distancing becomes clear: this tract does not represent a mere personal attack; it is not an overflowing of uncontrolled emotions and vituperation, nor is it simply an expression of personal rancour, or a petty quibbling motivated by Hall's insults to Milton's prose. This altercation, staged in diatribal form, goes beyond personal assault. Milton attacks not Hall the individual, but instead Hall, the representative of the established church. As Christopher Hill has pointed out, Milton was in many ways a radical and a revolutionary whose convictions were expressed in passionate terms to counter an entrenched orthodoxy:

When the orthodox in the seventeenth century heard the ideas of the radical underground they called for the whip and the branding iron. When Milton heard them he said they reminded him of the early Christians, and that the way to truth was through fearless discussion.[43]

Animadversions implicitly represents the impassioned defence of fearless discussion by a man willing to face possible imprisonment and even death for the sake of the principles that he upholds. Christopher Hill's unabashedly polemical evaluation is surely accurate in describing the spirit with which Milton wrote his polemical tracts:

It was only the strength of the radical movement and its vigorous defence by brave men like Milton, which gave the ideas a dozen or so years of uniquely free discussion before orthodoxy got the lid back on again.[44]

Seen in this light, *Animadversions* is not merely a personal diatribe in the popular sense of the word—i.e., a vituperative attack on a kind and well-meaning individual, Joseph Hall. Nor is it simply a duel between two different personae, assumed by the two combatants as masks to disguise little more than a personal squabble. Instead, it represents a vigorous attempt to express nonconformist Protestant ideas through Milton's trans-formation of the diatribal model. In Milton's hands this literary paradigm certainly demonstrates—to use Milton's own words in reference to the power of "grim laughter"—"a strong sinewy force in teaching and confut-ing" (*Animadversions*, pp. 663–04).

University of Michigan-Flint

NOTES

1. F. Anne Payne, *Chaucer and Menippean Satire* (Madison, 1981), p. 3.

2. See Barbara Kiefer Lewalski, *Paradise Lost and the Rhetoric of Literary Forms* (Princeton, 1985), for an encyclopaedic description and analysis of Milton's transformation of "a panoply of literary forms, with their accumulated freight of shared cultural significance" (p. 3) in *Paradise Lost*. See also Donald M. Rosenberg's astute analysis of Milton's political and social transmutation of a generic pattern—the country estate poem—in "Milton's *Paradise Lost* and the Country Estate Poem," *Clio* XVIII: ii (1989), pp. 123–34. I wish to express my gratitude to Professor Rosenberg, whose comments on the early drafts of this essay were of great help in shaping my present discussion.

3. John Milton, *Animadversions upon the Remonstrants Defence Against Smectym-nuus*, in *Complete Prose Works of John Milton*, 8 vols., ed. Don M. Wolfe et al. (New Haven, 1953–82), vol. I, pp. 670–735. Hereafter cited in the text as *Animadversions*.

4. Joseph Hall, *A Defence of the Humble Remonstrance Against the Frivolous and False Exceptions of Smectymnuus* (n.p., 1641). Hereafter cited in the text as *Defence*.

5. Previous critics have, for the most part, either disregarded *Animadversions*, or have assessed the work in essentially negative terms, objecting to what appears to be the author's lack of aesthetic distance, and to his violation of a sense of decorum in his approach both to Hall and to the subject of religious reform itself. One of the clearest statements of critical reservations is expressed by Rudolph Kirk, ed., "Preface and Notes," *Animadver-sions*, in *Complete Prose Works of John Milton*. 8 vols., ed. Don M. Wolfe et al. (New Haven, 1953–82), Vol. I. According to Kirk, Milton's argument is "unfair and inconsistent," his prose "difficult and obscure," (p. 654), his thought and method "scurrilous." He concludes: "though posterity is indebted to Milton for his self-defense, we can scarcely condone the language he initiated against a good man" (p. 655). Even critics who attempt to counter negative and dismissive assessment of the pamphlet continue to be troubled by the question of Milton's

rhetorical and emotional distance in the controversy. See, for example, Thomas Kranidas, "Style and Rectitude in Seventeenth-Century Prose: Hall, Smectymnuus, and Milton," *Huntington Library Quarterly* XLVI (1983), who speaks of Milton's stance at certain points in the tract as "admittedly embarrassing" (p. 264).

6. The few critics who have attempted with some consistency to counter prevailing negative assessments of *Animadversions* as a flawed, incoherent, and even reprehensible work, have used a number of strategies to account for and to defend Milton's rhetorical stance. In his astute analysis of Milton's and Hall's polemical personae, Kranidas ("Style and Rectitude") has attempted to "demythologize" Hall himself. He has demonstrated that the image of Hall as a completely innocent target of a vituperative attack is at least in part a rhetorical fiction which Hall establishes as a means to discredit his adversaries in the debate (pp. 237–42). Michael Lieb, Raymond Anselment, and Peter Auksi have focused particularly on the historical context of the debate and have made reference to contemporary literary and popular precedents or models within the equally—if not more—vituperative Protestant and Puritan polemical tradition, particularly as represented by the Marprelate tracts. Raymond Anselment, *"Betwixt Jest and Earnest": Marprelate, Milton, Marvell, Swift and the Decorum of Religious Ridicule* (Toronto, 1979), cites the justification offered both by the Marprelate polemicist (p. 33) and by Milton (p. 66) for the use of rough humor and satire as a means to seek the truth, pointing to Milton's own defence of "grim laughter" (*Animadversions*, pp. 663–4). See also Michael Lieb, "Milton's *Of Reformation* and the Dynamics of Controversy," in *Achievements of the Left Hand: Essays on the Prose of John Milton*, ed. Michael Lieb and John T. Shawcross (Amherst, 1974), pp. 73–4; and Peter Auksi, "Milton's 'Sanctifi'd Bitterness': Polemical Technique in the early Prose," *Texas Studies in Literature and Language* XIX (1977), p. 366.

7. Numerous critics have used the dialectic patterns of the philosophic (i.e. Platonic/Socratic) dialogue not as *explicit* but as *implicit* models against which all of Milton's anti-prelatical tracts including *Animadversions*, are measured and found wanting. See William B. Haller, *Liberty and Reformation in the Puritan Revolution* (New York, 1955), p. 57; and Kirk, "Preface and Notes," p. 655. Although neither critic explicitly compares the tract to the philosophic dialogue, both find fault with *Animadversions* on the grounds that Milton fails to sustain the kind of expected dialectical consistency which is one of the characteristics of the Platonic/Socratic dialogue. This line of argument is skillfully and ingeniously articulated by Stanley Fish, *Self-Consuming Artifacts: The Experience of Seventeenth-Century Literature* (Berkeley and Los Angeles, 1972), in his discussion of *The Reason of Church Government*. Because Fish uses dialectical consistency as a criterion, he concludes that *Of Reformation* is a "joke," and an—albeit sophisticated—exercise in self-cancellation (pp. 266–71).

8. I am indebted to Peter Auksi, University of Western Ontario, whose comments about Rudolph Bultmann's discussion of the diatribe led to my research into the German scholarship on this much neglected generic form.

9. Heather Dubrow, *Genre* (New York, 1982), vol. XLII, p. 2.

10. Alastair Fowler, *Kinds of Literature* (Cambridge, 1982), p. 88.

11. Joan Webber, *The Eloquent "I": Style and Self in Seventeenth-Century Prose* (Madison, 1968), p. 191.

12. See Haller, *Liberty and Reformation*, p. 57; Anselment, *"Betwixt Jest and Earnest,"* p. 73; Fish, *Self-Consuming Artifacts*, pp. 266–71.

13. See Lieb, "Milton's *Of Reformation*," and Anselment, *"Betwixt Jest and Earnest."* Lieb regards *Of Reformation*—and by implication *Animadversions*—as "too flexible, even unpredictable" to be part of "some predetermined polemical framework" (p. 64). According

to Anselment, *Animadversions* is a powerful tract which "departs from traditional polemic" (p. 74).

14. In the following discussion, I depart from almost all previous critical approaches to the diatribe in two key areas. First, I focus on the close interrelationship between its outer and inner form; that is, I demonstrate that the external, surface rhetorical features are used consistently as a means to express the inner form and function of the diatribe as a monologic and polemical discourse. With the exception of a few, brief comments by Capelle and several proforma statements by Stowers, previous critics have attempted to define the diatribe merely by enumerating its surface rhetorical features (i.e., by presenting little more than long lists of rhetorical devices) without taking into account its inner form and function.

Secondly, unlike previous critics, I do not see the diatribal paradigm as fixed or set. Instead, I treat the diatribal model as a flexible code, which is capable of alteration and transformation. Within each individual work, such a code functions not as a set scheme for respectful or servile imitation but instead as the diachronically fluid point of departure for a poetics in process. With few exceptions, previous critics of the diatribe have disregarded the potential flexibility of the generic model, and have attempted to see the diatribe as a fixed and unchanging rhetorical scheme or formula. See Stanley Kent Stowers, *The Diatribe and Paul's Letter to the Romans*, Society of Biblical Literature Dissertation Series, No. 57, ed. William Baird (Chico, Calif., 1981). Stowers's otherwise excellent summary and evaluation of critical approaches to the diatribe (pp. 1–78) is hampered by his implicit view of genre as an entirely synchronic—and therefore static—network of interrelated rhetorical patterns which writers reiterate unchanged, right down to the smallest rhetorical and syntactical detail. For an excellent discussion regarding the fluidity of generic codes, see Claudio Guillén, "On the Uses of Literary Genre," in *Literature as System: Essays Toward the Theory of Literary History* (Princeton, 1971), particularly p. 111.

15. Rosalie Colie, *The Resources of Kind: Genre-Theory in the Renaissance*, (Berkeley and Los Angeles, 1973), p. 4. See also Renato Poggioli, "Poetics and Metrics," *The Spirit of the Letter: Essays in European Literature* (Cambridge, Mass., 1965), who argues that such an "unwritten poetics" frequently exists, or has existed in the past, side by side with the written or official poetics of a particular age, a state of affairs that, in Poggioli's words, "has escaped the conscious attention of most literary scholars" (p. 345).

16. Most dictionaries in the English language give a definition only for the popular, nonliterary use of the term *diatribe* as a designation for abusive criticism. Even the *Oxford English Dictionary* provides only a perfunctory reference consisting of five words: "a discourse, disquisition, critical dissertation." The definition is clearly so broad as to be almost meaningless in a specifically generic context. Literary handbooks in the English language give the term *diatribe* at best short shrift, either omitting the term altogether, or presenting little more than the equivalent of the rather vague definition offered by the *OED*.

17. As an unofficial poetics, the diatribal model may be traced back to the third century B.C., where it reportedly first appeared in written form in the works—preserved only in fragments—of the Greek philosophers Bion of Borysthenes, and Teles. Epictetus, who lived during the first century A.D., is perhaps the most striking of the known representatives of the diatribe. His orally presented diatribes, transcribed stenographically by his student, Arrian, provide one of the first relatively complete, extant literary manifestations of the diatribal model. See Capelle, *Epiktet*, p. 25; Stowers, *Diatribe*, pp. 53–6; W. A. Oldfather, trans., *Epictetus: The Discourses as Reported by Arrian, the Manual, and Fragments* (Cambridge, Mass., 1946), pp. vii–xxx.

18. See U. Wilamowitz-Moellendorff, "*Der kynische Prediger Teles*," Excursus 3,

Antigonos von Karystos, Philologische Untersuchungen IV (1881), pp. 239–319; Ernst Weber, *"De Dione Christostomo Cynicorum sectatore,"* *Leipziger Studien* IX (1887), pp. 77–268; Paul Wendland and Otto Kern, *"Philo und die kynisch-stoische Diatribe,"* *Beiträge zur Geschichte der griechischen Philosophie und Religion: Festschrift Hermann Diels,* ed. Paul Wendland and Otto Kern (Berlin, 1895).

19. Until the eighteenth century, the discussion of prose genres was relegated to the rhetorical handbooks. As Renato Poggioli has commented in "Poetics and Metrics,"

> From Aristotle to Horace, from Vida to Scaliger, from Boileau to Pope, all *artes poeticae* . . . concern themselves only and always with versified structures. Their authors fail to discuss any nonpoetic genre: so, for instance, Boileau and Pope refuse to treat or even mention the romance and the novel, since the latter cannot qualify as legitimate, "regular," or "classical" forms for being written in prose. (P. 346)

As a popular prose model, the diatribe would, according to traditional views, be considered at best a nonliterary "subgenre." The subsequent loosening up of critical categories and the questioning of generic norms, first articulated by such critics as Johann Gottfried Herder and Friedrich Schlegel in the late eighteenth century, made it possible for such forms as the diatribe to be recognized as legitimate genres.

20. Rudolf Bultmann, *Der Stil der paulinischen Predigt und die kynischstoische Diatribe* (Göttingen, 1910); André Oltramare, *Les origines de la diatribe romaine* (Lausanne, 1926); Wilhelm Capelle and Henri Irénée Marrou, "Diatribe," *Reallexikon für Antike und Christentum,* ed. Theodor Klauser, 7 vols. (Stuttgart, 1957), vol. III.

21. See A. Hermann, "Dialogue," *Reallexikon für Antike und Christentum,* ed. Theodor Klauser, 7 vols. (Stuttgart, 1957), vol. III, pp. 930–38; Capelle, *Epiktet,* p. 211.

22. Irwin Edman, ed., "Introduction," *The Works of Plato* (New York, 1956), p. xii.

23. Ibid, pp. xix–xx.

24. See Mikhail M. Bakhtin, *Problems of Dostoevsky's Poetics,* ed. and trans. Caryl Emerson (Minneapolis, 1984): "At the base of the genre lies the Socratic notion of the dialogic nature of truth and the dialogic nature of human thinking about the truth. The dialogic means of seeking the truth is counterposed to *official* monologism, which pretends to *possess a ready-made truth"* (p. 110). A thorough exploration of the complex and often ambiguous interplay between the dialogic and the monologic aspects of Plato's entire philosophical oeuvre (particularly as represented by his later dialogues) would go far beyond the scope of the present essay.

25. Wilhelm Capelle, *Epiktet,* p. 213. The translation of Capelle's text is my own.

26. Ibid, p. 212.

27. None of the previous studies of the diatribe, except for that of Mikhail M. Bakhtin, *Problems of Dostoevsky's Poetics,* have attempted to deal with this aspect of the diatribal model. Even Bakhtin's very brief comments are ambiguous and contradictory. Bakhtin has interpreted the intense pseudodialogization erroneously as evidence of a polyphonic approach such as one finds in the menippean satire (p. 120). Nevertheless, by recognizing the simplification of ideas (p. 115), and by designating the diatribe as a precursor of the "ancient Christian sermon" (p. 120), Bakhtin implicitly acknowledges its primarily monologic nature.

28. See Epictetus, *The Works of Epictetus consisting of his Discourses in four Books, the Enchiridion, and Fragments,* 2 vols., trans. Thomas Wentworth Higginson (Boston, 1890). Epictetus adopts fictive voices (Zeus, book I: 1; a recalcitrant student, book III: 26; Socrates, book II: 12, and even a bird, book IV: 1), and stages hypothetical debates throughout the diatribes. See also the adoption of multiple fictive voices in the polemical prose of the Reformers, such as William Tyndale, with whose work Milton was familiar.

29. The use of multiple questions is so frequent in Epictetus that even a brief perusal of almost any of the diatribes will provide one or more examples of this device. See also the fragments of Teles in Léonce Paquet, *Les Cyniques grecs: fragments et témoinages* (Ottawa, 1975), pp. 139–64. See also the letters of Paul, and the polemical prose of the Reformers.

30. Capelle, *Epiktet*, pp. 214–5.

31. Capelle and Marrou, "Diatribe," pp. 1001–08.

32. Even a brief glance at polemical prose in the vernacular during the Reformation reveals that the diatribal model informs the writings of William Tyndale as well as those of such lesser known contemporaries as John Frith, Nicholas Ridley, John Bale, Thomas Becon, and John Bradford. Critical discussions of Reformation and Renaissance polemic have been hampered by the absence of a relatively unified point of departure for critical assessment. The adoption and transformation of the diatribal paradigm would provide a very fruitful point of departure for a comparative study of polemical writing from Tyndale to Milton.

33. See Kranidas, "Style and Rectitude": "Each side musters impressive evidence for its position. But at this stage of the debate—fifty years after Cartwright—it is unlikely that many were seeing the evidence for the first time" (p. 239).

34. Fish, *Self-Consuming Artifacts*, p. 271.

35. See also *Animadversions*, pp. 668. 670–71, 674, 718, for further striking examples.

36. Colie, *Resources of Kind*, p. 8.

37. See also *Animadversions,* pp. 681–02, for a startling analogy that Milton designates as "Kitchin phisik."

38. According to Anselment (*"Betwixt Jest and Earnest"*), "Despite the formal structure with its pretext of dialogue, the bishop has no active role" (p. 74).

39. In "Style and Rectitude," Kranidas comments: "Hall's rectitude *is* in fact theatrical. At the beginning of *An Humble Remonstrance* he presents himself as courageous and modest in the face of a libelous mob; he sustains the figure throughout" (p. 244).

40. Kranidas's contention that this is essentially an *"ad hominem"* argument, pitting one persona against another, is only partially correct ("Style and Rectitude," p. 255). In his analysis of Hall's and Milton's personae, Kranidas implicitly recognizes the fact that Hall stands for the status quo, and he even expresses this insight occasionally, without however carrying this line of argument to its logical conclusion. Kranidas sees Milton as rising above the *ad hominem* argument only in the lyricism of his prayer. Since the prayer, while ostensibly directed toward God, provides Milton with a further opportunity to castigate his enemies, it does not, to my mind, represent a "rising above" but instead an impassioned and skillful continuation of the debate.

41. Donald M. Rosenberg, "Milton's *Paradise Lost*," p. 124.

42. In his *Defence,* Hall frequently quotes in Latin and Greek and makes a point of referring to the intelligence and education of the Smectymnuans in a patronizing and belittling manner (p. 32). He accuses them of faulty translation and interpretation of texts and emphasizes the fact that he has privileged access to manuscripts which are unknown to them (pp. 100–01). See also Kranidas, "Style and Rectitude," pp. 244–47.

43. Christopher Hill, *Milton and the English Revolution,* (New York, 1973), p. 7.

44. Ibid, p. 7.

FROM POLEMIC TO PROPHECY:
MILTON'S USES OF JEREMIAH IN
THE REASON OF CHURCH GOVERNMENT
AND *THE READIE AND EASIE WAY*

Reuben Sanchez

I

MILTON'S SELF-PRESENTATION varies from prose tract to prose tract because of the type of argument he makes and the type of persona he creates for the better persuasiveness of that argument. The persona and decorum of a given tract, therefore, are particular aspects of Milton's response to an immediate occasion. In this essay I should like to consider how and why Milton fashions his persona after Jeremiah in two widely separated prose tracts, one written near the beginning the other near the end of the revolution: *The Reason of Church Government* (1642) and *The Readie and Easie Way* (1660, second edition).[1]

In the autobiographical prologue to Book II of *The Reason of Church Government*, Milton attempts to justify not only his right and obligation to participate in the immediate debate concerning episcopacy but also the manner in which he participates in that debate. His several references to Jeremiah indicate that he finds in that prophet an example of someone who attempts to justify the role he has been called upon to play, and an example of someone who shows concern over the very manner in which he must express himself. In *The Readie and Easie Way*, Milton refers to Jeremiah only once, but that reference—along with other, more subtle, parallels between Milton's text and Jeremiah's—indicates that the English author identifies himself with the Old Testament spokesperson as the lone prophet to whom no one listens. By likening his situation to that of Jeremiah, Milton also infers a parallel between his own historical moment and that in which the Old Testament prophet lived.

It might be helpful, therefore, to highlight some of the more significant events of the historical period in which Jeremiah lived and to recognize the role he played during that period of his nation's history.[2] At about the time of Jeremiah's calling in 627 B.C.E. (Jer. i, 1–3), King Josiah had undertaken a program of political and religious reform in Judah (2 Kings xxii). The death of Josiah in 609 ended the process of reform. Pharo Neco, who had Josiah killed, put Jehoiakim on the throne. Jehoiakim's son, Jehoiachin (also referred to as Coniah or as Jeconiah), ruled briefly in 598; in that year Nebuchadnezzar conquered Jerusalem and took Jehoiachin and many people into exile in Babylon. Jehoiachin spent the rest of his life in exile, his last few years as a pensioner to the Babylonian king Evil-merodach (Jer. lii, 3–34).

In 597 Nebuchadnezzar made Zedekiah king of Judah. Jeremiah remained in Jerusalem, and declared that the exiles would return someday but that they should not expect to return soon. For the time being, he warned, the exiles must submit to the will of Yahweh and not resist the Babylonians whom Yahweh used to punish the people (Jer. xxix). Between 598 and 588 a resistance movement developed in Jerusalem. Because Zedekiah was not strong enough to counteract this movement, he found himself opposing the Babylonians. The Egyptians, meanwhile, had promised aid to the resistance movement. When the Babylonians once again moved against Jerusalem, Yahweh instructed Jeremiah to predict the withdrawal of Egyptian support and the fall of Jerusalem. Shortly after Egypt withdrew its support, Zedekiah arrested Jeremiah for sedition, accused him of going over to the Babylonians (Jer. xxxvii:11–16), and had him thrown into a pit to die, though Jeremiah was rescued (xxxviii, 1–13). Zedekiah later arrested Jeremiah, this time for prophesying the doom of Jerusalem and the exile of Zedekiah (xxxii, 1–5). He remained in prison until Jerusalem fell in 587. Though initially allowed to remain in the city, he was later taken to Egypt against his will by the remaining members of the resistance movement (xlii–xliii). The people did not heed him in Jerusalem or in Egypt. Indeed, they believed that they were in exile because of their loyalty to Yahweh, a loyalty for which they believed the other gods punished them (xliv, 15–18). The book tells us nothing of Jeremiah's death, only that he finds himself in Egypt, written off as a failure by those to whom he preached.

The Book of the Prophet Jeremiah must have been one of Milton's favorite books, as is evidenced by the many references to Jeremiah in *De Doctrina Christiana*.[3] The only other prophet he refers to more often in *De Doctrina Christiana* is Isaiah. Early and late in his prose writing career, Milton was well versed not only in Jeremiah's teachings but in the historical context in which that prophet preached. In late 1641 and early 1642 Milton fashions his self-presentation after that of Jeremiah, particularly in terms of the response to the calling and in terms of the manner in which the vocation is fulfilled; in late March and early April

1660 Milton again fashions his self-presentation after that of Jeremiah, though he then recognizes that, in its broader outlines, Jeremiah's "history" may be about to repeat itself. Late in their careers, each prophet responds to a national disaster—the fall of Jerusalem, the imminent return of the Stuart monarchy—and each prophesies a possible future history for his nation. By comparatively analyzing the use of Jeremiah in two widely separated tracts, we can gauge the development of Milton's thought concerning both the nation's and the individual's relationships with God. This development can be described as Milton's movement from reliance on the public covenant early in his career to a later recognition that the public covenant is dependent upon the private covenant.

II

Milton returned from his tour of the Continent in August 1639, and shortly thereafter took up schoolteaching in London. As the 1630s drew to a close, England was rife with political and religious unrest. Charles I's decision to embark on the so-called Bishops' Wars (1639 and 1640), as well as his decision to dissolve the Short Parliament, which had been in session from April through May 1640, proved to be political blunders. He had no choice but to call for another parliament. The Long Parliament convened in November 1640 to deal with political grievances directed against Charles I and his minister, Strafford. With Strafford—and later Archbishop Laud—out of the way and Charles's political base seriously weakened, the Long Parliament turned its attention in 1641 to church reform. One of the bills it considered was the Root and Branch Bill, which was intended to eliminate the episcopal system of church government. The tract wars promptly began and continued throughout 1641. Among the defenders of episcopacy were Bishop Hall and Archbishop Ussher; among the opponents of episcopacy were the five Presbyterian ministers known by the acronym *Smectymnuus*—the "ty" standing for Thomas Young, Milton's tutor from 1618 to 1620. Even as Charles I was forced to sign the Bishops' Exclusion Bill in February 1642, tracts on both sides continued to be published, including Milton's fourth antiprelatical tract, *The Reason of Church Government*.

Milton's goal throughout the antiprelatical tracts is to wrest control of church and government away from the bishops. He attempts to persuade, but his strategy for persuasion—and even more, for seizing power—is to discredit the bishops and their argument. That strategy often involves the use of derision and invective directed against the bishops. Of course, Milton had intended to fulfill his calling by writing poetry; he did not wish to leave "the high region of his [the poet's] fancies" for "the cool element of prose." Though Milton relegated the writing of prose to a left-handed enterprise, he obviously thought well enough of his own role as prose writer to cease writing poetry, except for some occasional pieces, for almost twenty years. The delay in writing the national epic indicates that he considered his own prose writing as a worthwhile endeavor:

Although it nothing content me to have disclos'd thus much before hand, but that I trust hereby to make it manifest with what small willingnesse I endure to interrupt the pursuit of no lesse hopes than these, and leave a calme and pleasing solitarynes, fed with cherful and confident thoughts, to imbark in a troubl'd sea of noises and hoars disputes. . . . Let any gentle apprehension that can distinguish learned pains from unlearned drudgery, imagin what pleasure or profoundnesse can be in this, or what honor to deal against such adversaries.[4]

Polemical strategy requires Milton to establish his personal rectitude. Milton contends that he does not enter the debate for selfish reasons; rather, because of his sense of duty to God and country, he has been drawn into the debate, a debate in which he can gain little if any "pleasure," "profoundness," or "honor" in his attempt "to deal" with "such adversaries."

In his discussion of *Animadversions,* Thomas Kranidas suggests that the term *polemical* implies *personal* for seventeenth-century prose writers.[5] To present a convincing argument, the polemicist must establish his personal rectitude because it is essential to style and argument in seventeenth-century polemical prose (p. 241). In order to understand Milton's prose style in *Animadversions,* for example, we must first understand Joseph Hall's prose style because he, through his own self-presentation, initiates the decorum of the debate. Decorum in Milton's time, therefore, is a malleable principle of composition. When Milton enters the public debate concerning episcopacy in 1641, he must participate according to the decorum characteristic of that debate. The participants' tacit agreement to a decorum determined by context does not, of course, preclude creativity, particularly in terms of self-presentation. But the participant must find a suitable mode of discourse that would locate him within the accepted structures of discourse and yet distinguish him from the other participants, so that the mode of communication is both effective and interesting.[6]

Though Milton states in *Of Education* that decorum is "the grand master peece to observe" (YP II, p. 405), "the grand master peece" nonetheless varies from tract to tract. In the antiprelatical tracts in general, the decorum observed by Milton calls for a self-presentation appropriate to the debate concerning episcopacy. In *The Reason of Church Government,* in particular, Milton justifies his self-presentation by arguing that he follows Jeremiah's example.

Milton emphasizes not only Jeremiah's inability to remain silent but also the manner in which Jeremiah speaks, thereby attempting to justify his own language directed against the prelates:

Which might teach these times not suddenly to condemn all things that are sharply spoken, or vehemently written, as proceeding out of stomach, virulence and ill nature, but to consider rather that if the Prelats have leav to say the worst that can be said, and doe the worst that can be don, while they strive to keep to themselves to their great pleasure and commodity those things which they ought to render up, no man can be justly offended with him that shall endeavour to impart and bestow without any gain to himselfe those sharp, but saving words which would be a terror, and a torment in him to keep back. (YP I, pp. 803–04)

The end of this passage—"words which would be a terror, and a torment in him to keep back"—alludes to Jeremiah xx, 9. Harsh words are at times appropriate to the decorum of Jeremiah's book, to other prophetic books of the Hebrew Bible, and, for Milton, to the immediate polemical debate concerning episcopacy. Though Milton implies that the words are appropriate to "these times," they are also the result of "an inward prompting," from being "weary with forbearing," from the moment when the prophet can no longer remain silent but must attempt to fulfill the calling.

However, Milton elsewhere emphasizes the prophet's willing participation once he has been called. Being chosen and gifted is not enough, for the prophet-teacher must actively participate in the process of his own education. In *The Reason of Church Government*, Milton refers to Isaiah's description of his calling (Isa. vi, 6–7), but adds a qualification. The "eternall Spirit" to whom one must pray "sends out his Seraphim with the hallow'd fire of his Altar to touch and purify the lips of whom he pleases: to this must be added industrious and select reading, steddy observation, insight into all seemly and generous arts and affaires" (YP I, p. 821). Though the prophet has been called, he must further educate himself in order to fulfill the vocation more effectively. The prophet must recognize as well that when he does speak he will likely be rejected by those to whom he speaks:

But when God commands to take the trumpet and blow a dolorous or a jarring blast, it lies not in mans will what he shall say, or what he shall conceal. If he shall think to be silent, as *Jeremiah* did, because of the reproach and derision he met with daily, and *all his familiar friends watcht for his halting* to be reveng'd on him for speaking the truth, he would be forc't to confesse as he confest, *his word was in my heart as a burning fire shut up in my bones, I was weary with forbearing, and could not stay.* (YP I, p. 803, Milton's italics)

In the second sentence of this passage Milton quotes Jeremiah (xx, 10, 9), establishing parallels in terms of situation and the compulsion to speak. The first sentence of the passage places both spokespersons within a specific context: the prophet's warnings of impending disaster, a common motif in the Hebrew Bible. For example, Isaiah l, 1, Ezekiel xxxiii, 3–4, and Jeremiah vi, 17 associate the trumpet blast with the *voice* of the prophet as *watchman*. The speaker's trumpet blast as *warning voice* suggests a particular decorum in which the prophet must express himself—a decorum that characterizes the debate in which Milton participates in 1641–42.

To the ambitious young poet who wishes to write an epic poem, it might indeed have seemed a *burden* (a word Milton uses frequently in *The Reason of Church Government*) to take up the trumpet instead of the lyre. But as Milton points out, Jeremiah also considered it a burden:

This is that which the sad Prophet *Jeremiah* laments, *Wo is me my mother, that thou hast born me a man of strife, and contention.* And although divine inspiration must certainly have been sweet to those ancient profets, yet the irksomenesse of that truth which they brought was so unpleasant to them, that every where they call it a burden. (YP I, pp. 802–03)

Although "those ancient profets" may have considered inspiration "sweet," Jeremiah nevertheless curses the day he was born (xx, 14; *see also* xv, 10). Jeremiah's role as prophet is problematic in that, at times throughout his long career of approximately forty years, he complains about the way Yahweh treats him—expresses, as it were, a "small willingnesse" to fulfill his calling. The prophet's initial resistance to the calling is a common motif in the Hebrew Bible, but instances of resistance over a long period of time distinguish Jeremiah's characterization from the characterizations of other prophets in the Hebrew Bible. Jeremiah's frustrations with his people, his resentment at the way Yahweh treats him, and his moments of anger and self-doubt have enabled biblical scholars to describe what may be referred to as the *biographical* aspects of Jeremiah's text.[7]

A prayer precedes the verses in which Jeremiah curses the day he was born. Jeremiah is much more visibly frustrated and angry than Milton, yet his prayer resembles Milton's "small willingnesse" at being pulled away from his private studies into the public debate. The prayer begins in frustration, but ends with Jeremiah assuring himself that Yahweh has not abandoned him (xx, 7–12).[8] Jeremiah is not a prophet at peace with his calling, is not content merely to be Yahweh's unquestioning amanuensis.[9] Indeed, he accuses Yahweh of having deceived him. While the prayer does end on a hopeful note, the verses in which Jeremiah curses the day he was born immediately follow (xx, 14–18).

Jeremiah implies that the manner in which he communicates may seem indecorous: "For since I spake, I cried out, I cried violence and spoil" (xx, 8).[10] This manner of expression—the cry, or lamentation—calls attention to itself. It is a form of communication constraining the prophet to a specific genre and language.[11] A parvenu of society to begin with, Jeremiah must continue to express himself as he does at the cost of further alienating his listeners. He cannot help but lament because it is the only way he can express the deity's word. Decorum, therefore, determines the text's prophetic persona, determines the cacophony of the prophet's lamentation.

In *The Reason of Church Government* Milton suggests that the manner in which the prophet expresses himself can be misunderstood if not recognized as generated in a specific historical and linguistic context. He refers to "a troubl'd sea of noises and hoars disputes" and to "these times" in order to place his argument in a particular decorum, his words to be understood by understanding the times and the appropriate structures of discourse. But Milton distinguishes his own voice from the voices of others in that "sea of noises" by paralleling his own calling and lamentation to that of Jeremiah.

III

Shortly after the death of Oliver Cromwell in September 1658, the Privy Council accepted the nomination of his son Richard as protector.[12] Richard proved to be an ineffective leader, perhaps because he simply was not suited to the job, perhaps because, suited to the job or not, the problems his protectorate faced seemed insurmountable: a disenchanted army leadership, a divided government, rampant political corruption within his government, a naval war with Spain, combined with severe economic difficulties in England. Richard's protectorate deteriorated over the winter of 1658–59. In May 1659 the Rump Parliament (which Oliver Cromwell had dissolved in April 1653) was recalled; one of its first orders of business was to establish a financial settlement with Richard, who had been forced by the military to step down as protector. The nation's problems continued, however, and a dissatisfied military leadership dissolved the Rump in October, establishing the Committee of Safety—what amounted to rule by a military junta—from October through December 1659. General George Monck had negotiated the recall of the Rump Parliament, which convened again on 27 December 1659; but the Rump, like Richard Cromwell, proved ineffective. In early January 1660 Monck, who had been in Scotland, returned to England with his army and entered London on 3 February.

While Milton was writing the first edition of *The Readie and Easie Way* in early February, it may have appeared that the Rump would remain in power; indeed, in early to mid-February Monck himself seemed to support the Rump, although his sincerity is questionable. Certainly by the end of February and early March, however, the political climate had altered dramatically. Monck saw to it that the survivors of Pride's Purge, the "Secluded Members," were readmitted to the House of Commons on 21 February. Monck instructed them to effect yet another dissolution of the Rump (which they did on 16 March), to set in motion the election procedures for a new parliament (which they did, resulting in the Convention Parliament that convened on 20 April), to issue payments to the military and to approve his installation as commander-in-chief of the army (both of which they did immediately). There was speculation, of course, that the foregoing measures prepared for the return of the Stuart monarchy, although it is not certain whether that was Monck's intention. Milton hurriedly wrote the second edition of *The Readie and Easie Way* probably in late March and published it in early April.[13] Much had changed since he wrote the first edition in mid-February, and it seems likely that his optimism concerning the republic's chances for survival had been tempered by these changes.

In the second edition of *The Readie and Easie Way* Milton does not concern himself, as he does in *The Reason of Church Government*, with justifying his language or with explaining how he became involved in a public debate. Instead, he attempts to apply to his own time the lessons he has gleaned from biblical history. When Milton sets about to describe the historical moment, to participate in that moment, and to predict a possible future history for his nation, he turns to the Hebrew Bible, and particularly to the history offered by Jeremiah.

The attack on kingship and the concern with idolatry and punishment are two motifs Milton's text and Jeremiah's have in common. Jeremiah's denunciation of the kingships of Zedekiah, Johoiakim, and Jehoiachin/Coniah are particularly harsh (xxi, 1–xxiii, 8). It must be noted, however, that Jeremiah does not attack kingship per se but rather weak or evil kings, whereas much of Milton's text involves an attack on kingship as an institution (YP VII, pp. 409–29, 446–55). One of the kings whom Jeremiah singles out as evil is Jehoiachin/Coniah, whom Milton compares to Charles II in the first edition of *The Readie and Easie Way* (YP VII, p. 388). However, the reference to Coniah is of course conspicuously absent from the second edition. Although Jeremiah's Coniah did not return to Jerusalem, it may have seemed possible in late March 1660 that Milton's Coniah would shortly return to England.

Milton warns Englishmen that they are quite mistaken to consider themselves safe under kingship:

Certainly then that people must needs be madd or strangely infatuated, that build the chief hope of thir common happiness or safetie on a single person. . . . they who think the nation undon without a king, though they look grave or haughtie, have not so much true spirit and understanding in them as a pismire. (YP VII, p. 427)

Such Englishmen are as foolish as Jeremiah's contemporaries, who believe they will be safe in the sanctuary of the Jerusalem Temple. Jeremiah warns in the Temple Sermon that so long as the people are idolatrous they will not be safe even in the temple (vii). If the people do not "Amend [their] ways" Yahweh will destroy the temple itself (vii, 14–15). Jeremiah preaches, then, that idolatry can result in the loss of freedom because Yahweh will use other nations to punish the people (x, 17–25). He is especially concerned to warn the people about the idolatry of other nations, "the way of the heathen" (x, 1–16), a concern that also characterizes the text of Second Isaiah (40–55, especially 40–48), who may have been a younger contemporary of Jeremiah and preached to the exiles in Babylon (587–539 B.C.E.).

Like Jeremiah and 2 Isaiah, Milton associates idolatry with the loss of spiritual and civil freedom. Milton describes the return to kingship as a return to idolatry, and gives an example from biblical history to support his argument:

If lastly, after all this light among us, the same reason shall pass for current to put our necks again under kingship, as was made use of by the *Jews* to returne back to *Egypt* and to the worship of thir idol queen, because they falsly imagind that they then livd in more plentie and prosperitie, our condition is not sound but rotten, both in religion and all civil prudence; and will bring us soon, the way we are marching, to those calamities which attend alwaies and unavoidably on luxurie, all national judgments under forein or domestic slaverie: so far we shall be from mending our condition by monarchizing our government, whatever new conceit now possesses us. (YP VII, p. 462)

The argument that idolatry is an attendant condition to the loss of religious and civil freedom is not new for Milton in 1660. Yet the concern with idolatry and false security perhaps bear special and immediate significance for Milton on the eve of the Restoration. One might wonder whether Milton by this time did believe that the people were indeed capable of "mending" their "condition." One might wonder, therefore, whether the warning is simply rhetorical.

Milton warns of impending disaster, but he also implies that history need not repeat itself. It is "easie" to ensure liberty:

The way propounded is plane, easie and open before us; without intricacies, without introducement of new or obsolete forms, or terms, or exotic models; idea's that would effect nothing, but with a number of new injunctions to manacle the native liberty of mankinde; turning all vertue into prescription, servitude, and necessitie, to the great impairing and frustrating of Christian libertie: I say again, this way lies free and smooth before us; is not tangl'd with inconveniencies; invents no new incumbrances; requires no perilous, no injurious alteration or circumscription of mens lands and properties. (YP VII, p. 445)

When Milton wrote the second edition of *The Readie and Easie Way*, it could have been possible to interpret the unfolding political events as signaling the return of the Stuart monarchy, or it could have been equally possible to believe that the Convention Parliament would block any attempts at a Stuart restoration. It seems likely, however, that the optimism Milton displayed in the first edition of *The Readie and Easie Way* may have waned by the time he set about writing the second edition. His optimism in the above passage, therefore, is unrealistic. The passage itself is an expansion of a passage in the first edition (YP VII, p. 374). One result of the expansion is to undercut the optimism with a series of negatives: without / without / nothing / not / no / no / no. The nouns, verbs, adjectives, and adverbs undercut the optimism as well: intricacies / obsolete / exotic / injunctions / manacle / prescription / servitude / necessitie / impairing / frustrating / tangl'd / inconveniencies / incumbrances / perilous / injurious alteration / circumscription. Of course, "the way" is not easy, and that is Milton's point. By this time in his nation's history, he has learned that the private way, to paraphrase from another context, must be made subsequent *and* precedent to the public way (*Of Education*, YP II, p. 403).

There is still time to avoid disaster, Milton contends: "However with all hazard I have ventur'd what I thought my duty to speak in season, and to forewarne my countrey in time" (YP VII, p. 462). This passage is repeated verbatim from the first edition (YP VII, p. 387). But between the writing of the first and second editions the political changes that occurred in England could have been interpreted as threatening the survival of the republic. The warning in the second edition therefore seems rhetorical. Perhaps the warning may be thought of as a motif, for there are similar moments of rhetorical optimism in Jeremiah's text as well. In the story of the potter's shop (xviii, 1–11), for example, Jeremiah declares that disaster may be averted even before the fall of Jerusalem in 587 B.C.E. Of course, this passage is followed by Yahweh's declaration that because the people will not listen they will be punished (xviii, 12–17). Indeed, as in Milton's text, one might wonder whether the people can be persuaded to amend their ways and thereby avert disaster.

Jeremiah and Milton recognize that the people will not repent and that they will therefore be punished, albeit both prophets offer the possibility of repentance and forgiveness. The optimism displayed by Jeremiah and Milton, however, is not merely rhetorical. Milton does have hope for the future of his nation; he finds the exemplary model of hope in Jeremiah, who also describes and participates in his nation's history during a time of national disaster. Both prophets recognize that deity and nation must establish a new covenant. To understand more clearly why Milton would find Jeremiah's history relevant to his own, we might consider the historical circumstances in which Jeremiah writes and to which he responds, for the historical circumstances resemble those in which Milton writes and to which he responds in 1660.

During the final siege of Jerusalem in 587 B.C.E. Jeremiah, while in prison, does something that seems inexplicable. Yahweh instructs him to redeem his kinsman's land at Anathoth (xxxii, 6–14). Jeremiah obeys, taking care to ensure the legality of the transaction. Why, one must ask, would Jeremiah redeem his kinsman's land when he knows very well, since Yahweh has told him so, that Babylon will conquer Judah? Why would Yahweh have him perform such a seemingly useless act? Jeremiah does not question Yahweh's instructions; rather, he points out to Baruch that the chosen people will once again legally possess the land, but only after the land has been given over to Judah's enemies (xxxii, 28–36). Only after the Babylonian Exile, which is the death of the nation, will Yahweh bring the chosen people back to their land (xxxii, 37–44).

Jeremiah redeems the land according to the law stipulated in Leviticus xxv, 25, honoring the Moses-Sinai covenant (Exod. xix, 5–6). Even as the nation dies, then, the law remains binding. Perhaps most significantly, the symbolic act provides hope for Judah and for Israel; this hope does not rest solely upon the Moses-Sinai covenant, which the Israelites could not keep, but upon a new covenant. On the eve of the fall of Jerusalem, Jeremiah finds hope for the future. Out of the destruction of the city and the exile of the people, a new future in the form of a new covenant will be forged, this time not on stone tablets but on the human heart:

> Behold, the days come, saith the Lord, that I will make a new covenant with
> the house of Israel, and with the house of Judah
> . . . .
> But this shall be the covenant that I will make with the house of Israel; After
> those days, saith the Lord, I will put my law in their inward parts, and write it in
> their hearts; and will be their God, and they shall be my people. (xxxi, 31, 33)

The Moses-Sinai covenant is not rejected; the law still appertains. Nor is
the David-Zion tradition rejected (2 Samuel vii, 16); Yahweh will once
again forgive the people and protect them. The rebirth of the nation,
however, will occur only after the punishment of exile, and will not occur
in Jeremiah's lifetime.

In his response to the same national disaster, Ezekiel also uses the
heart as the image of future rebirth for the individual and the nation.
Yahweh will replace "the stony heart" with a "heart of flesh," thereby
establishing a new relationship with the individual and with the nation.
This "heart of flesh" will be accompanied by a "new spirit" that will enable
the individual to follow Yahweh's "statutes" and "judgements" (Ezek.
xxxvi, 26–27). The return from the Babylonian Exile is described as "a
new thing" in Second Isaiah, an act of creation by Yahweh (Isa. xliii, 19–
21), but "a new thing" that must nonetheless be accompanied by adherence to the Law (xliii, 23–24). Ezekiel, Second Isaiah, and Jeremiah teach
that the law still binds, but that it will be infused with a new spirit. These
prophets, all responding somehow to the same historical event, emphasize the old and the new. Ezekiel and Jeremiah, in their uses of the heart
as metaphor for rebirth, emphasize the public and the private, hence
signaling a shift to individual responsibility as prelude to public liberty, a
shift Milton will find especially useful on the eve of the Restoration.
Perhaps most useful to Milton—as he responds to the failure of the nation, and later as he writes the two epics and *Samson Agonistes*—is that
the shift renders the matter concerning (private) salvation and (public)
liberty contingent upon the individual's willingness to accept offered
grace.

In *The Readie and Easie Way*, Milton through allusions to the Hebrew Bible and the New Testament chooses to express his awareness of
the failure of the nation. He infers the possibility of a new covenant by
alluding directly to Jeremiah, and indirectly to Ezekiel, Matthew, and
Luke:

> Thus much I should perhaps have said though I were sure I should have spoken
> only to trees and stones; and had none to cry to, but with the Prophet, *O earth,
> earth, earth!* to tell the very soil it self, what her perverse inhabitants are deaf to.

Nay though what I have spoke, should happ'n (which Thou suffer not, who didst create mankinde free; nor Thou next, who didst redeem us from being servants of men!) to be the last words of our expiring libertie. But I trust I shall have spoken perswasion to abundance of sensible and ingenuous men: to som perhaps whom God may raise of these stones to become children of reviving libertie. (YP VII, pp. 462–463)

Near the beginning of the passage Milton cites Jeremiah xxii, 29: "O earth, earth, earth, hear the word of the Lord." He uses Jeremiah's words, but he also emphasizes the metaphorical quality of those words by suggesting that he would/does act "*with* the Prophet," not "*like* the Prophet." As the bard sings *with* "The multitude of Angels" in heaven or *with* the "Blest pair" in the Garden, in *The Readie and Easie Way* Milton participates in the exemplary, though in this instance ultimately futile, action he has chosen to describe.

One can of course see that the emphasis throughout *The Readie and Easie Way* is not so much on the government model(s) Milton offers, but on Milton's self-presentation. Describing *The Readie and Easie Way* as "an anti-utopian jeremiad," for example, James Holstun suggests that Milton "does not attempt to unite a community around some program of political innovation (like the Puritan utopist) or renovation (like the American Jeremiah). Rather, he creates for himself the identity of a lone prophet who withdraws from his community and stands prophesying its ruin."[14] Nor is this true only of *The Readie and Easie Way*, Holstun adds, for throughout his prose career Milton involves himself in a "process of self-memorialization and prophecy" (p. 260).

The quote from Jeremiah—"*O earth, earth, eaarth!*"—does highlight self-presentation: The lone prophet in the wilderness, certainly a persona Milton self-consciously fashions for himself in this and other tracts. Merritt Y. Hughes suggests that the passage, "to *som* perhaps whom God may raise of these stones to become children of reviving libertie" (emphasis mine), alludes to Ezekiel xxxvii.[15] Milton may therefore have a future community in mind, for Ezekiel prophesies that Yahweh will revive the dry bones of Israel, a prophecy that enables, perhaps requires, Milton to take cognizance of the "som." However vague the image of the "som" may be, it implies hope for the future rebirth of the community. Robert Ayers, too, suggests that Milton may have a future community in mind, for the reference to the "stones" alludes to specific passages in Matthew and Luke.[16] "Bring forth therefore fruits worthy of repentance," John the Baptist declares, "and begin not to say within yourselves, We have Abraham to our father: for I say unto you, That God is able of these stones to raise up children unto Abraham" (Luke iii, 8; *see also* Matthew iii, 7–9). On the one hand, as in Jeremiah and Ezekiel, Milton predicts impending destruction; on the other hand, as in Jeremiah and Ezekiel as well as in Matthew and Luke, Milton infers a possible revival through a *new* covenant established between God and individual.

IV

We can, in Milton's prose writing career, trace the development of his thought from dependence upon public covenant to revaluation of public covenant as dependent upon private covenant. Mary Ann Radzinowicz has described this revaluation in terms of Milton's conception of history, which develops in four stages—three stages seen in his prose career, the fourth seen in *Paradise Lost*. [17] The first stage, which begins with the antiprelatical tracts and ends with the divorce tracts, is distinguished by Milton's optimistic view that believers can indeed reform the church. The second stage begins after Milton's break with the Presbyterians over the divorce tracts and concludes with *The Tenure of Kings and Magistrates*. In this stage, Milton's emphasis shifts from church reform to social reform, or revolution. The third stage, beginning with *Eikonoklastes*, ends with the second edition of *The Readie and Easie Way*. In this stage, Milton believes that the majority of Englishmen have regressed and that a minority must defend liberty. He no longer believes that a reformed nation will redeem history. In the fourth stage the select minority gives way to the individual now responsible only for himself. Each stage marks a movement away from religious and secular order based on the group's ability to maintain a covenant—from church to state to small group to individual—a movement away from strong reliance upon a public covenant based on religious and secular statutes to willing acceptance of a private covenant written on the human heart.

Early in his prose writing career Milton is optimistic about the reward awaiting the nation if it maintains its covenant with God. For the young idealist, green years upon his head, the millennium actually approaches, and the chosen people must maintain the public covenant. Early in his career Jeremiah preaches that although the people have violated the Moses-Sinai covenant (chap. 2), Yahweh will forgive them if they repent and adhere to the covenant (iii, 12–22; iv, 1–2). In 1642 Milton does seem to believe that Englishmen may after all heed his words. That optimism characterizes Milton's work near the beginning of the Revolution, an optimism significantly tempered by events between 1642 and 1660. In the final part of his career, Jeremiah witnesses the destruction of his nation by Nebuchadnezzar, who functions as Yahweh's chosen instrument to punish the unfaithful (chaps. xxix; xxxii, 26–35). For the mature prophet-teacher, without an audience for his lamentation, Milton must respond to the failure of the nation's public covenant, a failure symbolized by the people "chusing them a captain back for *Egypt.*" With the nation's loss of liberty, however, Jeremiah and Milton choose to redefine liberty.

Milton felt that the English, like the Israelites before them, bore the responsibility for the loss of their own liberty. Through the reference to Ezekiel chapter xxxvii at the conclusion of *The Readie and Easie Way*, he presents the prospect of hope—a prospect, though, much qualified by his understanding of the quickly changing political atmosphere in February and March 1660:

But I trust I shall have spoken perswasion to abundance of sensible and ingenuous men: to som perhaps whom God may raise of these stones to become children of reviving libertie; and may reclaim, though they seem now chusing them a captain back for *Egypt,* to bethink themselves a little and consider whether they are rushing; to exhort this torrent also of the people, not to be so impetuos, but to keep their due channell; and at length recovering and uniting their better resolutions, now that they see alreadie how open and unbounded the insolence and rage is of our common enemies, to stay these ruinous proceedings; justly and timely fearing to what a precipice of destruction the deluge of this epidemic madness would hurrie us through the general defection of a misguided and abus'd multitude. (YP VII, p. 463)

The optimism expressed through the allusion to Ezekiel is of course overwhelmed by all that follows, most of which Milton adds to the second edition of *The Readie and Easie Way.* [18] Any hope expressed in the passage is tenuous at best: "I *trust* I shall have spoken perswasion . . . to som *perhaps* whom God *may* raise" (emphasis mine). The image in this passage is of a nation gripped in an *epidemic madness* and a *general defection.* By now Milton surely knows that the nation will not be persuaded.

Whereas sincere, albeit naive, optimism characterizes *The Reason of Church Government,* rhetorical optimism characterizes *The Readie and Easie Way,* an optimism that masks Milton's realistic understanding of the unfolding history in which he participates. In *The Readie and Easie Way* Milton does not bother to defend his language to his listeners, as he does in *The Reason of Church Government;* at the end of the revolution he acknowledges that few people if any listen to him. Yet in April 1660, as in early 1642, he declares his need and obligation to speak. Like Jeremiah before the fall of Jerusalem, Milton before the return of the Stuart monarchy at best has a fit audience though few. Whether or not he has an audience, the prophet-teacher must engage in lamentation. The refusal of the people to listen would not have been reason to be silent (*O earth, earth, earth!*). Once the prophet-teacher has chosen to fulfill his appointed role, he recognizes that the lamentation is the decorum appropriate to his calling.

California State University, Fresno

NOTES

1. *The Reason of Church Government*, probably written toward the end of 1641 and published in January or February 1642, was preceded by three tracts: *Of Reformation, Of Prelatical Episcopacy*, and *Animadversions*, all appearing in 1641. The first edition of *The Readie and Easie Way* was written and published in February 1660; the second edition was probably written in late March and published in early April 1660. *The Readie and Easie Way* was followed by one public tract: *Of True Religion*, appearing in 1673.

2. For the historical background of this period in Israelite history I have relied upon the following works: John Bright, *A History of Israel* (Philadelphia, 1981), pp. 316–39; Siegfried Herrmann, *A History of Israel in Old Testament Times* (Philadelphia, 1975), pp. 263–85; J. Maxwell Miller and John J. Hayes, *A History of Ancient Israel and Judah* (Philadelphia, 1986), pp. 391–415; Martin Noth, *The History of Israel* (London, 1965), pp. 269–99.

3. See Michael Bauman, *A Scripture Index to John Milton's "De Doctrina Christiana"* (Binghamton, 1989), pp. 74–78.

4. *Complete Prose Works of John Milton*, 8 vols., ed. Don M. Wolfe et al. (New Haven, 1953–82), I, pp. 821–822. All quotations from Milton's prose are from this edition, and subsequent volume and page references will appear in the text as YP.

5. Thomas Kranidas suggests that rectitude is an aspect of rhetorical strategy in seventeenth-century polemical prose: "Style and Rectitude in Seventeenth-Century Prose: Hall, Smectymnuus, and Milton," *Huntington Library Quarterly*, 46 (1983), 237–69.

6. See for example John Huntley's analysis of Milton's *bene dicendi* in *The Reason of Church Government:* "The Images of Poet & Poetry in Milton's *The Reason of Church Government*," in *Achievements of the Left Hand*, ed. Michael Lieb and John T. Shawcross (Amherst, 1974), pp. 82–120.

7. For a review of the "Biographical Interest" in Jeremiah, see Timothy Polk, *The Prophetic Persona: Jeremiah and the Language of the Self* (Sheffield, 1984), chapter 1.

8.   O Lord, thou has deceived me, and I was deceived: thou art stronger than I, and hast prevailed: I am in derision daily, every one mocketh me.

For since I spake, I cried out, I cried violence and spoil; because the word of the Lord was made a reproach unto me, and a derision, daily.

Then I said, I will not make mention of him, nor speak any more in his name. But his word was in mine heart as a burning fire shut up in my bones, and I was weary with forbearing, and I could not stay.

For I heard the defaming of many, fear on every side. Report, say they, and we will report it. All my familiars watched for my halting, saying, Peradventure he will be enticed, and we shall prevail against him, and we shall take our revenge on him.

But the Lord is with me as a mighty terrible one: therefore my persecutors shall stumble, and they shall not prevail: they shall be greatly ashamed; for they shall not prosper: their everlasting confusion shall never be forgotten.

But, O Lord of hosts, that triest the righteous, and seest the reins and the heart, let me see thy vengeance on them: for unto thee have I opened my cause.

(xx, 7–12, King James Version)

9. Michael Fishbane describes Jeremiah's prayer as a manifestation of the spiritual struggle within Jeremiah: "This remarkable prayer reveals a tragic moment wherein a prophet despairs but cannot fully rebel. Jeremiah struggles to suppress God's voice within him. But his realization that God's word is in his bones, and his recognition of divine protection in v, 11, point to the reunification of his will with God's. For Jeremiah's spiritual restoration lies in the full acceptance of his unique task in the world: to be a faithful and trusting divine messenger" (" 'A Wretched Thing of Shame, A Mere Belly': An Interpretation of Jeremiah xx, 7–12," in *The Biblical Mosaic: Changing Perspectives*, ed. Robert M. Polzin and Eugene Rothman [Chico, Calif., 1982], p. 181). Fishbane suggests that Jeremiah is spiritually torn between personal liberty and submission to the deity's will. Jeremiah must spiritually surrender in order to find peace—and this he finds difficult to do (p. 181).

10. All quotations from the Bible are from the King James Version.

11. Geoffrey Hartman discusses this prayer in terms of *language* and *genre:* "Jeremiah being a prophet, the status of language or of the cry is at least as important as the genre concept of prayer. Formal analysis can type 7–12 as a prayer. But if there were a genre called 'the cry,' surely we would consider it at least as fitting. I do not mean psychologically that Jeremiah cries from the depths of his soul; I mean something like 'whenever I speak, I shout' or 'I cry violence and plunder' " ("Jeremiah xx, 7–12: A Literary Response," in *The Biblical Mosaic: Changing Perspectives*, p. 190). The prophet's "cry," suggests Hartman, serves as the language through which the deity communicates with the people (pp. 193–94).

12. For the historical background of this period, I have relied upon Austin Woolrych's "Historical Introduction" in *The Complete Prose Works of John Milton*, VII, pp. 96–228.

13. For the dating of the second edition of *The Readie and Easie Way* see Robert W. Ayers' "Preface" in *The Complete Prose Works of John Milton*, VII, 398–400. For the dating of the first edition of *The Readie and Easie Way*, see Ayers' "Preface," VII, 343–45.

14. James Holstun, *A Rational Millennium: Puritan Utopias of Seventeenth-Century England and America* (Oxford, 1987), p. 260. For another, more recent, treatment of *The Readie and Easie Way* as jeremiad see Laura Lunger Knoppers, "Milton's *The Readie and Easie Way* and the English jeremiad," in *Politics, Poetics, and Hermeneutics in Milton's Prose*, ed. David Loewenstein and James Grantham Turner (Cambridge, 1990), pp. 213–25. Knoppers presents an interesting and persuasive argument concerning how Milton's response to the historical moment results in his unique use of, what has become by the eve of the Restoration, the popular and oft-used jeremiad. For background on the seventeenth-century jeremiad see the following: James Egan, " 'This is a Lamentation and shall be for a Lamentation': Nathaniel Ward and the Rhetoric of the Jeremiad," *Proceedings of the American Philosophical Society*, vol. 122, no. 6 (Dec., 1978), 400–10; Perry Miller, *The New England Mind: From Colony to Province* (Cambridge, Mass., 1953), pp. 27–39; Sacvan Bercovitch, *The American Jeremiad* (Madison, 1978).

15. Merritt Y. Hughes, *John Milton: Complete Poetry and Major Prose* (Indianapolis, 1957), p. 898n.

16. Robert W. Ayers, *Complete Prose Works of John Milton*, VII, 388n.

17. Mary Ann Radzinowicz, *Toward "Samson Agonistes": The Growth of Milton's Mind* (Princeton, 1978), pp. 69–108.

18. The first edition reads as follows: "But I trust, I shall have spoken perswasion to abundance of sensible and ingenuous men: to som perhaps, whom God may raise of these stones, to become children of libertie, and may enable and unite in thir noble resolutions to give a stay to these our ruinous proceedings and to this general defection of the misguided and abus'd multitude" (YP VII, p. 388).

CREATOR-CRITIC: AESTHETIC SUBTEXTS IN MILTON'S ANTIPRELATICAL AND REGICIDE POLEMICS

James Egan

I

MILTONISTS ARE FAMILIAR with the poet's involvement in the pamphlet wars of the 1640s over episcopacy and regicide, particularly his political contributions to debate and the rhetorical strategies he typically employed.[1] Milton's polemic certainly has conventional features given its nature as propaganda and because of his identification with many of the issues he strenuously debated. The conventional qualities of the polemic may also have inspired the longstanding critical assumption that formulaic attack and rebuttal impede aesthetic expression, in part because of the polemicist's public obligations to the cause he champions, an assumption that holds true for the majority of Milton's pamphlets.[2] Joan Webber's discussion of the prose style of the antiprelatical tracts, however, challenged the separatist notion that polemic mars the artistic integrity of the prose with its demonstration that Milton was poetically active even as he argued against prelacy.[3] Edward S. Le Comte, John F. Huntley, and Michael Lieb have supported Webber's position by identifying, respectively, the "poetic" qualities of *Areopagitica*, the "power of poetic ornament and style" in *The Reason of Church-Government*, and the ways in which Milton's treatment of history in *Of Reformation* expresses "in polemical form his earlier impulse to write an Arthuriad."[4] The most recent and comprehensive statement of the integrative argument and its premises has been made by David Loewenstein and James Grantham Turner: Loewenstein has linked Milton's "literary imagination" with his "historiographical" and "polemical" discourse, and Turner has examined the workings of Milton's "poetics of engagement."[5] I propose that the close correspondence of Miltonic prose and poetry can be further illustrated and clarified by reviewing the agendas and tactics of the significant literary subtexts in two disputations of the 1640s, Milton's quarrel with Joseph Hall in 1641–42 and his attack on King Charles I's *Eikon Basilike* in 1649.

Hall and Charles offered Milton an opportunity to address literary issues in which he was well versed, something his opponents normally did not grant him. He responded by making his polemic at once personal and public, aesthetic and propagandistic. Hall and Charles were either artists or pseudoartists, both of whom had produced powerful artifacts meriting considerable acclaim or recognition. As Milton measured the work of these antagonists, he recognized the relationship of their literary habits and preferences to the development of his own. To deal with Hall and Charles, he adopted the stance of creator-critic, justifying his position by virtue of his creative accomplishment and critical training. The artistic shaping provided by his own career sanctioned an ethos sufficient to identify, evaluate, and deconstruct the genres and modes of Hall and Charles. The literary reputations of these figures allowed Milton to indulge in devastating iconoclasm as he mimicked, reshaped, and formulated alternatives to their idioms, and those reputations sparked considerable creative deliberation as well. In the debates with Hall and Charles, Milton asserted his literary talents, principles, and credentials against those he disavowed. By answering the political arguments of his adversaries as he reflected upon the literary values we customarily associate with his poetry and drama, Milton formulated an aesthetic polemic, one which depended upon an artistic awareness of decorum, genre, the unities of time, place, and action, verisimilitude, and the nature of fiction. The *Animadversions* (1641), *An Apology* (1642), and *Eikonoklastes* (1649) each demonstrate the interaction of public agendas and aesthetic subtexts.

II

When Milton entered the Smectymnuan controversy in 1641, he confronted Bishop Joseph Hall, one of the most visible and influential spokesmen for the established church in the first half of the seventeenth century. Hall was a prelate of formidable intellectual powers and reputation as a disputant, a reputation earned by the versatile mockery he had employed in several earlier polemic skirmishes, yet his tactics against the Smectymnuans proved to be conventional and unimaginative. In *An Humble Remonstrance* (1641), for example, Hall summarizes two objections to the episcopal system of church government:

> I may not yet dissemble, that while we plead the divine right of episcopacy, a double scandal is taken by men otherwise not injudicious, and cast upon us, from the usual suggestions of some late pamphleteers.
> The one, that we have deserted our former tenet, not without the great

prejudice of sovereignty. . . . The other, that while we labour to defend the divine right of our episcopacy, we seem to cast a dangerous imputation upon those reformed churches which want that government.[6]

As he lists sectarian objections and musters a refutation, Hall has the opportunity to construct a dialogue, to maneuver his foes into a position whereby he can wittily expose their blunders in logic and flaws of character, but he opts for a literal exegesis, hoping to gain in clarity what he might lose in repartee. In their literality, their avoidance of rhetorical flourish or cleverness with the dialogue format, Hall's procedures come to resemble the vast majority of utilitarian, predictable prose written in the seventeenth century.[7]

To appreciate Milton's tactics, it is important to understand that he refused to underestimate his opponent's skill at conventional modes of disputation and realized that surpassing Hall would require versatility and considerable energy. Milton adopts in the *Animadversions* the debate format popularized by Martin Marprelate in the 1580s.[8] The verbal ingenuity and satiric sophistication of the Marprelate idiom offered him several advantages that Hall's traditional discourse did not allow the Bishop. Martin had often employed a literal exegetical mode against the Elizabethan prelates, and Milton does the same against Hall; abundant exegetical clarification and qualification prove Milton to be as capable a disputant as his opponent was. He also follows Marprelate by outflanking Hall's repetitive strategies, turning to wit and argumentative versatility in order to transcend the limits of normative polemic. Using the Marprelate mode for his own purposes, Milton demonstrates that he can reshape the traditional idiom of debate, that he can entertain as well as address public, doctrinal issues. The following selection typifies Milton's practice:

Answ. Wee see you are in choler, therefore till you coole a while wee turne to the ingenious Reader. . . . They are accus'd by him of uncharitable falshood, whereas their onely crime hath beene that they have too credulously thought him if not an overlogicall, yet a well-meaning man . . . for say *Remonstrant*.[9]

The Marprelate dramatic fiction of dialogue sustains the illusion that Milton controls Hall by revising his position until it is amenable to clever rebuttal, flippancy, and frivolity.[10] Milton deftly maneuvers Hall through editorial shaping and selective quoting in order to mock his victim, much as Marprelate had done to his antagonists. Through Martinist tactics, Milton becomes a creator who transforms Hall's pamphlet into a protodramatic script. As soon as the preface to the *Animadversions* ends, he plunges the reader into Hall's text abruptly, as though he were announcing the entrance of a dramatic character: "But now he begins" (YP I, p. 664). Here Milton displays another form of entertaining textual inventiveness:

Re.   Thus their cavills concerning *Liturgy* are vanish't.
Answ. You wanted but *Hey-passe* to have made your transition like a mysticall
         man of *Sturbridge*. (YP I, p. 692)

The allusion to vanishing and the jugglers at Sturbridge characterizes Milton's sharp, unpredictable wit, his power to mold the Remonstrant's tracts into an associative series of jibes and rejoinders (YP I, p. 692 n.2). Since the reader does not know what passage will be selected next or how Milton will treat it, the *Animadversions* generates a dramatic suspense. In situations such as the ones under discussion, Milton's comic dialogue provides a quasi-literary alternative to his opponent's unrelievedly serious polemic. The following instance suggests that Milton was sometimes able to achieve a sort of comic continuity with his wit:

Remonst. Hitherto they have flourish't, now I hope they will strike.
Ans.   His former transition was in the faire about the Jugglers, now he is at
            the *Pageants* among the Whifflers. (YP I, p. 697).

The jousting allusion recalls "the pageants and the whifflers who keep the way clear for a procession" (YP I, p. 697 n.1). This illustration was taken from a series of allusions, all of which associate the Remonstrant with the carnivalesque. Collectively, such references shape a protofictive comic plot by suggesting the continuity and consistency of Milton's strategy and by illustrating that he does not merely repeat the same jest but instead works imaginative variations on a theme. If Hall's disputative tactics were primarily utilitarian, even in his occasional sneering challenges to the Smectymnuan position or sarcastic rejoinders, Milton's are both instructive and capable of evoking "grim laughter." He counters the Bishop's occasional taunts with an extensive satiric fiction buttressed by a detailed apologia. Milton's innovative efforts to sophisticate and expand his attack with fictive and dramatic devices make Hall's formulaic habits seem static by contrast.

The thorough process of differentiation from Hall and his values also characterizes Milton's attack on his opponent's reputation as a Senecan stylist and a man of letters. The *Animadversions* reveals that Milton had studied Hall's idioms from an aesthetic perspective unusual among seventeenth-century tract writers. He mentions Hall's meditations, and his allusions to Hall's *Mundus Alter et Idem* (1605) indicate that he had a Latin copy at hand and did not depend upon Healey's English translation.[11] Milton's wordplay and mimicry are so integral to his aesthetic referendum on Hall that he becomes literary critic and satirist at once. Hall's tracts against the Smectymnuans, of course, provide many examples of the Senecan mode he had popularized. In this instance Milton takes satirical note of Hall's stylistic preferences:

Remonst. I doe gladly fly to the barre.
Ans. To the barre with him them. Gladly you say. (YP I, p. 666)

He mocks Hall with a terse verbal reenactment of his style, evoking that style only to deny it by sardonically agreeing with Hall's proposal, but in fewer words than Hall had used, and parsing the originally short statement into one that is not only clipped but, in context, parodic. The same stylistic parody recurs throughout the *Animadversions*, reminding the reader that Milton can easily turn one of Hall's most characteristic verbal mannerisms against him.[12] Milton makes reference as well to Hall's *Characters of Vertues and Vices* (1608), possibly the Bishop's most easily recognized literary idiom, one which he was widely credited with inventing. The *Characters* featured a series of pithy aphorisms which encapsulated a succinct moral message. Milton provides his own version of the antithetical, sententious mode of the *Characters* in the following exchange with the Remonstrant:

Remon. Brethren whiles yee desire to seeme Godly, learne to be less malitious.
Ans. *Remonstrant,* till you have better learnt your principles of Logick, take not upon you to be a Doctor to others.
. . . .
Remon. If Episcopacy have yoked Monarchy, it is the Insolence of the Persons, not the fault of the Calling.
Ans. It was the fault of the persons, and of no Calling, we doe not count Prelatry a Calling. (YP I, p. 673)

Milton's satirical *sententiae* mimic the abbreviated moral description and advice omnipresent in the *Characters*, with the result that the reader can easily recall a familiar literary idiom while examining the doctrinal matters at issue. The literary subtext of the exchange seems fairly direct: reenacting and reversing Hall's idiom allow Milton to turn against the Bishop the very genre which had gained fame for him. Milton acquires a dual advantage with this sort of mocking and punning. He evokes the Marprelate tradition, a familiar subject of literary and theological dispute at the very time when Hall published his verse satires, *Virgidemiarum*, in 1597. A Martinist revival in the 1640s, moreover, coincided with the conflict over Hall's episcopal pamphlets.[13] Milton's historical recognition of Hall's repu-

tation and his selection of an appropriate mode of parodic deflation enhance his creative-critical ethos.

The aesthetic referendum on Hall includes frequent reference to
Virgidemiarum, the collection of verse which had critically assessed contemporary Elizabethan poetic genres. Milton turns the tables with his
evaluation of the satiric medium Hall claimed to have pioneered. In a
postscript to *Virgidemiarum*, Hall had conceded that the targets and language of his attack were somewhat remote, observing that a "true and
naturall Satyre" will be "both hard of conceipt, and harsh of stile."[14] If Hall
had cultivated a recondite obscurity, Milton's wrath seems a good deal
clearer and more direct:

How can wee therefore expect sound Doctrine . . . from any covetous, and
honour-hunting *Bishop* that shall plead so stiffly for [money and worldly posses-
sions], while St. *Paul* thus exhorts, every *Bishop: But thou O man of God flye
these things.* As for the just policie . . . and those many Lawes which you say have
conferr'd these benefits upon you, it hath been nothing else but the superstitious
devotion of *Princes* and great men that knew no better, or the base importunity of
begging *Friers*, haunting and harassing the deathbeds of men departing this life in
a blind and wretched condition of hope to merit Heaven for the building of
Churches, Cloysters, and *Covents.* (YP I, p. 702)

The preface to the *Animadversions* had cited the need for an unambiguous
attack on impediments to salvation. Here Milton aims directly at substantive moral issues, and his satire parts company with Hall's because it strikes
at lofty targets: prelatical corruption and the delusions of tradition. Again
he defines himself in opposition to Hall, this time by demonstrating that his
reaction to moral outrage is a lucid, scathing indignation quite distinct from
the oblique, sometimes quibbling petulance voiced by the speaker of *Virgidemiarum*.[15] Though Milton implicitly evaluates the defects of Hall's satires as a critic might, he nevertheless maintains a creator's sensitivity to audience and its needs by varying the tenor of his own attack from indirection,
curt wit, and reversal, to lengthy, zealous denunciation, and back again.

As an alternative to Hall's preference for aphorisms, Milton provides
a metaphorical, visionary style of celebration illustrated in the lengthy
prayer of the *Animadversions:*

Thou has made our false *Prophets* to be found a lie in the sight of all the people. . . . Who is there that cannot trace thee now in thy beamy walke through the
midst of thy Sanctuary, amidst those golden *candlesticks*, which have long suffer'd
a dimnesse amongst us through the violence of those that had seiz'd them, and
were more taken with the mention of their gold then of their starry light; teaching

the doctrine of *Balaam* to cast a stumbling-block before thy servants, commanding them to eat things sacrifiz'd to Idols, and forcing them to fornication. (YP I, pp. 705–06)

The figurative devices of the passage, primarily assonance, consonance, alliteration, and allusion, contribute to an apocalyptic majesty very nearly poetic and certainly remote from Hall's literal, abbreviated Senecanisms. With imagery which recalls the Book of Revelation, Milton's style magnifies and dramatizes the vast significance of the moral issues under consideration. Milton's strategies in the *Animadversions*, then, point to a sophistication and an aesthetic perception not evident in Hall's tracts, for not only did Milton outflank Hall by working variations on the very polemical tactics Hall had favored, but he displayed a creator's awareness that satire might engage the reader more fully, might strengthen the satirist's ethos by articulating options to that which he parodies.

The anonymous pamphleteer who challenged the *Animadversions* with *A Modest Confutation* (1642) showed himself to be familiar with the matters of doctrine and discipline under dispute and alert to flaws in Milton's position, notably Milton's selective attribution of the faults of all prelates to the Humble Remonstrant.[16] The Confuter combined a logician's analytical skill with a broad vocabulary and an extensive range of literary and philosophical references, to the extent that Milton considered him worthy of a detailed answer. As though he had recognized the dramatic strategies and aesthetic subtexts of the *Animadversions*, the Confuter compares Milton to Marprelate: "*Martin Mar-Prelate* . . . is in the disgrace of our *Clergie* cited by the Papists, as a grave unquestionable Authour: and what place your *Animadversions* may once have in the Vaticane, is yet dubious" (p. 32). Continuing to engage Milton on literary grounds, he dismisses him as a mere libeler on several occasions, but in the process raises the question of the proper language of religious dispute. The Confuter introduces the issues of aesthetic motive and persona when he charges that "private and personall spleen . . . is the greatest matter" in the *Animadversions* (p. 5), and then insists that Milton had donned a "bright and new-varnisht *Modona* vizard" (p. 34) to mask his inner ugliness. He rebukes Milton's creative-critical ethos and aesthetic standards by calling him a "carping Poetaster" (p. 9), cautioning that only a "Critick" can be a "competent Judge of a terse Poeme" (p. 23). His claim that "envie and anger" befool Milton establishes a simplified characterization of him not unlike the raging satyr figure of Elizabethan satiric literature (p. 36).

To rebut the Confuter, Milton often speaks in a homiletic voice on the central themes of the prelatical controversy, thereby demonstrating his

understanding of the formulaic tactics and refutational demands of polemic. The *Modest Confutation,* however, offered many more direct opportunities for artistic deliberation than Hall's exegetical pamphlets had,
and he took full advantage of the occasion for reflective literary criticism.
Despite Milton's inability to confirm the *Modest Confutation's* authorship, the tenor of the Confuter's arguments and his detailed explanation of
Hall's toothless satire (pp. 9–11) made Hall himself a likely candidate, or
at least a privileged consultant. When Milton refers in *An Apology* to the
"big and blunted fame of his elder adversary" and promises to look on him
"at home, where I may finde him in the proper light of his owne worth"
(YP I, p. 869), he announces a higher priority than certainty of authorship,
namely his intention to employ Hall's reputation as a means of literary
clarification and self-definition. Such references also begin to generate an
aesthetic ethos of historical, critical, intellectually comprehensive authority, one which Milton's subsequent argument will consistently support, as
it does, for example, in his evaluation of Hall's *Mundus Alter et Idem,* a
fiction he considers ephemeral and morally directionless (YP I, p. 880).
Milton cites several works generically similar but intellectually superior to
Hall's, notably "*Plato in Critias,* and our two famous countrymen, the one
in his *Utopia,* the other in his *new Atlantis*"; More and Bacon, unlike Hall,
"chose . . . to display the largenesse of their spirits by teaching this our
world better and exacter things" (YP I, p. 881). This measurement of
Mundus in the literary context of the Utopian travel narrative indicates
that Milton's knowledge of both history and genre transcends that of an
ignorant, "carping Poetaster" and denies the Confuter's charge that "envie
and anger" reduce him to the literarily provincial. The Confuter gave
Milton another opening when he complained that the *Animadversions*
was a "*mime thrust forth upon the stage to make up the breaches of those
solemne Scenes between the Prelats and the Smectymnuans*" (YP I, p.
879). Milton responds with sarcastic conjectures about a mime and the
observation, "Nor yet doth he tell us what a Mime is, whereof we have no
pattern from ancient writers except some fragments, which containe many
acute and wise sentences" (YP I, p. 879). His subsequent definitions taken
from Laertius and Scaliger, together with his proof that the *Animadversions* cannot be a mime according to the more relevant theoretical positions, strengthen his ethos and give the Confuter a literary comeuppance.
When he accused Milton of being a "grim, lowring, bitter fool" (sig. A3),
the opponent had introduced the matter of persona. Milton replies that he
considered himself "to be now not as mine own person, but as a member
incorporate into that truth whereof I was perswaded" (YP I, p. 871), and
mockingly reiterates his point when he reminds the Confuter that "the

author is ever distinguisht from the person he introduces" (p. 880). Granted, Milton does not consistently distinguish his own voice from those of his pamphlet's various personae, but he reasonably contends that the *Animadversions* contains considerable variation and complexity, that it at least has literary qualities. A response of this sort demeans the Confuter with its implication that sophisticated considerations of voice simply do not apply to his tract.

The most significant opportunity for self-definition grows out of Milton's suspicion that the Confuter had been attempting to describe him by means of "odde ends which from some penurious Book of Characters he had been culling out and would faine apply" (YP 1, pp. 882–83). I would argue that the personal digression of *An Apology* may be read as a literary reaction to what Milton considered the generic defects of the Character. Contemporary theory holds that the Character has a "severely limited framework," that it is a "highly artificial form" with certain repetitive formulas. [17] Milton's digression attacks the Character from a similar perspective, providing an aesthetic referendum on the genre. He counters the abstract, abbreviated, speculative quality of the Character by citing his academic and aesthetic reputation, one which can be substantiated by public letters and documents, transforming his aesthetic ethos into a verifiable proposition, not an abstract or theoretical invention. The digression works as a deliberate antidote to the generic limitations of the Character, an idiom given to compression and snippets of sententious moral wisdom. Milton's full literary pedigree transcends clichés, platitudes, and aphorisms, the conventional wisdom the Confuter had implied about the anonymous author of the *Animadversions*. A blending of oratorical, critical, and autobiographical elements, the digression is very much the opposite of a Character. Where the Confuter had tossed out speculation, Milton cites fact; against the Confuter's generalizations, he offers rich detail; the atypical combination of personal and literary qualifications Milton refers to offsets the Character's tendency to reduce to the stereotypical. He has turned the Confuter's attempted Characterization into an alternative form of values clarification and a device for extrapolating a uniquely significant agenda.

Milton shows equal enthusiasm for measuring his opponent's notions of satire. He purports to have read the "sixth Satyr of [Hall's] Second book," a direct reference to *Virgidemiarum*, verifying his ethos by quoting directly from the passage in question (YP I, p. 915). He doubts the efficacy of toothless satires, dismissing them as "toothlesse teeth" (YP I, p. 916). Hall's definition of satire was contradictory, Milton concludes, because his creative-critical ethos was weak. An artist who "would be counted *the first*

English Satyr" could have "learnt better among the Latin, and Italian Satyrists, and in our own tongue from the *vision and Creed of Pierce plowman"* (YP I, pp. 915–16). Literary context again serves as satirical rejoinder, and Milton exploits his opponent's incoherent definition when he provides a clearer one: "For a Satyr as it was borne out of a *Tragedy*, so ought to resemble his parentage, to strike high, and adventure dangerously at the most eminent vices among the greatest persons" (YP I, p. 916). After deconstructing Hall's thesis, Milton tries to avoid the pitfalls of theory by establishing a reference point to be used when the reader considers Milton's treatment of his own target, a powerful bishop and the entrenched institution supporting him, so that a literary alternative fills the aesthetic void created by the negation of Hall's position.

Before finishing with Hall, Milton ridicules him for blunders in genre and decorum for which any competent artist should be culpable: "[The Confuter's] ninth Section is spent in mournfull elegy, certaine passionat soliloquies, and two whole pages of intergatories that praise the Remonstrant even to the sonetting of *his fresh cheeks, quick eyes, round tongue, agil hand, and nimble invention"* (YP 1, p. 928). Not only does Milton imply that the Confuter misunderstands generic conventions and cannot control them, but his mockery recalls Hall's own attack on popular Elizabethan poetic forms in his first satire.[18] Hall had invoked the critical principles of decorum, genre, the unities, and verisimilitude to support that attack.[19] The generic blurriness Milton points to in the *Modest Confutation* cannot fail to be comic, a literary "hotchpotch." Milton repays Hall in his own coin with an ironic subtextual reversal. The jest is obvious, yet a substantive concern underlies it: Milton suggests that inept art must be exposed by those who understand the principles of higher art, because such imposture can be dangerously deceptive as well as ludicrous. Milton's creative-critical ethos, in effect, extends well beyond mimicry and a talent for reversals into a polished familiarity with art's profound effects and powers.

III

When he accepted the Commonwealth's charge to answer Charles I's *Eikon Basilike* in 1649, Milton again used a polemic occasion for aesthetic deliberation. He realized that the *Eikon* depended heavily upon a "fictional character with an emotional rhetorical appeal."[20] Though the artistic merits of the king's book struck him as dubious at best, he was forced to acknowledge the popularity of a work which went through thirty-five editions in English by the end of 1649 and was destined to become one of the seventeenth century's most widely recognized texts.[21] John Gauden, probably the primary author of the *Eikon,* was anything but a literary professional, yet his phenomenal success, and the nature of that success, prompted Milton to assess his own literary motives and goals.

The *Eikon Basilike* drew upon literary or quasi-literary conventions and genres instead of the traditional formula of doctrinal debate and textual exegesis. Several primary images of the monarch unify the *Eikon* and evoke the historical circumstances of his execution. Charles either presents himself as a martyr, "warrior," ruler, and "rebel" or works plausible variations on these themes. Each of the four images derives from heroic prototypes deeply embedded in popular culture and mythology.[22] The king's autobiographical reminiscences of the Civil War and his role in it, essentially Foxean reworkings of medieval hagiography, end with a prayer or meditation designed to illustrate his martyrlike qualities. Despite the fact that Charles was a generally inept warrior who could not credibly provide the heroic chronicle of a soldier that Fairfax, Cromwell, and Ludlow could, he seems intent on being perceived as a military figure, albeit a reluctant and now defeated and penitent one, who led his army in a just cause and who suffers at the hands of barbaric enemies. His repeated professions of devotion to his kingdom often recall knightly oaths of fealty and thus an ancient heroic tradition. Moreover, Charles loses no opportunity to assert the historically persuasive fact that, despite his present circumstances, he remains king by divine right, and therefore stands disdainfully above the usurping parliamentary law which has brought him to trial. Clearly, the king cannot be an "outlaw," but he can very well be a "rebel" in his own way, as much a rebel as those who tried him, a royal prisoner whose assertion of kingly principles necessarily contradicts those of his momentarily victorious antagonists. The *Eikon* makes no direct references to the king's trial, yet contemporary accounts of his behavior add a folklorish quality to the text. Nancy Klein MaGuire describes Charles as alert to the theatrical possibilities of his own defense.[23] Mocking the judicial procedures of the court, Charles confirmed his status as rebel, a defiant character who did not break under the pressure imposed by his enemies. The *Eikon* capitalizes repeatedly upon the benefits the king derived from being both ruler and rebel, aggressor and victim. The closing chapters of the *Eikon,* finally, confirm earlier clues that it was intended as a royal conduct book, one which offers enough counsel and caution to evoke another familiar image of the ruler, that of Solomon-figure.[24]

The histrionic circumstances of the king's trial, though anecdotal, reinforce the nature of his text as a performance, a series of soliloquies and internal theatrics.[25] Charles the martyr indulges in bombast and blatant melodramatic exaggeration, particularly in his meditations. Yet his account cannot be characterized as totally introspective and self-glorifying, for Charles links himself in various ways with a broader historical context. He favors the image of apocalypse, referring often to "that cloud which was soon after to overspread the whole kingdom and cast all into disorder and darkness" (p. 34). His own values, the Book of Common Prayer and the historical tradition of royal authority among them, represent an established, conventional world order, one which had provided peace and stability dramatically unlike the anxiety and political restlessness which swirled about as his memoir reached its audience.

Since his persona was shaped around the heroic prototypes of martyr, warrior, sage ruler, and rebel, the monarch had devised a particularly appealing piece of "popular" political literature, popular because it is essentially conservative, focusing on the ruler's "innate goodness."[26] In addition to evoking conventional heroic images and a traditional world view, as most earlier Renaissance popular political literature had done, the *Eikon* seemed destined to please a wide readership for several additional reasons. Charles presented himself as knightly, a hero in an unjustly persecuted cause, and by so doing appealed to general popular enthusiasm for "chivalric stories."[27] Moreover, his confessional format and pathetic appeal, his creation of a familial persona helps to bridge the gap between common readers and "the world of their political masters," a world which was ordinarily "infinitely remote."[28] Thus, royal propaganda can be read as a form of personal contact between the monarch and his subjects, a topic of popular fascination.[29] Formulaic political theorizing and intellectual debate, in contrast, would likely not have shortened the cultural distance between Charles and his audience. Finally, the king's book would be prized as a personal memoir of a culture at least temporarily suspended by the revolution: Charles's autobiographical performance in the *Eikon Basilike* would allow his text, its blatant sentimentality notwithstanding, to fill the political vacuum his execution had created. The aesthetic lapses passed over by the *Eikon*'s many admirers, however, quickly caught Milton's attention and he considered them at length in *Eikonoklastes*. The opening pages of the tract define the polarities of his strategy, one which confronts the public issues at stake and their personal ramifications for Milton, the historical and aesthetic dimensions of the regicide controversy. At its most fundamental level, his refutation is not satiric, dealing as it does with facts, the historical record, and episodes of the Civil War fairly familiar to the nation, seemingly intending to set the record straight, or at least to consider fundamental questions on the public's mind. Milton refutes with a traditional polemic idiom, using forthright logic and a plain style in sharp contrast to the sentimentalism and hyperbole of Charles. This rational and plain presentation constitutes an alternative to Charles's worldview, an antidote which appeals to external evidence rather than internal perception.[30] Decorum affected Milton's choice of format: Charles had not written the sort of exegetical tome which Milton could mock as he had mocked Hall's. He needed objectivity to do battle with the ruler's indulgent, effusive "I," and a scholarly, conventional polemic medium permitted him to differentiate himself from Charles through less personal tactics.

Milton's preface points out that royalists had seized upon the "advantage of [Charles's] Book . . . to . . . either falsly or fallaciously [represent] *the state of things*" (YP III, p. 338; italics mine). As a countermeasure, he supposes it "a good deed rather to the living, if by better information giv'n them . . . they may be kept from entring the third time unadvisedly into Warr and bloodshed" (YP III, p. 338–39). These remarks cast Milton in the role of public historian confronting a crucial matter of worldview. To make his case, he invokes conventional political wisdom and obvious evidence against Charles. Thus, when refuting the king's claim that "*He call'd this last Parlament . . . by his own chois and inclination*" (YP III, p. 350), Milton supports his own assertion that such a claim is inaccurate with several pages of careful historical documentation.[31] He repeatedly counters Charles's meditative afterthoughts with a commonsense empiricism: "But to prove his inclination to Parlaments, he affirms heer *To have always thought the right way of them, most safe for his Crown, and best pleasing to his People.* What hee thought we know not; but that hee ever took the contrary way wee saw" (YP III, p. 356). He employs a principle of reversal, trying on this and many other occasions to objectify, to turn outward the inward-looking dramatic script of the royal meditation. Milton discredits some of Charles's prayers in the same way, insisting that the king's acts led to pervasive suspicion about his words. In effect, he frequently converts the quotation and reply format of polemic into a strategy of historical fact-finding which presents his audience with a reconstruction of recent political activity and with interpretive conclusions that a reader in search of the truth must at least consider. Such tactics, of course, sharply differentiate Milton's version of events from that of Charles.

The process of reversal which Milton employed to correct the distorted historical perspective of the *Eikon Basilike* extends into his attack on the aesthetic principles of Charles's text. Milton's preface claims that he will "read" the *Eikon Basilike*, noting that the king has "left behind him this Book as the best advocat and interpreter of his own actions" (YP III, p. 340). In so doing, Charles has elicited the powers and liberties of

Milton's ethos as creator-critic, giving him an aesthetic charge, an obligation to measure the *Eikon Basilike* by artistic criteria. The publication of
Milton's *Poems* in 1645 had secured his ethos: by 1649 he was the Commonwealth government's most accomplished and visible poet, who no
longer needed to justify himself and predict future accomplishment. Essential to Milton's satiric strategies are several aesthetic issues which the
success of the king's book had called to his attention.[32] Art and its motives,
processes, standards, and audience are not only unifying satiric metaphors
in *Eikonoklastes*, but reflective devices whereby Milton can assess his
own role as controversialist.

David Loewenstein has demonstrated Milton's reversal of Charles's
tragic theatrical tropes into comic ones and his claims to legitimate authority into tyrannical posturing.[33] In addition to this extensive parody of
dramatic tropes, Milton critiques the artistic integrity, genre, decorum,
and fictive verisimilitude of the king's book. Not only will Milton fictively
treat the king as if he were alive, but he will assume that Charles was the
actual author of the *Eikon*, though he knew that other hands were involved. As it did in the Smectymnuan controversy, when he attributed *A
Modest Confutation* to Hall, this strategy suggests Milton's enthusiasm for
examining carefully the literary tactics of an opponent's text as opposed to
the more precise yet impersonal question of authorship. By deconstructing and revising the monarch's book, Milton could more easily expose his pseudoart and its dark, seductive powers. Charles cannot succeed, Milton contends, because he misunderstands the literary idioms he
attempts to use; for example, "quaint Emblems and devices begg'd from
the old Pageantry of some Twelf-nights entertainment at *Whitehall*, will
doe but ill to make a Saint or Martyr" (YP III, p. 343). Aware of the king's
desire to be perceived as a martyr, Milton not only calls the genres of
martyrology and hagiography into question, but implies that dramatic and
masquing techniques, combined with the flair for the histrionic and melodramatic in Charles, defeat the monarch's own intentions. The king, of
course, lacks the integrity of an artist, for one of his successes was to "putt
Tyranny into an Art" (YP III, p. 344). Charles merely impersonates an
artist for the false motive of political gain; his "Art" abuses the very concept of art.

Milton directs a considerable amount of his aesthetic deconstruction
at the royal prayers and meditations. Denouncing those prayers as a
"privat Psalter" yet one which was published, Milton tries again to refute
Charles's claims to saintly martyrdom (YP III, p. 360). He labels Charles
as a pharisaic exhibitionist, the antithesis of the self-denying martyr, by
turning outward the inner drama of the king's meditations, thereby expos-

ing that drama as a fundamental violation of the decorum of personal prayer. Later, Milton questions the king's use of the Psalms and his attempted comparison of himself to David: Charles had appropriated "presumptuously the words and protestations of *David,* without the spirit and conscience of *David*" (YP III, pp. 381–82). This intimation of discrepancies points up another aesthetic shortcoming—Charles cannot appreciate the essential artistic harmony of inner self and outer image because a pseudoartist cannot see past externals. In a related case, when he claims that the king's "Homily hath more of craft and affectation in it, then of sound Doctrin" (YP III, p. 482), Milton makes a critic's identification of genre and then notes both the irony and the blasphemy of a religious idiom turned to purposes of deception and disruption.

Charles managed as well to commit a fairly wide range of other literary offenses, all of which illustrate his comprehensive failure as an artist. He praises the Earl of Strafford lavishly in language which, as Milton points out, falls short because Charles "with Scolastic flourishes beneath the decencie of a King, compares him to *the Sun,* which in all figurative use, and significance beares allusion to a King, not to a Subject" (YP III, p. 372). This verdict discredits the king's basic processes of internalizing and assimilating the raw materials at his disposal. Charles has created a fiction of Strafford's worth from evident public fact, but it remains an indecorous, deceptive fiction since, in Milton's view, Charles allowed Strafford to be punished for crimes for which the monarch was the "chiefe Author" (YP III, p. 372). Later, Milton takes exception to the king's "fansie," his faculties of perception and imagination: "It being now no more in his hand to be reveng'd on his opposers, he seeks to satiat his fansie with the imagination of som revenge upon them from above" (YP III, p. 563), with the implication that the king's creative faculties have finally been corrupted beyond hope. Charles is less than a hack—he is an idle babbler, wildly fantastic, probably demented. Charles's ineptitude had always pointed to a fundamental incoherence, and now that incoherence dominates his vision. The king cannot meet the artist's obligation to express truth more profound than mere facts. Before offering this negative rationale, however, Milton has worked extensively to make it credible.

He speculates early on, "I begun to think that the whole Book might perhaps be intended a peece of Poetrie" (YP III, p. 406), calling attention to the *Eikon Basilike*'s lack of clear identity as an art form; the royal meditation seems a blur, a confused generic muddle, perhaps deliberately so. Milton continues, "I retract not what I thought of the fiction [that it was 'smooth and cleanly'], yet heer, I must confess, it lies too op'n" (YP III, p. 406). He cites historical information here to question Charles's fiction that he "*stai'd at White Hall till* [he] *was driven away by shame more than feare*" (YP III, p. 406). Since Charles lacks artistic skill and a sense of audience, he can do no more than shape what Milton sarcastically labels an "op'n" fiction, a lie, in short, and not a credible verisimilitude. Political context undercuts the verisimilitude of another kingly fiction: "He ascribes *Rudeness and barbarity worse then Indian* to the English Parlament, and *all vertue* to his Wife, in straines that come almost to Sonnetting" (YP III, pp. 420–21). The word "almost" again raises questions of genre and decorum—Charles substitutes sentimentality and rancor for the clarity and historical perception necessary to convince the reader of his fiction's truth. On other occasions, the king's intentions do not require critical deciphering, for they are plainly dishonest, for instance, when he invokes philosophy's principles "as masks and colours of injurious and violent deeds" (YP III, p. 413), an abuse of fiction for manipulative purposes.

Throughout *Eikonoklastes*, Milton reiterates the charge that inept, indecorous fictions follow inevitably from Charles's fundamental lack of artistic integrity. He observes that a certain section of the *Eikon* "was above his known stile and Orthographie, and accuses the whole composure to be conscious of som other Author" (YP III, p. 393). Suspect authorship indicts the king's pseudoart as an elaborate falsehood, one which might be expected from a morally dubious author. Referring to Charles's "borrowing" from the Psalms, Milton warns, "For such kind of borrowing as this, if it be not better'd by the borrower, among good Authors is accounted *Plagiarie*" (YP III, p. 547). Art here acts as a metaphor of the king's personal corruption, a corruption which underlies not only borrowing from the Bible, but a spectrum of literary offenses ranging from blatant theft to perversion of art's highest principles and powers. The monarch's distorted reading of historical events "declares it well to be a fals copy which he uses" (YP III, p. 564), and that "fals copy" points to deceit and internal decay. The king, however, is more than a mere plagiarist— his mutated versions of providential activity mark him as a blasphemer, an artist willing to falsify the divine message. Milton punctuates his distrust of royal integrity by reminding his readers of the ominous discrepancies hidden in the words of a false artist: "We know his meaning; and apprehend how little hope there could be of him from such language as this" (YP III, p. 431). Charles has turned language into a sophisticated medium of deceit; words themselves, truthful or at least neutral in the hands of others, are infected by his inner contamination.[34]

David Loewenstein has argued that Milton "casts down" and "refashions" the image of the king.[35] This refashioning is, I would suggest, another measure of Milton's creative powers. He capitalizes upon Charles's allusion to the Civil War and the chaos it unleashed to present an alternative tale of Charles as the demonic force responsible for the nation's trials. In refashioning the king, Milton sets his political behavior against his inner motives, sculpting a new character from the public record. With his allusion to "evasions [and] pretenses . . . in the mists and intricacies of State" (YP III, p. 382), Milton turns the king's mention of mists to another purpose and links him with a far more infamous ruler and rebel. When he reviews the king's early negotiations with Parliament and the army, Milton mentions that Charles repeatedly "tempts" his foes (YP III, pp. 383–84), constructing from historical details a satanic scenario of the king as a demonic presence looming over British history.[36] The capture of the royal letters by the army fits equally well into the satanic scenario when Milton describes the letters as full of "suttleties and mysterious arts in treating" (YP III, p. 538), an attempt to equate Charles with the powers of sorcery and the black arts. Imagery of disguise further refines the satanic portraiture. Of Charles's turning himself over to the Scots, Milton notes that "Providence was not couzen'd with disguises, neither outward nor inward" (YP III, p. 545), nor could the king expect to gain ground by slipping "out of op'n Warr into a new disguise" or by resorting to "the old circulating dance of his shifts and evasions" (YP III, p. 545). Here Milton plays on the archetypal image of Satan as a shape-shifter, a trickster of many false identities, one who summons a dark ritual, "the dance of his shifts and evasions." He connects Charles with the eventual characterization of Satan in heaven, finally, by means of two notations, that "*not evill Counselors*, but he himself hath been the Author of all our troubles" (YP III, p. 547), and that Charles "to himself was grown the most evil Counselor of all" (YP III, p. 549). Both evoke Satan's own rebellion, in which he was the primary culprit, and its sorry consequences for his followers. Each reference reverses the monarch's depictions of himself as a ruler and a divine-right rebel in a just cause.

Milton expends an equal amount of creative energy on forming an image of his audience and the truth about them, connecting that image with the pseudoart of the royal text in perhaps the most detailed assessment of audience in the prose. Milton's early perception of his readership oscillates between hope and doubt. He notes approvingly that the "general voice of the people almost [hissed Charles] and his ill-acted regality off the Stage" (YP III, p. 355), yet he must concede that the king has made his point, no matter how tyrannical his behavior: "By so strange a method amongst the mad multitude is a sudden reputation won" (YP III, p. 345). Irrespective of the shortcomings of Charles's rhetoric and his perversions of aesthetic ideals, Milton cannot dismiss the *Eikon Basilike*'s immense popularity and the implications of that popularity. His Jeremiac voice must acknowledge the power of diabolic pseudoart and articulate the bitter paradox that, although he may clearly state the truth, his words will largely fail to persuade. Yet even if the people deny the "magnifi'd wisdom of *Zorobabel*" (YP III, p. 585) and prove themselves no more than "inconstant, irrational, and Image-doting rabble" (YP III, p. 601), Milton can still justify his articulation of truth as the worthiest of goals. He incorporates the audience into his aesthetic scheme when he characterizes the English nation as an easily pacified lot who will settle for anything that can be construed as art, no matter how feeble a claim the text may make. Milton places his faith in "The rest, whom perhaps ignorance without malice . . . hath for the time misledd," the fit audience though few (YP III, p. 601).

Loewenstein maintains that Milton thought of the *Eikon Basilike* as a spiritually, emotionally, and intellectually "dead" text, but Milton's treatment of audience in *Eikonoklastes* suggests that his perception may be more subtle.[37] It is reasonable to conclude that he feared the king's book as a darkly powerful enticement with a demonic half-life and an enduring appeal for a broad audience. Milton might very well have considered his own iconoclasm as a "compelling means to effect historic redemption," but I would contend that the subtext of *Eikonoklastes* reads somewhat differently, that Milton had learned some hard lessons about artistic integrity and truth, and about his own aesthetic priorities.[38] *Eikonoklastes* can be interpreted as a referendum, an assessment of Milton's own critical sensibilities and values, his perception of audience, and of the limits of polemic persuasion. *Eikon Basilike* demonstrated the vast potency of popular genres, images, and stereotypes and the demands of the popular audience. Milton came to recognize the nature of such icons, but refused to succumb to them, for he realized that his responsibility was to the truth. The Jeremiac laments of *Eikonoklastes* record Milton's dismay at the inability of the people to appreciate and share his political vision and artistic criteria.

He discovered that the *Eikon Basilike* was a melodramatic popular romance with a particularly vexing irony: in light of its overwhelming appeal, the *Eikon*'s literary offenses testify to the power of art even in its bastardized form. Milton drew Charles's false aesthetic closer in order to evaluate and finally reject it. He now realized that he could not pander to the values of a "popular" audience and that a popular audience would almost certainly not grasp or support his arguments. Milton knew what a popular audience demanded in 1649—maudlin sentimentality, delusionary art, a false view of the past. He refused such demands. The process of self-definition in *Eikonoklastes* called for him to distance and liberate himself through distinct literary statements. With his admonitions, rationalizations, and oversimplifications, Charles had tried to play the Solomon-like ruler. Milton's dialectic exposes the king's proverbial lore as preposterous foolishness directly at odds with the public evidence of history. If the tragic posturing of the *Eikon* had encouraged engagement with and empathy for the suffering monarch, Milton's satirical reconstructions encourage an aesthetic distance from him. Milton's reading of the royal fable extends pathos into the pathetic. The ritualistic rhetoric of the reassuring and the traditional contained in the *Eikon* is countered by the paradoxical, unsettling version of the Civil War, the faults of the monarch, and the weaknesses of his subjects contained in *Eikonoklastes*. Whereas Charles had asked his readers to react emotionally and to bond with him, Milton calls for an analytical reading of history, an ironic interpretation of the royal fable, and a safe distance from its teller, all challenging demands. In making such demands, Milton came to appreciate popular art and popular literary tastes starkly different from his own values. Milton gained a recognition of aesthetic issues in 1649 that he did not possess when he debated Joseph Hall in 1641–42, and his aesthetic revaluation led to that recognition.

The interaction of political and literary agendas in the *Animadversions, An Apology,* and *Eikonoklastes,* then, calls attention to the sophisticated workings of Miltonic debate in the 1640s. The most significant way in which Milton's sensibilities as a polemicist exceed those of his opponents is his cultivation of historical occasions as opportunities for sustained aesthetic deliberation. But even these deliberations have a public side, for Milton carefully articulates historical, doctrinal, and literary alternatives for his audience. Each pamphlet, finally, is a fully developed exercise in literary self-definition through a dialectic of opposites. In the *Animadversions* and *An Apology* Milton records his objections to the obscurity and random quality of the late Elizabethan verse satire with which Hall was closely associated, and illustrates in both tracts his own critical position that "Satyr as it was borne out of a *Tragedy,* so ought . . . to strike high." His opposition to the aesthetic limitations of the Senecan style, his doubts about its appropriateness for celebration and exaltation generate a rationale for the elaborate, metaphorical periodicity which differentiates Milton's pamphlets from those of his contemporaries in the episcopal controversy. The most detailed critical commentary embedded in the debate with Hall, Milton's rebuttal of the Character, implies a weighing of the reductive tendencies of the aphoristic mode itself. Milton's critique makes clear that his literary sense of self derives from values quite distinct from those of the proverbial and the epigrammatic: plenitude, grandeur, the unique and not the formulaic. His attack on Hall's literary credentials was sharp, but Milton did not challenge the Bishop's aesthetic integrity in the same way that he challenged the king's in *Eikonoklastes*. With its shrewd evocations of the meditation, the romance, the conduct book, the knightly, and the familial, the *Eikon Basilike* represented to Milton the betrayal of art's highest powers in the interests of distortion, deceit, and popular appeal. He understood that answering Charles in kind meant denying his own principles. In 1649 definition by contraries meant an allegiance to austerity and the public record of the Civil War, but also an ironic, demanding, unsettling reading of historical events. If Milton could not subdue the "revolting counterpart" to his own aesthetic beliefs, he could at least refuse to imitate what he detested.[39]

The University of Akron

NOTES

1. Representative examples of historical and rhetorical scholarship include the following: Arthur Barker, *Milton and the Puritan Dilemma, 1641–1660* (Toronto, 1942); Christopher Hill, *Milton and the English Revolution* (New York, 1977); Thomas Kranidas, *The Fierce Equation: A Study of Milton's Decorum* (The Hague, 1965); Keith W. Stavely, *The Politics of Milton's Prose Style* (New Haven, 1975); Don M. Wolfe, *Milton in the Puritan Revolution* (New York, 1941).

2. A current version of the separatist argument can be found in Richard Helgerson, *Self-Crowned Laureates: Spenser, Jonson, Milton, and the Literary System* (Berkeley and Los Angeles, 1983), pp. 273–80.

3. Joan Webber, *The Eloquent "I": Style and Self in Seventeenth-Century Prose* (Madison, 1968), pp. 192–218.

4. Edward S. Le Comte, "*Areopagitica* as a Scenario for *Paradise Lost*," in *Achievements of the Left Hand: Essays on the Prose of John Milton*, ed. Michael Lieb and John T. Shawcross (Amherst, 1974), pp. 121–35; John F. Huntley, "The Images of Poet and Poetry in Milton's *The Reason of Church-Government*," p. 85; Michael Lieb, "Milton's *Of Reformation* and the Dynamics of Controversy," p. 56. After *Achievements of the Left Hand* had seconded the integrative argument in 1974, Miltonists continued to support the position in the 1980s. See, for example, Christopher Grose, *Milton and the Sense of Tradition* (New Haven, 1988), p. 27; and Thomas Kranidas, "Milton's *Of Reformation*: The Politics of Vision," *ELH* XLIX (1982), pp. 497–513.

5. David Loewenstein, *Milton and the Drama of History: Historical Vision, Iconoclasm, and the Literary Imagination* (Cambridge, 1990), p. 2; James Grantham Turner, "The Poetics of Engagement," in *Politics, Poetics, and Hermeneutics in Milton's Prose*, ed. Loewenstein and Turner (Cambridge, 1990), pp. 257–75.

6. Joseph Hall, *An Humble Remonstrance*, in *The Works of Joseph Hall*, 10 vols., ed. Philip Wynter (1863; rpt. New York, 1969), vol. IX, pp. 289–90.

7. See Thomas Kranidas, "Style and Rectitude in Seventeenth-Century Prose: Hall, Smectymnuus, and Milton," *HLQ* XLVI (1983), pp. 237–69, and Richard McCabe, "The Form and Methods of Milton's *Animadversions Upon the Remonstrants Defence Against Smectymnuus*," *ELN* XVIII (1981), pp. 266–72. Kranidas points to Hall's experience and expertise as a disputant, while McCabe illustrates Milton's familiarity with the Bishop's tactics in *A Common Apologie* (1610). McCabe correctly contends that the *Animadversions* was "a deliberate attempt to turn Hall's weapons against himself" (p. 266). My subsequent argument will demonstrate how pervasive Milton's strategies of reversal are in both the *Animadversions* and *An Apology*. He sought not merely to match the episcopal champion, but to transcend and thus confound him with a broad array of devices.

8. James Egan, "Milton and the Marprelate Tradition," in *Milton Studies VIII*, ed. James D. Simmonds (Pittsburgh, 1975), pp. 103–21. Though modern scholarship typically portrays Hall as a hapless underdog in the Smectymnuan controversy, there is no indication that Milton considered him so. The preface to the *Animadversions*, of course, characterizes Hall's prelatical rhetoric as complex and dangerous.

9. *Complete Prose Works of John Milton*, 8 vols., ed. Don M. Wolfe et al. (New Haven, 1953–82), vol. I, pp. 693–94. Hereafter cited as *YP*.

10. Martin Marprelate's fictive tactics have also been discussed by Raymond A. Anselment, *"Betwixt Jest and Earnest": Marprelate, Milton, Marvell, Swift and the Decorum of Religious Ridicule* (Toronto, 1979), pp. 33–48. For an argument which parallels mine, see Thomas N. Corns, "New Light on the Left Hand: Contemporary Views of Milton's Prose Style," *Durham University Journal* XLI (1979–80), p. 178.

11. Richard McCabe, *Joseph Hall: A Study in Satire and Meditation* (Oxford, 1982), pp. 152, 338. See also YP I, p. 696 n.14.

12. See Thomas N. Corns, *The Development of Milton's Prose Style* (Oxford, 1982), p. 39. Corns concludes that the *Animadversions* contains an "atypical proportion of short sentences," a conclusion compatible with my position about Miltonic parody of Hall's abbreviated syntax.

13. Egan, pp. 106–07.

14. *The Poems of Joseph Hall*, ed. Arnold Davenport (Liverpool, 1969), p. 97.

15. Milton may have decided that Hall was a trifler because *Virgidemiarum* was so wide-ranging, from Elizabethan tragedy, to ostentatiousness, fashions and clothing, social mannerisms, and academic life. These and several other topics were treated in what Milton likely considered a nominal fashion.

16. *A Modest Confutation*, in William Riley Parker, *Milton's Contemporary Reputation* (1940; rpt. New York, 1971), p. 6. Future citation will be from this edition. For a full discussion of *A Modest Confutation*'s authorship, see Frank Livingstone Huntley, *Bishop Joseph Hall 1574–1656: A Biographical and Critical Study* (Cambridge, 1979), pp. 124–29. Huntley identifies Robert Dunkin as the author.

17. Ronald J. Corthell, "Joseph Hall's *Characters of Vertues and Vices:* A 'Novum Repertum,' " *SP* LXXVI (1979), p. 30; Benjamin Boyce, *The Theophrastan Character in England to 1642* (Cambridge, Mass., 1947), pp. 19, 99.

18. Ejner J. Jensen, "Hall and Marston: The Role of the Satirist," *Satire Newsletter* IV (1967), p. 73.

19. Ronald J. Corthell, "Beginning as a Satirist: Joseph Hall's *Virgidemiarum Six Bookes*," *SEL* XXIII (1983), p. 56.

20. Joan S. Bennett, "God, Satan, and King Charles: Milton's Royal Portraits," *PMLA* XCII (1977), p. 441.

21. *Eikon Basilike: The Portraiture of His Sacred Majesty in His Solitudes and Sufferings*, ed. Philip A. Knachel (Ithaca, 1966), p. xv. Future citation will be from this edition.

22. Peter Burke, *Popular Culture in Early Modern Europe* (New York, 1978), p. 150.

23. Nancy Klein MaGuire, "The Theatrical Mask/Masque of Politics: The Case of Charles I," *Journal of British Studies* XXVIII (1989), pp. 1–22.

24. Burke, p. 151.

25. Richard Helgerson, "Milton Reads the King's Book: Print, Performance, and the Making of a Bourgeois Idol," *Criticism* XXIX (1987), p. 9.

26. Bernard Capp, "Popular Literature," in *Popular Culture in Seventeenth-Century England*, ed. Barry Reay (London, 1985), pp. 210–11.

27. Capp, p. 206.

28. Bruce Boehrer, "Elementary Structures of Kingship: Milton, Regicide, and the Family," *Milton Studies* XXIII, ed. James D. Simmonds (Pittsburgh, 1987), pp. 97–117. See also Capp, p. 209.

29. Capp, p. 209.

30. For a more complete analysis of the plain style of the regicide tracts, see Corns, *The Development of Milton's Prose Style*, pp. 87–89, and "Milton's Prose," in *The Cambridge Companion to Milton*, ed. Dennis Danielson (Cambridge, 1989), p. 194.

31. Timothy J. O'Keeffe, "The Imaginal Structure of John Milton's *Eikonoklastes*," *Ball State University Forum* XI (1971), p. 35. As O'Keeffe notes, historical documentation is omnipresent in the tract.

32. Cf. Loewenstein, *Milton and the Drama of History*, pp. 51–73. Loewenstein also examines some of the complex aesthetic implications of Milton's position. My own argument supports his, but its direction differs.

33. Loewenstein, pp. 60–70.

34. See Lana Cable, "Milton's Iconoclastic Truth," in *Politics, Poetics, and Hermeneutics in Milton's Prose*, pp. 135–51, for a full analysis of the idols of metaphors and words Milton confronted in *Eikonoklastes* and the semantic implications of such idols. We share several premises, but our analyses differ.

35. Loewenstein, pp. 67–73.

36. Cf. Bennett, "God, Satan, and King Charles," pp. 446–56. Though I generally concur with Bennett's detailed tracing of satanic prefigurations in Charles, I consider Milton's use of diabolic allusions as a counterthrust to the king's rebel allusions in *Eikon Basilike*. Milton, in short, creatively extrapolates the rebel image into the satanic.

37. Loewenstein, p. 61. The *Eikon Basilike* clearly lacked the animistic spirit Milton had praised in *Areopagitica*, yet his meditation suggests that he had come to appreciate the dark energy which did animate the *Eikon*.

38. Loewenstein, p. 72. See also Ernest B. Gilman, *Iconoclasm and Poetry in the English Reformation: Down Went Dagon* (Chicago, 1986), pp. 152–54, and Corns, *The Development of Milton's Prose Style*, p. 103. Loewenstein and Gilman argue for the efficiency and power of iconoclastic rhetoric, while Corns cautions that Milton appears in 1649 to "recognize the relative powerlessness of the creative writer to influence events through the application of his art and the . . . limitations of creative and unorthodox prose in shaping the crisis in which he finds himself." My arguments support those of Corns.

39. Turner, "The Poetics of Engagement," in *Politics, Poetics, and Hermeneutics in Milton's Prose*, p. 266.

"ANOTHER ROME IN THE WEST?":
MILTON AND THE IMPERIAL REPUBLIC,
1654–1670

Andrew Barnaby

WHEN IN *Areopagitica* Milton asserts that even Adam's prelapsarian rationality was established upon the necessity of choosing ("for reason is but choosing"), he suggests that human reason is by its very nature a moral faculty as much as it is a cognitive one.[1] Deriving from the condition of human freedom which it alone can manifest, rational choice defines the possibility of obedience—both to God and to the law of reason itself—where obedience functions paradoxically as the sign of the workings of an active virtue that perfects the very meaning of freedom and rationality.[2] For Milton, of course, the redemptive possibilities contained in the workings of this *recta ratio* are not confined to the individual knower. Indeed, they function in a broader, collective context as well, where the private activity of rational choice affects the ethical and religious life of the community at large and even promises to help restore human polity to the providential order of history.[3]

Because the redemptive operations of reason necessarily take root within a communal context, decisions about the constitution of collective life, about actual or idealized forms of human political organization, themselves function as part of the working out of this providential order. Given Milton's concern with these matters, it is hardly surprising that his *Readie and Easie Way*, written on the eve of the Restoration in 1660, figures the debate over governmental settlement in moral terms. The tract, that is, rewrites the issue of settlement—an issue that had dogged the commonwealth since its inception—as a question of the very possibility of redemption, where right knowing and proper choosing in political matters are seen to carry a collective soteriological burden. Milton seeks to force this perspective on the reader by reducing the issue to its simplest terms; he therefore represents the decision about government as a choice between maintaining the commonwealth, and so aligning English political order with God's purposes for history, and restoring monarchy, and so returning England to a degenerate political status—to a kind of political idolatry—by which the conditions of human fallenness are perpetuated.

Early in the tract, Milton aptly sums up his sense of the absolute division between these positions—between godly and degenerate polities—with what seems to be the conflation of two gospel passages. In reviewing the people of England's righteous action in deposing Charles I, he notes that they had to make a choice between totally opposed alternatives: "we could not serve two contrary maisters, God and the king" (YP VII, p. 411).4 The primary biblical contrast Milton draws on here is adapted from Matthew vi, 24, where Christ says: "No man can serve two masters. He will either hate one and love the other or be attentive to one and despise the other. You cannot give yourself to God and money." In Christ's contrast, the opposing alternatives (God *or* money) make absolute, and mutually exclusive, claims upon their respective adherents. Milton adopts the conditions of choice set forth in this passage but applies them in the context of a second passage, one which posits a different kind of opposition: "Give to Caesar what is Caesar's, but give to God what is God's" (Matt. xxii, 21). Milton would certainly have delighted in the distinction made in this passage between the claims of God and the claims of human kings (or tyrants), and the tract draws much of its energy from the force of that distinction: to choose Caesar (or a restored Stuart king) is to refuse God as the proper master by which the political status both of England as a whole and of its individual members should be defined.

We might note, of course, that in this second passage the opposing claims, while quite distinct, are not mutually exclusive. Indeed it seems that politically speaking, in the gospels at least, one *can* serve two masters, both God and Caesar.5 Milton, however, uses the context of the second passage (a contrast between the claims of God and the claims of kings) but inscribes within it the conditions of choice (mutual exclusivity) set forth in the first. He suggests thereby that political action exists in the context of strictly demarcated alternatives, ones, moreover, defined by God. One cannot have a king and serve God as well, for, according to Milton's reading of scripture, what God demands of his people is a commonwealth (YP VII, pp. 424–25, 429, 449–50). Within the tract's larger argument, then, even as the conflation of passages urges the rejection of Caesar as a sign of one's acceptance of God as true political master, it also opens the door to a rather different claim: that to reject Caesar is necessarily to choose what is, in effect, an anti-Caesarean political settlement—the republic—as the manifestation of one's proper allegiance.

Godly rule and Roman-styled republicanism may at first seem like strange bedfellows. But, as we shall see in greater detail, Milton pursues the connection even further. For in the specific context of the *Readie and Easie Way* as well as in the broader context of his 1650s' republicanism, Milton's England is to manifest its allegiance to God by becoming "another Rome in the west." Milton employs this topos of the *translatio imperii* not only to figure the as yet unfulfilled imperial aspirations of the fledgling republic but also, and more crucially, to equate these aspirations with the more glorious mission of restoring godliness to history through the agency of the elect nation.[6] For Milton in the 1650s, ancient Rome is a compelling figure for his political agenda both because its imperial orientation can so easily be assimilated into Christianity's as well as England's own imperial ideologies and because this imperial vision—tied as it is to republican political organization—would seem to provide an effective counter to the resurgence of support for Stuart monarchy. The association of the English commonwealth with the ancient Roman republic functions, in short, as part of Milton's claim, itself bound inseparably to his personal aspirations to the Virgilian epic inheritance, that England is to be a central participant in, even the main catalyst to, an imperial design that can only have God, not the next Stuart, as its ruler.

This essay will be concerned, then, with Milton's use of republican Rome, understood as the exemplar of the imperial republic, to figure the redemptive promise of history as it is to be carried out through the agency of the English commonwealth. It will focus primarily on how Milton makes or, perhaps more accurately, *represents* this claim in relation to the issues of governmental settlement in the years of the Protectorate (especially in the year of its demise, 1660). But in the essay's final section we shall also explore Milton's response to the failure both of republican polity and of his own earlier epic vision in the wake of the Restoration. We shall find that in *Paradise Regained* Milton undercuts the very figural design he had set forth in the 1650s for England's imperial and his own poetic inheritance by representing Rome precisely as the wrong exemplar upon which to stake the claim of national election, the claim, that is, to serve as the primary vehicle to Providence's true imperial design.

I

Among the many derisive responses to the *Readie and Easie Way*, the anonymously penned *Censure of the Rota* was particularly insightful in recognizing how Milton's reframing of the governmental issue as a question of collective redemption had forced him to situate republican settlement within a providential (even millennial) framework that by 1660 had certainly lost much of its appeal. "You rest Scripture most unmercifully," its author commented, "to prove that though Christ said, His King-dome was not of this world, yet his Common-wealthe is."[7] Milton had left himself vulnerable to the charge because even while he scoffed at Christian monarchy's divine pretensions (rejecting, for example, monarchy's claim to represent God's kingdom by reminding his readers that "the kingdom of Christ our common King and Lord, is hid to this world" [YP VII, pp. 429; cf. John xviii, 36]), he sought to define the commonwealth as a special point of convergence between God's will and human history and even as the means to the realization of the promised kingdom. But despite his assertion of the godliness of the free commonwealth, the exact nature of the relation between republican polity and its own aspiration to embody history's providential design remained unclear.

In his magisterial work, *The Machiavellian Moment*, J. G. A. Pocock suggests that the conceptual distance between secular order and sacred time was one of the central difficulties facing virtually all revivals of classical republicanism in the Renaissance. Pocock notes that Italian humanist writers of the fifteenth and sixteenth centuries revived and adapted a vocabulary drawn from republican models of antiquity both alongside and as an alternative to a more dominant vocabulary of Christian, theocratic, and particularly monarcho-centered views of political order. According to Pocock,

the revival of Aristotelian [political] philosophy carried with it the problem of reconciling the Hellenic view that man was formed to live in a city with the Christian view that man was formed to live in communion with God; but it was only when the republic, in its particularity as Rome or Florence, claimed (for whatever reason) an autonomous history of its own that it began opening new gaps between the two schemes of values.[8]

The problem was perhaps especially acute for that body politic (like Milton's England of 1649–1660) trying to define itself in a way that rejected much of its own past. For the difference between the eternal and transcendent city of God and the mutable, sublunar city of man would at that moment be most visible and most vexing.

Milton's attempt in the *Readie and Easie Way* to rekindle anti-monarchical flames by asserting the English commonwealth's special claim to embody some godly order entangles him in just this traditional republican confusion over how to adjudicate the claims of these rival cities. The conceptual dilemma facing him is particularly apparent in a passage concerning how the threat of the Restoration exposes republican England's failure to live up to its godly promise:

[T]o creep back so poorly as it seems the multitude would to thir once abjur'd and detested thraldom of Kingship . . . not only argues a strange degenerate contagion suddenly spread among us fitted and prepar'd for new slaverie, but will render us a scorn and derision to all our neighbours. And what will they at best say of us and of the whole *English* name, but scoffingly as of that foolish builder, mentiond by our Saviour, who began to build a tower, and was not able to finish it. Where is this goodly tower of a Commonwealth, which the English boasted they would build to overshaddow kings, and be another *Rome* in the west? (YP VII, pp. 422–23)

Coming as it does in the midst of a call to his compatriots to present a united front against the tyrannical ambition of human kings, Milton's allusion to the tower of Luke xiv seems a bit misplaced. Christ's brief parable of the unfinished tower is intended as a harsh lesson of the cost of discipleship, for by it he seeks to force his listeners to consider the strength of commitment demanded of those who would truly follow him:

A great multitude accompanied him [Jesus]; and he turned and said to them, "If any one comes to me and does not hate his own father and mother and wife and children and brothers and sisters, yes, and even his own life, he cannot be my disciple. Whoever does not bear his own cross and come after me, cannot be my disciple. For which of you, desiring to build a tower, does not first sit down and count the cost, whether he has enough to complete it? Otherwise, when he has laid the foundation, and is not able to finish, all who see it begin to mock him, saying, 'This man began to build, and was not able to finish.' . . . So therefore, whoever of you does not renounce all that he has cannot be my disciple. Salt is good, but if salt loses its flavor what good is it for seasoning? It is fit for neither the soil nor the manure heap; it has to be thrown away." (Luke xiv, 25–35)

As James Holstun has recently remarked, this is "not the ideal text for encouraging the political solidarity of a disintegrating republican collective."[9] And we might add that not only does Christ address discipleship in distinctly private terms, going so far as to set the true disciple apart from communal participation, but he also seems to reject the idea of human community altogether, as if it were just one of the many worldly things that distract the true disciple from a proper concern with a decidedly otherworldly calling.

Milton's allusion to this passage certainly retains much of the moral fervor of Christ's challenge to would-be disciples. Nevertheless, its function in the *Readie and Easie Way* seems to work against the antiworldly, antipolitical intimations of the original. The recollection of the tower parable in Milton's tract emerges in a distinctly collective appeal: as Milton uses it, the tower serves as an analogy "of a Commonwealth," and not of a private moral calling. And whereas in Luke, Christ seems to be driving away the "great multitude" of followers by taunting them with the suggestion that the required commitment may be beyond their reach, Milton, despite an obvious frustration with the English "multitude," still holds out the possibility, indeed the hope, that they will recognize and embrace their special calling.

This calling, moreover, is a challenge to collective, specifically worldly and political, action. Hard on the heels of the gospel echo, Milton's reference to the great republican exemplar, Rome, seems intended to remind the English of the special conditions of their discipleship, namely, firm commitment to a great civil cause. The completion of the work of the commonwealth, in fact, is a task to which they have already committed themselves precisely as a sign of their calling, and as the particular charge of their discipleship.

Milton's recasting of the gospel passage, in effect, not only assigns it specific governmental implications but also rewrites the challenge of discipleship as a reminder to the English people—the citizens of the commonwealth—that they are already disciples. Moreover, they are disciples precisely because it is they who have been called (not driven away), and called upon to complete God's work in history. Choosing in this sense is really God's prerogative more than it is man's, for the experience of discipleship has become the experience of election, and of the elect *nation*. Milton's passage recalls the issue of discipleship as it is set forth in the gospels not because the English are now in a position to consider its conditions *before* committing themselves to it; rather, he is simply reminding the English that certain conditions are prescribed for those whom God calls (or elects) to be disciples. For Milton, being a disciple is merely a public, communal version of that rational choosing that defines the possibility of redemption: that is, it is less a matter of deciding for oneself and more one of obeying those injunctions God has set forth, the conditions by which the elect will show themselves obedient to God's choices. And in the case of political settlement, according to the *Readie and Easie Way*, what God has prescribed for his people is the rejection of "gentilish" (unchosen?) kingship, and the establishment of a commonwealth.

In adding these political implications to the issue of discipleship, Milton seems to be rechanneling Luke xiv through a connected passage in Matthew v, a passage in which Christ's charge of discipleship is similarly rendered by the metaphor of "salt." But here, by contrast, the charge is expressed as a more public, worldly activity, one in which the human city becomes the very sign of the divine city that will subsume it:

You are the salt of the earth. But if salt loses its taste, how can you restore its flavor? It is good for nothing, and can only be thrown out to be trampled under people's feet. You are the light of the world. A city on a hill cannot be hid. Nor do men light a lamp and put it under a bushel, but on a stand, and it gives light to all in the house. Let your light so shine before men, that they may see your good works and give glory to your Father who is in heaven. (Matt. v, 13–16)

Explaining the special nature of their calling, Matthew's Christ calls the apostles to a distinctly communal discipleship, the fulfillment of whose conditions will serve both to announce the arrival of the promised kingdom and, eventually, to spread its truth to all nations. As we noted earlier, in the context of the *Readie and Easie Way* Milton's England is to take up this divine mission by becoming "another *Rome* in the west." This allusion to the *translatio imperii* serves to interlace the grander imperial aspirations of the commonwealth—modeled on the great republican exemplar, Rome—with the gospel's own challenge of discipleship; that is, the *Readie and Easie Way*'s recasting of the biblical paradigm of discipleship seeks to equate the full mission of discipleship—the final unfolding of God's kingdom—with the dual imperative of the great republic, both civic and imperial.

Christ's call thus becomes in Milton's revision a challenge to the English people to accept the burden of discipleship, at the heart of which lies the dual inheritance of the elect nation (Israel) and the imperial republic (Rome), both subsumed within the evangelical spirit of Christianity. Within this context, the mantle of empire bequeathed by Rome to its true disciple, *republican* England, also declares England's election to serve as both sign of and means to the unfolding of God's kingdom. The figure of the imperial republic, that is, serves as both the symbolic expression and literal vehicle by which the city of man becomes the city of God; for through republican settlement the promised kingdom (or is it God's commonwealth?) may at last be realized.

II

That Milton's version of this gospel idea should take a secular form is not so surprising given the rhetoric of English republicanism in the 1650s. During the years of the Protectorate, James Harrington, for example, had drawn on Machiavelli's republican typology as a way of exploring the possibilities of a "commonwealth for encrease" in connection with England's special status as God's chosen nation. His *Oceana* (1656) went so far as to reconceptualize Machiavelli's expansive republic (Rome) in the guise of the millennial commonwealth, with imperial conquest figured as a sacred duty to be performed by the elect nation as a way of precipitating what Pocock calls the "culmination of western history . . . the restoration of the kingdom of grace."[10]

Even before Harrington's *Oceana*, Milton himself had evoked the Roman republic's imperial heritage as part of his assertion of the special, godly calling of the young English republic. In his *Second Defence of the English People* (1654), his projection of this calling rises to a great imperial prospect in which England's godly task becomes the advancement of the cause of liberty across the globe:

I seem now to have embarked on a journey and to be surveying from on high farflung regions and territories across the sea, faces numberless and unknown, sentiments in complete agreement with mine. Here the manly strength of the Germans, hostile to slavery, meets my eye; there the lively and generous ardor of the Franks, worthy of their name; here the well-considered courage of the Spaniards; there the serene and self-controlled magnanimity of the Italians. . . . And, like Triptolemus of old, I seem to introduce to the nations of the earth a product from my own country, . . . the renewed cultivation of freedom and civic life that I disseminate throughout cities, kingdoms, and nations. (YP IV, pp. 554–56)

Milton's imagined scene here, and indeed the tract as whole, owe much to the ancient Romans' own mythical self-fashioning of their republic as the grand liberator of subject peoples. Largely fabricated from the perspective of the loss of the citizens' own liberty in the wake of the civil wars, the myth of the republic's just *imperium* sought to justify Roman expansion as the destined vehicle by which law, freedom, and justice were to be spread to all nations.[11] In Milton's surveying of those disparate peoples paradoxically captivated by his liberating pronouncement, the English republic inherits Rome's role as the vehicle of liberty's destined dissemination among the "nations of the earth." And it is the corroborating testimony of these newly liberated nations that serves to bridge the gap between republican values and the quest for empire, and thereby to mark imperial expansion as the working out of history's providential design.[12]

Milton's echoing of the Roman imperial heritage in this passage extends to the Virgilian epic tradition, and in particular to that tradition's attempt to justify imperial conquest as the epic nation's fulfillment of its providentially ordained mission. In his panoramic depiction of liberty's triumph, Milton condenses various elements of Anchises' prophecy of Rome's imperial destiny (*Aeneid* VI, 679–892). In the underworld Aeneas comes upon his father surveying ("lustrabat": 681) the great multitude of his descendants, a plenum that includes the innumerable tribes and peoples hovering above the river Lethe ("*hunc circum innumerae gentes populique volabant*": 706).[13] After a brief lesson in the transmigration of souls (722–51), Anchises leads Aeneas up a hill ("*tumulum capit*") from where they can better oversee the vast procession of the faces of those preparing to be reborn into history ("*unde omnes longo ordine posset / adversos legere et venientum discere voltus*": 754–55).

Milton's borrowings from this scene include the activity of surveying ("*perlustrare*"), the procession of "faces numberless" ("*vultus innumeros*") and the height from which he makes his survey ("*sublimis*"), a vantage that seems to draw together both Anchises' ascent up the "tumulum" and the hovering ("*volabant*") of the souls above Lethe.[14] Moreover, in connecting the prospect of the "*vultus innumeros*" with his own journey into those "farflung regions and territories across the sea," Milton seems to be adapting Anchises' prophetic account of that great transmigration of souls (of the "*innumerae gentes populique*") which marks the restoration of history to its true order. But Milton's imagined crossing of the bounding waters is a heroic achievement that belongs primarily to himself, and to the one nation whose special place in history it is his task to make known. Thus his journey aligns him, and England, not just with Virgil's hovering nations— those souls preparing to return to history's destined course—but also with the heroic Aeneas, whose own journey ("o'er what lands, [and] what wide seas") has become part of Anchises' vision (692–93). Milton conflates the two journeys in order to stress, more strongly than Virgil even, that the forwarding of destiny is the epic task assigned to God's chosen nation, even as its mission is to extend ultimately to all nations.

Milton brings together these various strands of Anchises' prophecy just before the conclusion of his own prophetic vision, a moment which includes his most direct allusion to the Virgilian scene: "Now, surrounded by such great throngs, from the Pillars of Hercules all the way to the farthest boundaries of Father Liber, I seem to be leading home again everywhere in the world, after a vast space of time, Liberty herself, so long expelled and exiled" (YP IV, p. 555). We again find echoes of Anchises' great assembly of the "innumerable tribes and peoples," engaged in that vast procession (Virgil's "*longo ordine*") which unfolds the true course of history (Milton's "vast space of time" / "*longo intervallo*"). In Virgil's work, the revelation of that historical sequence culminates with a description of the imperial domains to be conquered by the Romans in the time of Augustus:

This is he whom thou so oft hearest promised to thee, Augustus Caesar, son of a god, who shall again set up the Golden Age amid the fields where Saturn once reigned, and shall spread his empire past Garamant and India . . . In truth, . . .

Alcides never did range o'er such space of earth . . . nor he who guides his car with vine-leaf reins, triumphant Liber, driving his tigers down from Nysa's lofty crest. (791–805; translation slightly altered)

In adapting this passage, Milton retains Virgil's Alcides (Hercules) in a witty reference to the landmark that now bears his name ("*Herculeis columnis*," the Pillars of Hercules), a landmark that itself symbolizes a great portion of the epic geography Milton here envisions. He also borrows Virgil's unconventional name for Dionysus, "Liber," undoubtedly for the same reason Virgil does: both employ the pun—Liber / liber(tas)—to depict imperial conquest as a divinely guided mission and to equate its proper unfolding under the auspices of the chosen nation with the restoration of republican values, a moral restoration defined by the triumph of liberty (Virgil's "*victor Liber*"). [15]

Milton's passage figures the geographical contours of Roman imperial conquest as a crossing of time and space that marks the return of liberty to history from its ignoble exile. His transumption of the Virgilian scene thus stands as the rhetorical counterpart of the great transmigration recorded there, the process by which the heroic souls of the past are given new bodies and are thereby restored to the body of history. Toward the close of the tract, Milton will draw more specific analogies between Roman heroes and the heroes of his own republic, going so far as to suggest that the ancient Romans are reincarnated in their contemporary English counterparts (YP IV, pp. 669–82). And in more sweeping fashion, his final paragraph will include his most open proclamation of England's epic ancestry, a heritage given new life in England's own heroic exploits and celebrated by the new epic poet. [16]

But the transmigration of the soul of Roman history into England's historical flesh is not so simple a matter. Indeed, Milton finds it necessary to remind his compatriots that the work of destiny, so clearly inscribed in the mission of the republic, can be forestalled by moral weakness; such is the lesson both of Rome's own final decline and of the failure of subsequent attempts among the Italians to revive their republican heritage (YP IV, pp. 683–84). Thus, even as he concludes the tract with a celebration of England's special calling, he warns his readers that the task of the English republic is still far from complete:

If after such brave deeds you ignobly fail, . . . be sure that posterity will speak out and pass judgment: the foundations were soundly laid, the beginnings . . . were splendid, but posterity will look in vain, not without a certain distress, for those who were to complete the work . . . It will seem to posterity that a mighty harvest of glory was at hand, together with the opportunity for doing the greatest deeds, but that to this opportunity men were wanting. (YP IV, p. 685)

The paired mention of the "mighty harvest" and of the need for men to carry out such work recalls a passage in Matthew, where Christ first proclaims the unfolding of God's kingdom and then assigns the apostles their central place in that labor: "'The harvest is great but the laborers are few, so ask the Lord of the harvest to send out laborers to gather his harvest.' He summoned his twelve disciples and gave them authority. . . . These twelve Jesus sent out" (Matt. ix, 37; x, 5). Drawing on this passage at the close of the *Second Defence*, Milton not only figures true discipleship as an active, worldly response to Christ's call to the chosen to serve as vehicles for the dissemination of the kingdom, but he also intertwines the challenge of discipleship—the completion of God's work in history—with the proclamation of England's epic status as the heir of the Roman republic.

At the close of the *Second Defence*, then, the gospel's call to discipleship completes Milton's vision of the English republic's inheritance of the Roman imperial mantle. The visionary extension of liberty to the nations of the earth—the imperial republic's epic task—reveals itself as the work of God's chosen laborers, whose harvesting promises the restoration of a republican golden age that itself seems to point toward the final unfolding of God's kingdom. The gospel's call to discipleship thus becomes in Milton's reworking both a religious and a political call, or, perhaps more accurately, a religious goal announced in and, in effect, precipitated by a particular form of political organization.

Six years later, on the eve of the Restoration, the figure of the imperial republic still seems to function for Milton as a sign of England's special status as God's chosen nation. And if in the *Second Defence* he looks back to Virgil as a way of envisioning this charge, in the *Readie and Easie Way* he seems to recall his own earlier epic moment. That is, imagining England as "another *Rome* in the west" recalls the promise of 1654. With his allusion to the *translatio imperii* Milton again connects the gospel's call to discipleship with republican settlement by equating the promise of the republic—empire—with the evangelical mission of the apostles to spread God's kingdom to all nations.

But even as he recalls his earlier epic vision, Milton also recollects his warning that the work is as yet incomplete. So he continues the passage with which we began:

Where is this goodly tower of a Commonwealth, which the English boasted they
would build to overshaddow kings, and be another *Rome* in the west? The foundation indeed they laid gallantly; but fell into a wors confusion, not of tongues, but of
factions, then those at the tower of *Babel;* and have left no memorial of thir work
behinde them remaining, but in the common laughter of *Europ.* (YP VII, p. 423)

Echoing a line from the final passage of the *Second Defence* ("the foundation was soundly laid"), Milton reminds his readers of the heroic prospects
of 1654. But the memory becomes a rebuke, for he evokes it in order to
connect England's failure to complete the settlement of republican polity
to a greater failure to heed the proclamation of its epic labor. It is as if
Aeneas had turned his back on Anchises' prophetic charge.

What had been but a vaguely imagined chastisement in the earlier
tract ("posterity will speak out and pass judgment") becomes in the *Readie
and Easie Way* the more tangible, and more humiliating, rebuke of the
"common laughter of *Europ.*" Despite this difference, however, the connection between the two tracts remains strong. For even this harsher
image has its roots in the *Second Defence*, where Milton had projected
England's reputation among foreign nations as a potential source of shame
should the republic fail. He asked his readers there to keep in mind "what
foreign nations think and say of us, the high hopes which they have for
themselves as a result of our liberty, so bravely won, and our republic, so
gloriously born," immediately adding that "if the republic should mis-
carry, . . . surely no greater shame and disgrace could befall this country"
(YP IV, p. 673). The mention of the hopes that other nations have "for
themselves as a result of [English] liberty" suggests Milton's keen sense of
England's special place in a sweeping historical movement, as if the for-
tunes of some universal liberty depended on the labor of a republican
England called to action beyond its own political boundaries. With republican foundations still incomplete in 1660, Milton's recollection of 1654
shows a Europe not simply mocking England's epic vaunts but also regis-
tering its feeling of abandonment. In what seems almost a parody of the
kind of imperial moment depicted in Livy and other Roman writers, a
"laughing Europe" mocks England's boasts even as it sees its own hopes of
liberty dashed by England's failure to live up to its great promise.

III

We might note that the ridicule of the very nations England has
imagined itself liberating is but one sign of its failure. The allusion in the
passage to the unfinished tower of Luke adds to England's shame by
connecting Europe's chastisement to Christ's: from both sides the would-
be disciple—now epic nation—is reminded of its failure to carry out the

primary charge of its discipleship. The mention of that other great biblical tower, Babel, accentuates this divine rebuke, as God's own mockery of the vain builders of Genesis chapter xi seems to resound in Europe's laughter. [17]

But this divine mockery is itself rewritten in the final poems as a more sweeping condemnation of all merely human aspirations to empire. And Books III and IV of *Paradise Regained* are particularly harsh in their denunciation of classical Rome as an exemplary model for godly political endeavor. Again drawing on book VI of the *Aeneid,* Milton depicts Satan leading Jesus "up to a mountain high" (*PR* III, 252) from where he will behold the great "prospect" (263) of empire Satan sets before him. Though including two empires, both Parthia (III, 267–385) and Rome (IV, 25–108), the epic geography of the scene encompasses much the same area held by Virgil's Augustus (*Aeneid* VI, 791–805): the Parthian empire extends "As far as Indus east" (III, 272) and Rome reaches westward to Mauritania ("the realm of Bocchus to the Blackmoor sea") and Cadiz ("Gades") (IV, 72, 77), regions framing the Pillars of Hercules. [18] Satan attempts to persuade Jesus to pursue empire as the means of fulfilling his as yet unspecified mission on earth, a mission seemingly connected to the political status of God's chosen people. The temptation culminates in Satan's exhortation to follow the Roman imperial model in "aim[ing] . . . at no less than all the world" (IV, 105). In response, Jesus condemns the decadence of Roman customs, and especially the lapse of Roman political morals by which the citizens of the republic have surrendered their freedom both to their own base desires and to their tyrannical rulers (IV, 109–45).

Moreover, the denunciation extends beyond Rome's internal tyranny to include the tyrannical nature of Roman imperial rule. There is some ambivalence in this criticism, however, for Jesus seems to acknowledge that Roman conquest once held out the promise of extending true republican values to the conquered: he refers to the Romans before the morally enervating civil wars as "That people victor once, . . . who once just, / Frugal, and mild, and temperate, *conquered well*" (IV, 132–34; italics mine). But the values of the early republic—those justifying world dominion—have since deteriorated, and Rome now "govern[s] ill the nations under yoke, / Peeling their provinces, exhausted all / By lust and rapine" (135–37). With some sense of regret for a lost ideal, Jesus' words indict Rome for its failure to uphold the promise of just *imperium* as a pattern for other nations. [19]

Despite this separation of epic heroism from the Roman imperial model, however, Milton yet reaffirms the connection he has always envisioned between the dominion of God's elect and the final, universal un-

folding of the promised kingdom. Jesus concludes his rejection of the
temptation to Rome with two similes from Daniel which figure a godly
imperium spreading itself across the globe as the culmination of history:

> Know therefore when my season comes to sit
> On David's throne, it shall be like a tree
> Spreading and overshadowing all the earth,
> Or as a stone that shall to pieces dash
> All monarchies besides throughout the world,
> And of my Kingdom there shall be no end.   (IV, 146–51)[20]

The two similes represent a conflation of the key images in Nebuchadnezzar's dreams (Dan. chaps. ii, iv), which Daniel interprets as revealing
"what is to take place in the final days" (ii, 28). So Daniel both narrates and
interprets the first dream:

This is what you saw: a statue of extreme brightness stood before you, terrible to
see. . . . While you were gazing, a stone broke away, untouched by any hand, and
struck the statue, struck its feet of iron and clay and shattered them. Then iron and
clay, bronze, silver and gold, all broke into pieces as fine as chaff on the threshing
floor in summer. The wind blew them away, leaving not a trace behind. And the
stone that had struck the statue grew into a great mountain, filling the whole
world. . . . In the days of those kings, the God of heaven will set up a kingdom
which will never be destroyed, and this kingdom will not pass into the hands of
another race: it will shatter and absorb all the previous kingdoms and itself last
forever. (ii, 31–35, 44)

Christian exegesis traditionally interpreted the scene as revealing Christ's
final victory over the four great human empires, of which Rome (the iron
and clay) was usually taken as the last and greatest.[21] By applying the
prophecy to himself in the context of Satan's temptation, Milton's Jesus
registers the ultimate rejection of Rome as a model for his godly task. For
he not only sees Rome as a false type of his own future empire, but he also
views its destruction as a sign that will mark the beginning of his own
imperial advance.

By relocating Satan's depiction of imperial Rome in the context of
Daniel's prophecy, Milton's Jesus shatters the very image of Roman
imperium as a model of the epic mission of God's chosen laborers, called
to serve as vehicles for the dissemination of the kingdom. And the passage
seems also to mark the final shattering of the symbolic foundation of
Milton's own epic ideal. In 1660, we saw, Milton connected his vision of
republican England's special status to the Virgilian epic tradition by reference to the *translatio imperii*. But this topos of imperial inheritance is
itself included in the shattering of *Paradise Regained*. For the very notion

of the classical *translatio* was understood by Christian writers to have originated in Daniel's prophecy of the four empires.[22] Jesus' rejection of the temptation to Rome thus figures Milton's own final rejection, indeed the symbolic destruction, of the figurative possibilities contained within his epic inheritance, and in his own earlier writings.[23]

In the *Readie and Easie Way*, Milton seems to be at a critical juncture in his own grasp of these possibilities. Even as his allusion to the *translatio imperii* establishes Rome as a model for England's godly task in history, the mention of Babel marks the beginning of a process of associating Roman *imperium* with ungodly conquest. This strange juxtaposition seems to mark a kind of nostalgia for a fading epic ideal. When in the tract Milton asks where that new Rome is of which such great boasts have been made, one can hear the calling into question of his own earlier epic vaunting. In 1654 he worried of the "lack of men" truly committed to his epic vision; in 1660 he may be more concerned with the moral appropriateness of the vision itself.[24]

The figure of discipleship manages to sustain this vision for a final moment. And at this stage in the tract, imperial Rome is still part of his claim that England's discipleship is to be national, this-worldly, and politically active. But as the Roman model falls away, so, too, does Milton's notion of discipleship as a catalyst of divine *imperium*.[25] Moral reform is still attached in the *Readie and Easie Way* both to the proper functioning of human political order (YP VII, pp. 427–28, 442–44, 448–49, 456–61) and to the process by which Christ's promised reign becomes a reality (pp. 444–45). But the activity of discipleship is finally defined as an expression of private spiritual regeneration rather than as an attempt to precipitate the divine unfolding of history through human political action. If, as Arthur Barker once claimed, the tract finally engages in a "Platonic search for that ideal city whose pattern is laid up in heaven," then we see in the *Readie and Easie Way* the failure of discipleship as the trope by which the two cities of Renaissance republicanism may be brought into equilibrium.[26] One still chooses discipleship, but its meaning awaits God's choices for history.

University of Vermont

NOTES

1. *Areopagitica*, in *Complete Prose Works of John Milton*, 8 vols., ed. Don M. Wolfe et al. (New Haven, 1953–82), vol. II, p. 527; unless otherwise noted, all quotations from

Milton's prose are from this edition, and subsequent volume and page references will appear in the text as YP.

2. So in *Paradise Lost* both God (III, 95–125) and Adam (V, 100–21; IX, 343–63) explain the workings of reason in these terms. References to Milton's poetry are to *The Poems of John Milton*, ed. John Carey and Alastair Fowler (London, 1968).

3. For discussion of Milton's views on these matters, see, for example, Joan S. Bennett, *Reviving Liberty: Radical Christian Humanism in Milton's Great Poems* (Cambridge, Mass., 1989), and David Loewenstein, *Milton and the Drama of History: Historical Vision, Iconoclasm, and the Literary Imagination* (Cambridge, 1990), especially chapters 1–2.

4. Milton composed two editions of the *Readie and Easie Way* between February and April, 1660. I shall quote from the second edition (YP VII, pp. 405–63).

5. Stella Revard points out that Royalists in the latter 1640s argued precisely for this reading of the passage; see her "Milton and Classical Rome: The Political Context of *Paradise Regained*," in *Rome in the Renaissance: The City and the Myth*, ed. P. A. Ramsey (Binghamton, N.Y. 1982), p. 411.

6. The *translatio imperii* sought to describe the rise and fall of empire as a progressive historical transfer of power and civilization from one imperial center to the next. As countless writers depicted it, this providentially designed movement of history properly followed the course of the sun, and thus continually moved westward: see Ernst Robert Curtius, *European Literature and the Latin Middle Ages*, trans. Willard R. Trask (New York, 1953), pp. 28–30.

7. *Censure of the Rota Upon Mr Miltons Book, Entituled, the Ready and Easie Way to Establish a Free Common-Wealth* (London, 1660), p. 10.

8. J. G. A. Pocock, *The Machiavellian Moment: Florentine Political Thought and the Atlantic Republican Tradition* (Princeton, 1975), p. 84.

9. James Holstun, *A Rational Millennium: Puritan Utopias of Seventeenth-Century England and America* (Oxford, 1987), pp. 258–59.

10. "Historical Introduction," in *The Political Works of James Harrington*, ed. J. G. A. Pocock (Cambridge, 1977), p. 73. For a more general discussion of the conceptual connection made in the Renaissance between republican political organization and imperial aspirations, see Pocock, *Machiavellian Moment*, chapter 7. For Harrington's own description of this promise, see Lord Archon's speech in *Oceana* (*Political Works*, pp. 320–33); for discussion, see Pocock, *Machiavellian Moment*, chapter 11, and Holstun, *Rational Millennium*, pp. 209–19.

11. Livy, for example, concluded his narration of the Second Macedonian War with a fanciful description of the wonder felt by the newly liberated peoples of Greece in response to the Roman consul's proclamation of freedom at the Isthmian games in 196 B.C.:

> The herald's pronouncement was heard with a joy so great that men could not comprehend its full significance . . . and the tumult of applause that arose, and was so often repeated, made it abundantly clear that no boon could be more welcome to that vast gathering than the gift of liberty. . . . There really was, it seemed, a nation on earth prepared to fight for the freedom of other men, and to fight at her own expense, and at the cost of hardship and peril to herself; a nation prepared to do service not just for her near neighbors, for those in her part of the world, for lands geographically connected with her own, but even prepared to cross the sea in order to prevent the establishment of an unjust dominion in any quarter of the globe, and to ensure that right and justice, and the rule of law, should everywhere be supreme. (*Ab*

Urbe Condita XXXIII, 32–33, trans. Henry Bettenson in *Rome and the Mediterranean* [Harmondsworth, Middlesex, 1976], pp. 126–27)

12. Just as Livy's Greeks bear witness to the Roman republic's willingness to "cross the sea" to fight against "unjust dominion," so Milton envisions a similar spectacle of freedom initiated by his own imaginary advance into "territories across the sea." Upon hearing the proclamation of their freedom Livy's Greeks respond with a "tumult of applause"; so Milton's captive host properly recognizes the source of its liberation by "mak[ing] haste to applaud" (YP IV, p. 555).

13. Virgil's Latin text, with English translation, from *Virgil*, 2 vols., trans. H. Rushton Fairclough (Cambridge, Mass., 1934); references are cited by line number.

14. Milton's Latin text from the *Works of John Milton*, 18 vols., ed. Frank Allen Patterson et al. (New York, 1931–38), vol. VIII, p. 12.

15. It comes as no surprise that Milton does not include in his borrowing the figure of the emperor whose presence marks the culmination of Virgil's epic vision. Nevertheless, at the end of the *Second Defence* Milton's championing of Cromwell as the center of the commonwealth appears to echo Augustus' own self-portrayal as the *"pater patriae,"* and as restorer of republican values: see YP IV, pp. 671–72; cf. Augustus, *Res Gestae*, 34–35, in *Res Gestae Divi Augusti: The Achievement of the Divine Augustus*, ed. P. A. Brunt and J. M. Moore (Oxford, 1967), pp. 34–37.

16. So Milton marks his own text's place in the epic tradition he wishes to emulate:

I have borne witness, I might almost say I have erected a monument that will not soon pass away, to those deeds that were illustrious, that were glorious, that were almost beyond my praise . . . Moreover, just as the epic poet, if he is scrupulous and disinclined to break the rules, undertakes to extol, not the whole life of the hero whom he proposes to celebrate in his verse, but usually one event of his life (the exploits of Achilles at Troy, let us say, or the return of Ulysses, or the arrival of Aeneas in Italy) and passes over the rest, so let it suffice me too . . . to have celebrated at least one heroic achievement of my countrymen. The rest I omit. Who could extol all the achievements of an entire nation? (YP IV, p. 685)

17. God's laughter at the folly of Babel is not part of the biblical account itself; rather, it is a detail of that larger exegetical tradition Milton so frequently draws on in his writing: so, for example, in his *Lectures on Genesis*, Luther connects the account of God's rebuke of Babel's builders with the divine laughter recounted in Psalms ii, 4. In giving his own account of this scene in *Paradise Lost* (XII, 24–62), Milton strongly emphasizes this divine mockery by mentioning both God's "derision" and the "great laughter" of heaven in a space of eight lines (52–59).

18. Barbara Lewalski notes that "the traditional Protestant commentary upon the temptation of the kingdoms provides bases for Milton's identification of Rome as the chief kingdom offered to Christ" (*Milton's Brief Epic: The Genre, Meaning, and Art of Paradise Regained* [Providence, 1966], p. 276). We should note that Milton's Rome also extends eastward to encompass Parthia itself as well as India (*PR* IV, 73–76).

19. The connection between the sight of Rome and the temptation to false heroic action recalls the poem's earlier description of Jesus' own youthful aspiration "to subdue and quell o'er all the earth / Brute violence and proud tyrannic power" (I, 218–19). These lines echo Anchises' famous proclamation that it is part of Rome's destiny "to tame in war the

proud" (*Aeneid* VI, 853), except that for Jesus Rome is the prime example of the "tyrannic power" he means to oppose (I, 217).

20. Both this passage and a related one in *Paradise Lost* (XII, 370–71) echo those moments in the *Aeneid* (I, 257–75; VI, 781–84) where Rome's endless *imperium* is prophesied.

21. The interpretive backdrop of Milton's scene is described by Lewalski, pp. 267–79. We might note that in Daniel the image of the great tree (Dan. iv, 7–19) refers to Nebuchadnezzar's own empire rather than to God's.

22. This traditional connection, along with later adaptations of the prophecy to post-Roman *translatio*, is discussed by Samuel Kliger, "The 'Urbs Aeterna' in *Paradise Regained*," *PMLA* LXI (1946), 487–89.

23. The entire temptation-to-the-kingdoms sequence in *Paradise Regained*—especially as it builds on the earlier depiction of Jesus' own imperial ambitions (I, 196–233)—strangely recalls Milton's own youthful aspiration as recorded in the *Reason of Church Government* (YP I, pp. 808–23) and elsewhere. We thus sense that Milton subtly equates Jesus' rejection of Satan's offer with his own nostalgic surrendering of past temptations to see in Rome's imperial greatness a figure for his and England's epic destinies.

24. In an unpublished essay entitled "Milton and the New World," David Armitage has suggested that Milton came to reject his earlier epic vision because he saw the commonwealth's own imperialist projects—most notably the Protectorate's "Western Design"—as failing to live up to the ideals of the godly mission he had proclaimed in 1654. From Milton's perspective, according to this thesis, the military failing that ended the Western Design—the embarrassing defeat of the English at the hands of the Spanish in 1655—registered the republic's moral failing and a divine rebuke for its mixing of delusions of imperial grandeur with pretensions to liberate the enslaved people of the earth. For a similar account of Milton's dismay over British colonialist ventures, see David Quint, "The Boat of Romance and Renaissance Epic," in *Romance: Generic Transformations from Chrétien de Troyes to Cervantes*, ed. Kevin Brownlee and Marina Scordilis Brownlee (Hanover, N.H. 1985), pp. 187–88, 194–96.

25. For discussion of the tract's final rejection of Roman-styled republicanism, with its orientation toward imperial expansion, see Andrew Barnaby, "Machiavellian Hypotheses: Republican Settlement and the Question of Empire in Milton's *Readie and Easie Way*," *CLIO* XIX (1990), 251–70.

26. Arthur Barker, *Milton and the Puritan Dilemma, 1641–1660* (Toronto, 1942), p. 288.

RULE, SELF, SUBJECT:
THE PROBLEM OF POWER IN
PARADISE LOST

David Weisberg

DURING THE SEVENTEENTH CENTURY in Europe, and particularly in England, the great transformation from a religious to a secular, state-oriented society was beginning to affect every aspect of human activity. The transformations in the forms and structures of social organization, power relations, and knowledge all increasingly emphasized a new, modern notion of the individuality of human beings, while at the same time individuals were being subjected to expanding networks of examination, surveillance, and control.[1] It is precisely within this complex framework of developing state-oriented social organization, power, and individuality that *Paradise Lost* manifests itself as a transitional work situated at the historical moment when both religious and secular-rational spheres of knowledge conflicted with and interanimated each other. In many parts of the poem, characteristically secular and modern forms of power relations are represented in the descriptions of the characters' interactions, yet in other parts, power itself is self-consciously explained within a premodern, theological world view. The transitional quality of *Paradise Lost* lies in the gap between its representations of power and human autonomy and its own (or Milton's, if you wish) theorization of those representations. Yet the very details in which those representations show themselves to be incommensurate with the poem's philosophy attest to Milton's intellectual and artistic sensitivity to the momentous social transformations of the seventeeth century.

The purpose of this paper is to address this transitional significance of *Paradise Lost* by asking an old, rather careworn question about the poem in a new way: the old form of this very important question was usually centered on concepts such as man's free will, choice, causality, predestination, determination, God's omnipotence, etc. More importantly, the question usually took the form of a problem of contradictory forces or principles seeking resolution, either in Milton's own working out of these contending concepts in his poetry and in certain prose works, especially *The Christian*

Doctrine, or else in the reader's or critic's act of interpretation. A recent (1982) article by R. D. Bedford gives a good indication of the persistence of this type of questioning:

> It will readily be acknowledged that at the heart of the middle books of the poem lie questions of freedom, causality, determinism—and hence of responsibility—questions to which both Milton as poet and we as readers are forced to offer various shifts and stratagems. One of these characteristic questions is that if Adam's fall is in any sense caused . . . then it logically can not be avoided. If . . . Adam's choice is not caused, then the only alternative must be that it is an arbitrary event, an accident, for which no more responsibility can be adduced than for a necessitated act. Either way, we do not have what the poem seems to demand: a clear conception of free will acting with full responsibility and accountability.[2]

Bedford's resolution—in the Boethian concept of a God outside of temporal relations—is nicely attuned to the problematic he and the Miltonic critical tradition have set up, but what, if anything, does it offer us in the way of relating such vital problems in Milton's masterpiece to our own contemporary critical concern with issues of freedom and choice? Of course, it is a valuable and legitimate task of criticism to attempt to contextualize Milton's concepts of free will and predestination within an earlier tradition which was part of Milton's cultural milieu.[3] Yet, on the other hand, it is necessary to observe that the persistence of the question in this particular form actually precludes any type of resolution or examination except one drawn from that same tradition. It is something like going around in a hermeneutic circle of ever-constricting circumference. And the resolution found through recourse to tradition can often be more problematic than the original Miltonic question: is the Boethian concept of God out of time any less maddening and convoluted a problem than the workings of free will and predestination in *Paradise Lost?* Perhaps it would have been reassuring for Theodoric the Ostrogoth, but it can hardly satisfy us.

As Thomas Kranidas has demonstrated, "there is in Milton a very strong strain of caution towards and even opposition to the traditional."[4] In the spirit of Milton's warnings against excessive use of traditional authority, Kranidas asks: "What if we approach the troublesome sections of the poem with an attempt to understand rather than label, with an attempt to make the section imaginatively operative rather than relatable to something else in literary history?"[5]

What I propose, in a similar spirit, is a new interrogation of a set of themes which have up to now been designated by those terms pointed out earlier. In an attempt, which diverges sharply from the tradition of Milton criticism, to make "imaginatively operative" the functioning and representation of freedom and will in *Paradise Lost*, I would like to use a correspondingly nontraditional set of critical assumptions formulated in the works of Michel Foucault, especially in the relations he sketches out between forms of power and "the modes of objectification which transform human beings into subjects."[6] The purpose of this interrogation is not to find a resolution to the old problematic in a contemporary guise, but rather to open up certain aspects of *Paradise Lost* to a series of issues that seem key to the historical development of our own, present experience. The remarks and observations that follow are necessarily in a somewhat preliminary and provisional form, since they attempt to follow quite closely a set of investigations that Foucault himself referred to as "fragmentary researches"[7] made up of "uncompletable drafts."[8]

There are three moments in *Paradise Lost* that might serve to mark out the limits of the problematic I wish to address. The first is an absolutely startling image of Satan in hell:

> So strecht out huge in length the Arch-fiend lay
> Chain'd on the burning Lake, nor ever thence
> Had ris'n or heav'd his head, but that the will
> And high permission of all-ruling Heav'n
> Left him at large to his own dark designs,
> That with reiterated crimes he might
> Heap on himself damnation, while he sought
> Evil to others, and enrag'd might see
> How all his malice serv'd but to bring forth
> Infinite goodness, grace and mercy.   (I, 209–18)[9]

There are several interesting points to note here: first, there is the minute detail of Satan moving his head together with the reference to a very broad series of actions, the "reiterated crimes" whose narration takes up a considerable portion of the entire poem.

Both the physical detail and the large narrative actions are presented as originating in the body and mind of Satan; that is, Satan raises his own head, and he acts according to "his own dark designs." Satan is an actor, an agent, a subject at least in the grammatical sense that he is the active noun of a clause. However, it is clear that his actions, from the heaving of his head to his whole life story, are very strongly influenced by some other agency outside his mind and body. This influence is specified as "permission," as a being left "at large." This influence is also an action: an action "of all-ruling Heav'n." Thus, the scene describes two types of action, one concerning a detailed physical body and also a series of crimes that this body-mind commits, the other an action that greatly influences and that comes not from a body or mind per se, but rather a place, a very influential place. Further, there is the indication of a final result concerning these two types of action: Satan commits his crimes according to his own design and intention, but the result is the opposite of what he seemingly intends. "Goodness, grace and mercy" result from "all his malice." Thus, the influencing action, in the end and perhaps all along, gets what it wants. In fact, it totally dominates the actions of the other, of Satan, from his bodily movements to his dark designs.

It is vital to distinguish here a relationship of domination from a state of determination: there is no determination in this remarkable scene, there is only a kind of invisible, even momentarily liberating domination. Satan is an actor whose actions are greatly, or even totally, influenced by another's actions, but Satan's actions are not *caused by* the other, by heaven. The notion of "permission" entirely rules out determination, since a determining agent would never have a need to permit or forbid anything. A prisoner or captive, for example, might be permitted to participate in a certain activity, but a prisoner's actions are never determined; an individual is, in fact, made a prisoner precisely because his actions cannot be determined, but can only be restricted or influenced. Let us say, for now, that the relationship between Satan and heaven is one of domination, that this domination seems total, that the domination is one over actions large and small that are intended and created by a mind-body, and that the domination is successful in that it gets the seemingly desired results.

The second moment in *Paradise Lost* that will help define the limits of our problematic is an episode in Book III that Carrol B. Cox has characterized as "angels acting outside the presence of divine or human agents"[10]—Uriel meeting and speaking with a Cherub, who is actually Satan in disguise. Satan is on his way to Eden, when he reaches the Sun and sees "a glorious Angel" (III, 622):

> Glad was the spirit impure; as now in hope
> To find who might direct his wandering flight
> To paradise the happie seat of Man,
> His journies end and our beginning woe.
> But first he casts to change his proper shape,
> Which else might work him danger or delay:
> And now a stripling Cherub he appeers.   (630–36)

The angel that Satan encounters is described by the narrator as the "Regent of the Sun" (III, 690):

> Th' Arch-Angel *Uriel*, one of the seav'n
> Who in Gods presence, neerest to his Throne
> Stand ready at command, and are his Eyes.   (648–50)

Satan, now in disguise, invents a story in order to fool Uriel into telling him the way to Paradise:

> Unspeakable desire to see, and know
> All these his wondrous works, but chiefly Man.
>   . . . .
> Hath brought me from the Quires of Cherubim
> Alone thus wandring. Brightest Seraph tell
> In which of all these shining Orbs hath Man
> His fixed seat.
>   . . . .
> So spake the false dissembler unperceiv'd;
> For neither Man nor Angel can discern
> Hypocrisie, the only evil that walks
> Invisible, except to God alone,
> By his permissive will.   (662–63; 666–69; 681–85)

Uriel is "beguil'd" (III, 689) by Satan's ruse and responds:

> Fair Angel, thy desire which tends to know
> The works of God, thereby to glorifie
> The great Work-Maister, leads to no excess
> That reaches blame, but rather merits praise.
>   . . . .
> To witness with thine eyes what some perhaps
> Contented with report hear onely in heav'n.   (694–97; 700–01)

Uriel offers a brief account of the creation, and then gives Satan the exact information he requires: "That spot to which I point is *Paradise*" (III, 733).

I have quoted at some length because I would like to make a series of observations about this scene that emerge from a close reading of the narrative actions rather than from any philosophical or theological discussions, either in *Paradise Lost* or in Milton's other works, about the relationships of God to his angels. My analysis of forms of power represented in the interplay of *free* and influenced actions in the poem follows Foucault's assertion that "power exists only when it is put into action" and that "what defines a relationship of power is that it is a mode of action which does not act directly and immediately on others. Instead it acts upon their actions: an action upon an action."[11] I will discuss the implications of Foucault's analytic of power in greater detail later in this paper; let's return to the episode of Uriel and the false cherub and look more closely at five important aspects of the passages quoted above.

First: it is clear that Satan adopts a specific strategy in his attempt to extract vital information from Uriel. Once again, we can see that Satan is acting according to "his own dark designs" and that in adopting a strategy of imposture, he hopes to influence the actions of another, of Uriel. In order to adopt such a strategy, Satan must have a certain kind of knowledge about Uriel: he must know first of all that if he simply shows himself undisguised to Uriel, he will fail to get the information and that such a course of action "might work him danger or delay." He must also know that it is possible, or even probable, that he can deceive the "Regent" angel. Satan knows the limits of Uriel's wisdom, or perception, or field of experience. Satan's knowledge seems somewhat specific in that he chooses his guise in the very particular form of a cherub: Satan has a range of angels whose form he can feign, but he chooses the angel-form he thinks will be most effective. The text even gives us a close description of Satan's disguise (III, 636–44) to emphasize the effectiveness of his choice. Thus, there is a close connection in this scene between a strategy to gain information, and the knowledge needed to choose such a strategy. In fact, there are two types of knowledge at stake: a knowledge of an angel's ability to perceive, and also an empirical knowledge, a knowledge of geographic space which Uriel commands, which Satan knows Uriel commands, and which Satan wants to get from Uriel. The scene is a confrontation over forms of knowledge, and knowledge here is both a thing to be won, and a strategy by which to win it.

Second: Uriel is a "Regent," one who rules or governs in the place of, or by the authority of, a sovereign. Uriel's relation to God is one of close proximity, "neerest to his Throne," "ready at command," and he serves as God's "eyes." As much as any angel can be, Uriel (along with the other six who serve in a similar proximity) seems the most competent or able to perform a governing function, and by means of sight, at least, he assists or informs heaven in its governance. Further, if heaven is a governing agency that influences and acts upon the actions of others, then Uriel, as a regent, will to some degree also be able to exercise power, to influence the actions of others.

Third: Satan devises a story in which he offers as an explanation for his physical presence before Uriel, at the Orb of the Sun, and for his wish to know the way to paradise, a "desire to see and know" God's "wondrous works." He wandered alone from his place in heaven, the "Quire" of cherubim, to seek out these works. Here, the false cherub is making a plea to be allowed firsthand knowledge of the creation, knowing or assuming that Uriel will accept such a request. His story must contain two kinds of information: an explanation that involves his physical body's presence in a particular space, and an explanation of his inner thoughts, his "desire." The explanation is also a differentiating story in that it sets him uniquely apart from the other cherubim who are "contented with report" of the creation and who do not wander alone seeking to fulfil a "desire to see, and know."

Fourth: Uriel's approval of the Cherub's stated mission, which Uriel thinks "merits praise," takes a specific form—it is a praise of the cherub's individuality. Of course, Satan's strategy here is somewhat risky, since it is clear that Uriel might consider the cherub's desire "excess / that reaches blame." The possibility of the failure or success of Satan's strategy rests upon Uriel's acceptance or rejection of the cherub's individuality; either way, the strategy and the response not only emphasize the notion of individuality but also create it: the scene is individualizing and unique and involves a story that invents (for the first time in heaven?) a specific form of individuality—a desiring-to-see-and-know individuality that a governing regent angel approves of and assists in its quest for empirical knowledge of the most "wondrous" creation of the "Work-Maister." The fact that the cherub is false, that the story Satan tells is an imposture, actually reinforces the inventedness of this specific form of individuality.

Fifth: the text offers an explanation for Uriel's failure to detect Satan's imposture, but this explanation does not in any way discount the specific form of individuality invented in the encounter. In fact, the notion of a type of individual who cannot "discern / Hypocrisie," which was a common topos in seventeenth-century literature, reinforces another type of specific individual differentiation, this time not of a false-but-possible praiseworthy Cherub but rather of Satan himself.[12] "Neither Man nor Angel can discern / Hypocrisie." The problem that this statement raises is: if Satan, though fallen, is still an angel, then he cannot discern hypocrisy, and if he cannot discern it, he certainly could not assume a hypocritical stance. In fact, one might consider Satan's unique knowledge of hypocrisy, and not his revolt from heaven, as his most singular characteristic, his true mark of specific individuality, since the poem contains numerous examples of both falling and disobedience. In any case, Satan is a hypocritical individual and this absolutely differentiates him, at least in this scene, from all the other characters, angels and human, except, of course, God. "God alone" sees hypocrisy, and Satan alone commits it. Further, the word hypocrite comes from the Greek *hypokrites*, which means *actor* in the sense of an actor on the stage. Satan is an actor playing a role, and once again we find that his action is influenced by God's "permissive will." As discussed in relation to the scene of Satan in hell, permission is not a kind of action deployed in a situation of determination. Thus, we might say that the role Satan is playing here is not determined by God, not authored by heaven, but rather by Satan, and that heaven permits him to play this role since it can eventually be used in heaven's overall strategy aiming at the final result of "goodness, grace and mercy."

The type and degree of heaven's influence in the cherub scene is dramatically different from the dominating influence operative in the scene in hell. Here, Satan acts upon his own body in the process of transforming himself. The influencing action of heaven does not seem to affect Satan's choice of transformation, which we have seen is predicated on a type of knowledge about Uriel's field of experience. Also, Uriel does not seem to be influenced by his relation to heaven as Regent. Although he is God's "eyes," he does not share God's knowledge of hypocrisy. As a regent who governs in the absence of a sovereign, he acts separately from that sovereign, he has his own type of knowledge, his own ability and experience, however wide-ranging or limited that experience might be. For both Satan and Uriel, their relation to heaven, as a governing or influencing place, is neither one of determination nor, in this scene, of domination. It is a much less totalized relation which, nevertheless, is still one of influence: their actions are influenced by the actions of heaven but not dominated by those actions.

To reiterate and summarize the five main points made about this scene:

1. Knowledge: the scene displays a confrontation over specific forms of knowledge, both empirical and psychological. Knowledge is both a strategy employed and something to be gained or won.

2. Government: heaven is a governing place and Uriel's function as Regent indicates that this government takes on specific forms in specific agents with different degrees of governing ability and governing knowledge.

3. Differentiation: the scene involves a process of differentiation in which the possibility of a unique cherub different from all other cherubim is articulated by Satan and accepted by Uriel.

4. Individuation: the scene is highly individualizing; there is a creation of a highly specific form of desiring-to-see-and-know individuality. The fictive quality of Satan's cherub story emphasizes the inventedness of this type of individuality.

5. Influence: the scene demonstrates an influence of actions on other actions in a form distinct from that of either determination or domination.

Heaven deploys a strategy which, in pursuit of its goal of grace and goodness, permits a wide range of possible independent actions.

The third moment in *Paradise Lost* that will help mark off the parameters of an analysis of power relations involves Adam. Thus the three moments—satanic, angelic, and human—more or less cover the range of character types, excluding God, in the poem.[13] If God or heaven functions as the locus and final reference point of all power relations, then an examination of how heaven itself "justifies" its power or actions, either theologically or philosophically, either speaking for itself (in the middle books of the poem) or through an inspired prophetic narrator, would indeed be a suspect method for examining how power operates in the poem's representations of action.[14] In other words, as Carrol B. Cox notes concerning the Uriel-cherub episode: "Milton's immediate concern in [this] episode, of course, was hardly to elaborate a 'heavenly sociology.' But for that very reason [it] may exhibit Milton's spontaneous assumptions—assumptions that would be more grounded in his own tacit social experience rather than in any self-conscious theology."[15]

Since "power is not to be taken to be a phenomenon of one individual's consolidated and homogeneous domination over others . . . [and] must be analysed as something which circulates. . . . [and] is never localized here or there,"[16] then neither God in heaven nor heaven's self-articulated notions of free will are the proper objects for an analysis of power relations in the poem. Power per se cannot be analyzed *in* heaven or God, but only in what Foucault would call "power effects."[17] It is necessary to look at how actions, both speaking actions and physical actions, are affected in the poem. To look for any essence of power, or any theory of relative determination or free will produced from the point of view of a governing realm or agency, is to remain within the bounds of a traditional "juridico-discursive" theory of power against which Foucault explicitly develops his "analytic" of power.[18]

In Book X, Adam issues a "sad complaint" (719) when he begins to perceive "the growing miseries" (715) and the awesome implications, far beyond his own mortality, of the breaking of the prohibition against eating the fruit.

> Did I request thee, Maker, from my Clay
> To mould me Man, did I sollicite thee
> From darkness to promote me, or here place
> In this delicious Garden? as my Will
> Concurd not to my being, it were but right
> And equal to reduce me to my dust,

> Desirous to resigne, and render back
> All I receav'd, unable to perform
> Thy terms too hard, by which I was to hold
> The good I sought not. To the loss of that,
> Sufficient penaltie, why hast thou added
> The sense of endless woes? inexplicable
> Thy Justice seems; yet to say truth, too late,
> I thus contest; then should have been refus'd
> Those terms whatever, when they were propos'd:
> Thou didst accept them; wilt thou enjoy the good,
> Then cavil the conditions?   (X, 743–59)

The action being represented here, in the most general sense, is Adam speaking. In *Paradise Lost* Adam and Eve are most distant from their biblical representations in precisely their ability to speak, question, explain, and attempt to justify their own actions. What is especially interesting here is Adam's assumption that he himself played a constitutive part in his own creation. His initial question, rhetorically addressed to God, implies that it might have been possible for Adam to "request" or "sollicite" God to give him corporeal form, and that God, ignoring a "Will" that somehow preexisted Adam's bodily creation, had created Adam without Adam's consent. Whether or not Adam's assumption is accurate is not really important: what is significant is that Adam perceives himself as a "Will" separate, in time and space, from his body, a "Will" "concurd not to" his "being," and a will that could have intervened, perhaps unsuccessfully, in its own embodiment.

This notion of Adam's possibly influencing a heavenly action is reiterated when Adam realizes that the "terms" of his existence in Eden "Should have been refus'd . . . when they were propos'd" but that he now "contest[s]" the terms too late—he has already accepted the "conditions," including most importantly the prohibition, and feels he must suffer a "penaltie." Once again, whether or not Adam could have refused the terms of the prohibition is not the question: rather, Adam's sense of having an influence on a heavenly action is reinforced. In fact, the speech itself is another act of contestation, not of his own creation or the terms of the prohibition, but of the form of the "penaltie." Adam is quite willing to relinquish his body back into dust, but he considers the "sense of endless woes" an inordinate punishment. Thus, Adam situates three key narrative moments of the poem—his creation, the prohibition, and the punishment—as actions that "should have been" or might be influenced, either by silence (not requesting creation), refusal, or a plea for mollification. At least in this moment of the poem, Adam considers himself part of a power relation in which he perceives the possibility of change.

According to Foucault:

Power is exercised only over free subjects, and only insofar as they are free. By this we mean individual or collective subjects who are faced with *a field of possibility* in which several ways of behaving, several reactions and diverse comportments may be realized. . . . there is no face to face confrontation of power and freedom which is mutually exclusive . . . but a much more complicated interplay. In this game freedom may well appear as the condition for the exercise of power . . . *without the possibility of recalcitrance, power would be equivalent to a physical determination.* (italics mine)[19]

The above passage suggests that for Adam there is both "a field of possibility" and "the possibility of recalcitrance" within and around which the most important actions of the poem unfold. In fact, the entire function of the prohibition in the text is to set up such a field of possibility—to eat or not to eat—and a consequent recalcitrance—to eat is to disobey. But before going on to discuss the centrifugal importance of the prohibition, there is another crucial dimension to Adam's complaint that must be addressed in order to understand the relation between Adam's actions and heavenly governance.

As previously noted, Adam's question "Did I request thee, Maker" is rhetorically addressed to God, specifically in his function as Adam's creator. Obviously, the "I" refers to the speaker, to Adam, and the "thee" to God. However, God is not present in the scene, for despite God's stated "omnipresence" the poem clearly distinguishes between scenes where God as a listening and responding interlocutor is palpably present, as in Book VIII where Adam and God discuss the possibility of a companion for Adam, and scenes like the above where "Adam to himself lamented aloud" (X, 845). The dialogue quality of Adam's speech here is less a function of an omnipotent intelligence "listening in" from outside than a Bakhtinian notion of dialogics in which the intended listener or reader of any spoken or written word is always present and influential in the formation of an utterance, no matter how seemingly monologic in rhetorical form. What I want to stress here is that God's influential presence, as it manifests itself in the internal logic of Adam's complaint, is not a result of God's power to be everywhere at once, but is much more like the influence of a human or earthly individual for whom, internally or imaginatively, one intends a speech or word, even when that individual is not physically present to hear or read it.

As the complaint progresses, there occurs an unusual shift in pronoun reference:

> I thus contest; then should have been refus'd
> Those terms whatever, when they were propos'd:
> *Thou* didst accept them; wilt thou enjoy the good,
> Then cavil the conditions?   (X, 756–59) (italics mine)

The "thou" first appears in such a position that it could possibly refer to either God or Adam—if terms were proposed, it seems that both parties would in a sense accept the working out of the final form of those terms. In fact, since the "I" two lines before is so strongly stressed as referring to Adam in an act of contestation, the "thou," when it first appears, is quite jarring, and it is only as the "thou" continues to appear in the place of the "I" that it becomes certain that the "thou" is Adam addressing himself in the second person.[20] During the course of the entire complaint (X, 720–844) Adam refers to himself in the first, second, and third persons, and to God in the second and third persons. Most significantly, however, Adam begins to refer to himself predominantly in the second person exactly at the point where he laments that he "should have" refused the terms and conditions of his existence in Eden and where grammatically God and Adam can exist together, if only for the space of a line, in a single word.

The pivotal shift in which Adam moves from ostensibly addressing God to literally addressing himself signals a parallel change in the content of the complaint. After the "I" becomes the "thou" Adam, instead of contesting the three key moments of creation, prohibition, and punishment, submits:

> God made thee of choice his own, and of his own
> To serve him, thy reward was of his grace,
> Thy punishment then justly is at his Will.
> Be it so, for I submit, his doom is fair.   (X, 766–69)

From this point on, until the end of the complaint, Adam refers to himself only as "I," and God is relegated back into a stable and clearly distanced third person. In fact, the shifting pronouns become fixed in the very line of submission where "I" reappears, to stay, as the subject of the verb "submit." Literally, through a process in which Adam occupies every grammatical subject position, and in which both God and Adam seem to occupy the same grammatical subject position in a moment of transition, Adam reclaims his own identity in a self-proclaimed act of becoming a subject in one sense of the word—one who is subjected to a punishment, a rule, a governance. Not only does this shifting of position take place grammatically, but also through a self-questioning in which Adam asks himself: "what if thy Son / Prove disobedient, and reprov'd, retort / Wherefore didst thou beget me?" (X, 760–62). Adam places himself hypothetically in the position of a father and a creator in order to understand his own position in relation to God.

Adam's complaint traces a process of verbalization in which the very act of becoming an "I," of making his will "concur" to his being, is also a process of becoming the governed subject of a will or power outside himself. This process, I would like to suggest, is closely related to what Foucault has described as a specifically Western form of rationality and power that

categorizes the individual, marks him by his own individuality, attaches him to his own identity, imposes a law of truth on him which he must recognize and which others have to recognize in him. It is a form of power which makes individuals subjects. There are two meanings of the word *subject:* subject to someone else by control and dependence, and tied to his own identity by a conscience or self-knowledge. Both meanings suggest a form of power which subjugates and makes subject to.[21]

Adam's complaint, as an act through which a speaking subject reveals the truth of his self-identity *and* his submission to a form of power, can be interpreted as a type of confession, as the term is used in Foucault's *The History of Sexuality*, in both the particular, Christian sense and as a description of a general method that has been incorporated into modern psychiatric, philosophical, literary, and legal discourses and practices:

The confession is a ritual of discourse in which the speaking subject is also the subject of the statement; it is also a ritual that unfolds within a power relationship, for one does not confess without the presence (or virtual presence) of a partner who is not simply the interlocutor but the authority who requires the confession, prescribes and appreciates it, and intervenes in order to judge, punish, forgive and reconcile; . . . a ritual in which the expression alone, independently of its external consequences, produces intrinsic modifications in the person who articulates it; . . . it unburdens him of his wrongs, liberates him, and promises him salvation.[22]

Adam, through the ritual of confession that begins in the complaint as an act of contestation, reveals a complex interplay of power relations between himself and the heavenly governance in response to whose strategy his confession unfolds. Here it is quite evident that the concepts of determination, domination, and free will are wholly inadequate to describe such an interplay: rather, contestation, questioning, self-knowledge, and the dialogic internalization of a listening presence are all necessary aspects of the very specific forms of subjectivity with which *Paradise Lost* invests its characters and structures its narrative acts.

It could be argued that the three moments I have chosen in the attempt to outline a range of power relationships and strategies in the poem are somewhat incidental to the central scenes of the narrative, to the descriptions of God and the creation, to the great struggles of Satan and his army against Michael and Gabriel, to the temptation of Eve by the serpent, and to the fall of Adam and his education through which he becomes aware of future events that his and Eve's actions will set in motion. Even if one wishes to discount, for the methodological reasons I have set forth, any explicit theories or theologies of power in the poem, surely the best place to look for power relations is in the fantastic panoramas of physical and psychical struggle that Satan, Michael, Adam, and Eve experience, resist, and finally withstand, though not without loss, the loss of Paradise. Instead, I have concentrated on three relatively minor episodes: Satan lifting his head from the burning lake, Satan slipping past Uriel on a ruse, and Adam moaning about the severity of God's punishment. In ignoring what the poem is really about, I have not directly confronted the problems of free will and determination and have offered a series of observations that hinge more on details, narrative and stylistic, than on the great themes of the poem. Yet it seems to me that the most astonishing thing about *Paradise Lost* is that from a severely restricted set of narrative motifs found in the first three chapters of Genesis, Milton generated over ten thousand lines of extremely detailed and varied narration. In fact, it is precisely with the details, and not with the great biblical themes of creation, temptation, and fall, that Milton transformed an ancient, mythic story into a historically situated, undeniably seventeenth-century work of art.

As Max Weber observed in his classic study of modern society, in *Paradise Lost* "even a superficial glance shows that there is here quite a different relationship between the religious life and earthly activity than in either Catholicism or Lutheranism. . . . One feels at once that [the] powerful expression of the Puritan's serious attention to this world, his acceptance of his life in this world as a task, could not possibly have come from the pen of a medieval writer."[23] For Weber, the significant, particular difference of English Puritan thought, "[e]ven in literature motivated purely by religious factors,"[24] is an attention to the worldly as a realm that can be affected and transformed through human activity. In *Paradise Lost* the significant difference is in the thousands of particularities that wrest it away from a more ancient or medieval worldview, in those places in the text where a task to accomplish a particular action involves a nexus of motivations and strategies that only have meaning in the human, socially constructed world, and fall into total pointlessness if viewed simply as part of God's plan.

There are thousands of centers in *Paradise Lost*, as many centers as there are details. To return, then, to the central episodes I have examined, we can begin to sketch out a model of the "field of possibility" for action and for actions influencing actions:

Satan in hell: there is a kind of totalizing domination that works through the technique of permission, a heavenly strategy that permits a subject to act according to its own "designs" as long as that design can be used in achieving heaven's overarching aim. One might use the metaphor of the *prison* here, to describe a situation where one's physical body is confined, but thought is free, and where certain actions are allowed as long as those actions lead either to the prisoner's rehabilitation, or to the good of society or creation as a whole.

Satan and Uriel: although the technique of permission figures here, it appears as a kind of influence much less totalized and localized than domination. Specific knowledges, material and psychological, figure importantly, both as strategies and desired objectives. There are also processes of differentiation and individuation at work; the strategies used are dependent on each actor being aware of the other as a unique individual whose very individuality is invented, even if fictively, in the act of confrontation. Here, an apt metaphor might be that of *government*, in which a certain notion of order and control is not dependent on any particular person or site, but rather is diffused in a network of relationships of varying degrees of influence, control, domination, knowledge, and ability. Once again, there is an overall strategy and goal—order and the well-being of all—but the strategy is not so much "to permit" but rather "to structure the possible field of action upon others. . . . [I]n the sixteenth century . . . 'Government' did not refer only to political structures or to the management of states; rather it designated the way in which the conduct of individuals or of groups might be directed."[25]

Adam's complaint: the subject becomes aware of its own subjectivity—that is, its own self-conscious identity *and* its being subject to some power clearly outside of itself—in a confessing discourse. The confessor-authority is only "present" as an internalized, dialogic interplay of subject positions. Thus, a power relationship is established which both ties Adam to God's rule at the same time that it ties him to himself, as a separate individual who can contest and refuse, but who comes to submit on his own, speaking to himself, without any perceivable, direct influence from the entity to which he submits. Clearly, this type of situation is far from the prison; it is rather a form of self-governance, a kind of relationship a person has to himself or herself which arises from a government of individuation.

The metaphors which I am using to characterize these three moments correspond, to a certain degree, to the "three modes of objectification which [according to Foucault] transform human beings into subjects" in the modern, Western world:

1. Confinement in a prison is a type of "dividing practice." "The subject is either divided inside himself or divided from others. This process objectifies him. Examples are the mad and the sane, the sick and the healthy, the criminals and the 'good boys.' "

2. A government which relies on and commands specific knowledges, both of the material world and psychic experience, for the efficacy of its rule, is tied to "the modes of inquiry which try to give themselves the status of sciences; for example the objectivizing of the speaking subject in . . . philology and linguistics. . . . of the productive subject in the analysis of economics . . . of the sheer fact of being alive in natural history or biology."

3. A government of individuation involves "the way a human being turns him- or herself into a subject."[26]

Obviously, these three modes are highly interconnected and extremely generalized, yet even in this very schematic form they give a good indication of the complexity of power relations, of how the modern individual experiences simultaneously a sense of individual autonomy and of being "governed" by powers outside him- or herself, and of how both experiences are clearly dependent on each other.

Of the three narrative actions that Adam identifies as susceptible to influence or change—his creation, the prohibition, and the punishment— it is the prohibition against eating the fruit of the Tree of Knowledge which most directly structures the principal thematic manifestation of the "field of possibility" within which the processes of objectification that create the modern individual subject take place. In an informative article that attempts to demonstrate Milton's "cultural anthropologist" attitude toward the prohibition and its representation in the poem as an irrational, ritualistic taboo, Michael Lieb notes that

Milton postulates a situation in which a command is issued in order to impose upon man a deliberately arbitrary injunction that by its very nature runs counter to the dictates of human reason.[27]

. . . .

Despite the complex logical superstructure of doctrinal explanation and rational discourse that characterizes Milton's epic, *Paradise Lost* retains, and even intensifies, the subimperative sense of myth that pervades the Jahwistic account of Genesis.[28]

Lieb's account of the prohibition as nonrational and mythic, like Bedford's account of the contradiction between predetermination and free will as "Boethian," demodernizes Milton's text and seeks to explain its apparent incongruities in archaic terms. However, Lieb's analysis might be a good starting point for asking a somewhat more difficult question about the prohibition. Instead of saying that the prohibition is either logical or illogical, we might better note that the prohibition certainly does not exhibit the kind of rationality upon which Milton's religio-philosophic explanations depend. Then we can ask, instead of a yes/no rationality question: what kind of rationality does the representation of the prohibition use, or evoke? In other words, it is important, as I have pointed out earlier, to locate the difference between explanation and representation in *Paradise Lost*, but then the next step should always be to interrogate that difference and determine how the representations in the poem operate on some other type of rationality distinct from the explanations. In fact, from a twentieth-century sociological or philosophical point of view, many of Milton's *rational* arguments which depend on biblical citation for authority could hardly stand as a model against which the *irrationality* of his representations might be evaluated. Even in his own day, there were clear challenges to Milton's type of explanatory rationality and mode of argumentation, most notably from a Hobbesian perspective.[29]

As Foucault has noted in his critique of the "juridico-discursive" representation of power, the negative notion of prohibition and repression that is normally used to characterize how power works

is quite inadequate for capturing what is precisely the productive aspect of power. In defining the effects of power as repression, one adopts a purely juridical conception of such power . . . power is taken above all as carrying the force of a prohibition. . . . If power were never anything but repressive, do you really think anyone would be brought to obey it? What makes power hold good, what makes it accepted, is simply the fact that it doesn't only weigh on us as a force that says no, but that it traverses and produces things, it induces pleasure, forms knowledges, produces discourse. It needs to be considered as a productive network . . . much more than as a negative instance whose function is repression.[30]

From such a perspective, we might now want to formulate the problem in positive terms. As a kind of rational act distinct from explanation, the prohibition has a goal in a strategy, in heaven's strategy: in order to obtain its goals, and as a consequence of its power, what does the prohibition produce in the poem? what attitudes or actions does it incite? how does it affect the very movement of the narration? what type of discourse does it bring into being?

In the space remaining I can only begin to indicate some avenues of inquiry concerning this type of interrogation of the prohibition. Since I am concerned here with the act of prohibiting, rather than with the effects of disobeying the prohibition (itself a question needing a new type of analysis), I turn to the scene in Book VIII where Adam recounts his first encounter with a God who tells him:

> This Paradise I give thee, count it thine
> To Till and keep, and of the Fruit to eat:
> Of every Tree that in the Garden grows
> Eat freely with glad heart; fear here no dearth:
> But of the Tree whose operation brings
> Knowledge of good and ill, which I have set
> The Pledge of thy Obedience and thy Faith,
> Amid the Garden by the Tree of Life,
> Remember what I warn thee, shun to taste,
> And shun the bitter consequence; for know,
> The day thou eat'st thereof, my sole command
> Transgrest, inevitably thou shalt dye;
> From that day mortal, and this happie State
> Shalt loose, expell'd from hence into a World
> Of woe and sorrow. Sternly he pronounc'd
> The rigid interdiction, which resounds
> Yet dreadful in mine ear, though in my choice
> Not to incur; but soon his cleer aspect
> Return'd and gracious purpose thus renew'd.   (319–37)

The first thing to notice is that, although at the heart of the passage lies the "interdiction," Adam is told to *do* more things than he is told not to do: till, keep, eat freely, remember, and know. In fact, though God refers to a "sole command" the passage as a whole suggests that all the remarks are intended to support the command; for example, Adam must "know" what God is saying and he must "remember" it, or else the command will be useless, since God intends the command to be a "Pledge of . . . Obedience," not a test of memorization. Thus, the command, negative in form, requires a positive knowledge and an active shunning: there are many trees in the Garden, and Adam must be careful not to inadvertently eat from the wrong one.

Not only does the command require a positive knowledge, but it also requires a type of knowledge which divides things: fruits to enjoy and fruits to shun; knowledge of good and knowledge of ill; a happy state and a world of woe; plenty and dearth; life without end and a mortal day; a rigid interdiction and a gracious purpose. If it is the fruit of the tree which brings the knowledge of good and ill, then it is the act of prohibiting which first brings to Adam's awareness that such divergent knowledges exist. In its narrative unfolding as a speech act between God and Man, the interdiction and the positive commands that support it create a world already divided into a field of possibility. It is not so much the prohibition itself but rather its active transmission that creates a "dividing practice," functioning as a kind of grid through which Adam will be able to know the world and learn how to live in it.

The interdiction passage is embedded in Adam's speech to Raphael in which Adam tries to account for his own "beginning" (VIII, 251). As discussed in connection with Adam's complaint, there is the indication that Adam feels as if his own bodily creation were something he might have had some control over. Here, he asks "how came I thus, how here? / Not of myself; by some great Maker then" (VIII, 277–78). As if in answer to his question he has a dream:

> Each Tree
> Load'n with fairest Fruit that hung to th' Eye
> Tempting, stirr'd in me sudden appetite
> To pluck and eat; whereat I wak'd, and found
> Before mine Eyes all real, as the dream
> Had lively shadowd: Here had new begun
> My wandering, had not hee who was my Guide
> Up hither, from among the Trees appeer'd,
> Presence Divine. Rejoycing, but with aw
> In adoration at his feet I fell
> Submiss.   (VIII, 306–16)

As a kind of prelude to the annunciation of the interdiction which begins two lines later, this passage involves Adam in a basic epistemological division: dream and reality. Not only will the world be divided between the dream and the actual, but the dream will be subordinate to the real as a shadow, as dependent on the real. When God appears "among the Trees" the division and hierarchy have already been set; God is of the real, not the dream. Thus, when God delivers the interdiction it will clearly be anchored in the primary real and Adam will not question whether or not the God he speaks to is a product of his own mind, a shadow in a dream, or a vision. The question whether Adam is self-made or made by a Maker outside himself is related to his ability to discern internal dream from outside reality; in turn, the efficacy of the prohibition also rests on this necessary division between subjective, secondary vision and primary objective reality. Adam must be certain of both the factuality of the speaking God's prohibition and the objective, factual existence of a specific tree.

In his dream, Adam sees fruit hanging on the trees. Seeing the fruit stirs his appetite, and he is tempted "To pluck and eat." He awakes, sees the real trees that he immediately distinguishes from the dream trees, is about to "wander" again, then sees his "Guide" who is also his Maker. What is most interesting here is the creation or evocation of a desire through the visual perception of a seemingly inherently desirable object. But here it is impossible to say if the fruit is desirable because it will satisfy an appetite that was already latent, or if the sight of the fruit itself causes the desire to exist. In any case, the fruit and the desire for the fruit, along with the temptation to eat it, cannot yet be clearly divided. When the "Guide" appears "among the Trees," he is physically in the location of desire-desired object. Adam immediately falls at his feet "Submiss," in an archetypal gesture of submission. Thus, God's palpable presence displaces the fruit-as-desire as the object of Adam's attention; Adam is guided by God to become a subject—one who is subjected to rule from outside—instead of just a subject—one who controls oneself, who is the author of one's own thoughts and actions.

What becomes established by the prohibition is the clear division between desire and the fruit. God must tell Adam, in a command, not to eat the fruit of a single tree. Presumably, there is nothing about the tree itself that would indicate its prohibited nature. As Lieb points out, traditional commentary on the tree tended to view the tree itself as harmless; it is a symbol or "Pledge" of obedience, not a bearer of intrinsically intoxicating or harmful fruit (VIII, 248). Thus, the act of prohibition separates the fruit from any desire-evoking properties it may contain. In other words, in order for the prohibition strategy to operate as a pledge it is necessary that any desire Adam feels for the fruit come from Adam himself. If Adam is expected to negotiate and choose between conflicting desires, it is because the desires are his and are not inextricable from the objects that might arouse them. Adam must be securely placed in a system where desire, objects desired, and knowledge of which objects should or should not be desired, are clearly delineated, just as dream and reality, and good and ill, are also strictly divided.

The three modes of objectification—dividing practices, knowledges that claim the status of factuality or science, and the attitude or relation a person has to his or her self—are all clearly and complexly present in the scene of prohibiting. If anything, the act of prohibition is part of a process of subjectification which the heavenly strategy requires in order to achieve its goals. As God says to his Son:

> What pleasure I from such obedience paid,
> When Will and Reason (Reason also is choice)
> Useless and vain, of freedom both despoild,
> Made passive both, had serv'd necessitie,
> Not mee. (III, 107–11)

Whether heaven's ultimate goals are either goodness and grace, or simply God's "pleasure," the power God wields operates through specific methods, such as domination, influence, permission, and prohibition, and through specific knowledges of the material world and the workings of the mind. In the poem it is these methods and knowledges that create subjects (and readers) who are aware of the contradictory position of one who simultaneously chooses for oneself and is ruled from outside. This type of contradiction is precisely indicative of the modernity of *Paradise Lost* and must serve as the framework through which its manifold and complex web of narration and explanation is examined in order to place the poem within a "genealogy"[31] of our present and the historical forces which have made us what we are, which form our own field of possibility and the conditions for its transformation.

University of Delaware

NOTES

1. For the overarching theoretical treatment of the historical transformation of European society in regard to processes of rationalization and the institutions of civil society and the state, see for example Max Weber, "Religious Rejections of the World and Their Directions," in *From Max Weber*, eds. H. H. Gerth and C. Wright Mills (New York, 1958); Jürgen Habermas, *The Structural Transformation of the Public Sphere*, trans. Thomas Burger (Cambridge, Mass. 1989); and the works of Michel Foucault cited below.

2. R. D. Bedford, "Time, Freedom, and Foreknowledge in *Paradise Lost*," in *Milton Studies* XVI, ed. James D. Simmonds (Pittsburgh, 1982), p. 61.

3. Dennis Richard Danielson's *Milton's Good God: A Study in Literary Theodicy* (Cambridge, 1982) is perhaps the most thorough attempt to contextualize *Paradise Lost* within seventeenth-century debates concerning the contradictory notions of a benevolent God and the existence of evil. This paper, in contrast, views the poem not in terms of a comprehensive theodicy but rather in terms of a network of represented narrative actions of which the theodicy is only a part.

4. Thomas Kranidas, "A View of Milton and the Traditional," in *Milton Studies* I, ed. James D. Simmonds (Pittsburgh, 1969), p. 16.

5. Ibid., p. 22.

6. Michel Foucault, "The Subject and Power," in Hubert L. Dreyfus and Paul Rabinow, *Michel Foucault: Beyond Structuralism and Hermeneutics* (Chicago, 1983) p. 208.

Two recent studies have attempted either to move Milton criticism out of the tradition, or to engage the tradition with recent critical theory. Christopher Kendrick's *Milton: A Study in Ideology and Form* (New York, 1986) works through a Jamesonian-Marxist interpretation; William Myers's *Milton and Free Will* (New York, 1987) attempts to combine a humanist-philosophical examination of the idea of free will and autonomy with certain contemporary critical concerns, but basically "involves a defence of traditional notions of truth, the self and God" (p. 4). The present study, relying primarily on a Foucauldian analytic, necessarily involves an implicit challenge to both of these approaches.

7. Michel Foucault, *Power/Knowledge*, trans. Colin Gordon et al. (New York, 1980) p. 78.

8. Michel Foucault, "Omnes et Singulatim: Towards a Critique of Political Reason," in *Tanner Lectures on Human Values*, vol. II, ed. S. M. McMurvin (Salt Lake City, 1981), p. 225.

9. All book and line references are from *The Complete Poetry of John Milton*, ed. John T. Shawcross, rev. ed. (New York, 1971).

10. Carrol B. Cox, "Citizen Angels: Civil Society and the Abstract Individual in *Paradise Lost*," in *Milton Studies* XXIII, ed. James D. Simmonds (Pittsburgh, 1987), p. 165. Cox's article seeks to locate in *Paradise Lost* a representation of a social structure which "is neither a Monarchy, nor a feudal hierarchy, but something much closer to Dickens's London or Austen's bourgeois gentry than to either Dante's heaven or Homer's Olympus" (p. 165). While serving as an impetus for a good deal of my argu' ıent about the Uriel-cherub scene, Cox's article remains bound up in notions of the "abstract individual" and "compulsory freedom" that are quite distant from my concerns with power and specific processes of subjectification.

11. Foucault, "The Subject and Power," pp. 219–20.

12. Perhaps the most extended narrative exploitation, in the seventeenth century, of the problem of the individual who cannot perceive a lie yet nonetheless is able to lie and is involved in elaborate deceptions is in Aphra Behn's *Oroonoko*. For the problem of telling the truth and discerning lies in seventeenth-century narrative in general see Michael McKeon, *The Origins of the English Novel: 1600–1740* (Baltimore, 1988), pp. 65–128.

13. The narrator, as a character who is implicated in the representations of power relations, raises specific questions that involve a distinct set of problems. In the self-proclaimed role of he who will "justifie the wayes of God to men" (I, 26), the inspired prophetic voice takes a mediating position between the human and the divine, thus creating a privileged sphere for the poet as a historical, moral force. While recognizing the importance of this self-conscious authorizing, this paper is limited to a discussion of power relations as manifested through the actions of the characters who palpably struggle with each other, and themselves, in their bodily presence in the poem.

14. Michel Foucault, *The History of Sexuality*, vol. I, trans. Robert Hurley (New York, 1980), p. 86: "[P]ower is tolerable only on condition that it mask a substantial part of itself. Its success is proportional to its ability to hide its own mechanisms. . . . [Its] secrecy is not in the nature of an abuse; it is indispensable for its operation."

15. Cox, "Citizen Angels," p. 165.

16. Foucault, *Power/Knowledge*, p. 90.

17. See the chapter "Truth and Power" in *Power/Knowledge* for a discussion of the importance of an analysis of *effects* rather than power or *truth* per se.

18. For Foucault's most concise explanation of and methodological justification for developing an "analytic" of power in opposition to the traditional "juridico-discursive theory" of power see "Two Lectures" in *Power/Knowledge* and *The History of Sexuality*, pp. 81–91.

19. Foucault, "The Subject and Power," p. 221.

20. In Book VIII, God and Adam address each other as both "thee" and "thou," thus compounding the subject-referent confusion of the "thou" in the complaint.

21. Foucault, "The Subject and Power," p. 212.

22. Foucault, *History of Sexuality*, pp. 61–62.

23. Max Weber, *The Protestant Ethic and the Spirit of Capitalism*, trans. Talcott Parsons (New York, 1958), pp. 87–88.

24. Ibid., p. 87.

25. Foucault, "The Subject and Power," p. 221.

26. Ibid., p. 208.

27. Michael Lieb, *"Paradise Lost* and the Myth of Prohibition," in *Milton Studies* VII, ed. Albert C. Labriola and Michael Lieb (Pittsburgh, 1975), p. 237.

28. Ibid., pp. 233–34.

29. See the chapter "Thomas Hobbes and the Revolution in Political Thought" in Christopher Hill, *Puritanism and Revolution* (London, 1958) for a discussion of the significant difference between two distinct forms of political rationality in Milton and Hobbes.

30. Foucault, *Power/Knowledge*, p. 119.

31. Ibid. See page 83, for a concise definition of his concept of *genealogy*.

SELF-RAISED SINNERS AND THE SPIRIT OF CAPITALISM: *PARADISE LOST* AND THE CRITIQUE OF PROTESTANT MELIORISM

Catherine Gimelli Martin

PERHAPS NO ASPECT OF *Paradise Lost* has been more consistently debated than the significance of its closure. While Dryden considered its sense of an ending deficient in redemptive optimism, Arthur O. Lovejoy later argued with almost equal success that it demonstrated Milton's acceptance of the optimistic doctrine of the *felix culpa*.[1] Yet despite these differing emphases on its joyfulness or resignation, critics have consistently tended to agree with Max Weber's view of the poem's ending as a triumphant affirmation of the spirit of "worldly asceticism" which provided the driving force of the Protestant ethic. In this still-dominant view, Adam's reeducation usefully prepares him for a renunciation of the pleasures of Eden and an acceptance of the more rigorous restraints of the "paradise within," a regimen based upon the values of self-control, hard work, and thrift that will allow him to prosper *ad majorem Dei gloriam*.[2] Such conclusions seem particularly convincing in light of the fact that Milton's early work concerns itself with something very like the formulation of a Protestant ethic. As Marshall Grossman notes, a major strain of this work reveals how "Milton remembers that 'God even to a strictness requires the improvement of these his entrusted gifts,' and he accepts the burden of 'dispos[ing] and employ[ing] those summes of knowledge and illumination, which God hath sent him into this world to trade with' (*RCG*, CP, 1: 801)."[3]

Despite the general validity of these remarks, the stubborn fact remains that nowhere in the finale or the development of Milton's post-Restoration poem is there any inkling of an acceptance of the Platonic dichotomies fundamental to the Protestant ethic, let alone any unmitigated assertion of optimism concerning the fate of the human elect on earth. Instead, Milton consistently overturns and inverts the premises of philosophical dualism not only in *Paradise Lost*, but even in much earlier efforts, where Grossman finds that he "turns the synchronous and essentialist doctrine of Plato into a model for the cultivation of the soul through

109

labor in the intellectual soil of the sensible world. Where Plato outlines the escape of what is always already the philosophical soul from the mire of its corporeal forgetting, Milton seizes the material beauty that reawakens the idea and works to transform it." Thus significantly, although he considers Milton's attempt at dialectical transcendence a failure ("the 'sublation' of the concept is always purchased at the cost of its abstraction from concrete, material substance"), Grossman's identification of this *species* of failure as Marxian suggests its great philosophical distance from the more familiar, Weberian form of the Protestant ethic, one that Milton seems never to have affirmed at all.[4] Assuming that in its early development the Protestant ethic contains many forms *in potentia*, much of Milton's prose and poetic ouevre actively points to the fact that he sought to undermine rather than to justify a dominant strand of Puritanism which "in accordance with the converging traditions of Christianity and Platonic idealism, reasserts the old dualistic patterns of Western thinking—reality and ideality, matter and spirit, body and soul—and radicalizes them in terms of the Calvinistic division of humanity into the elect and the reprobate."[5] While the Weberian model of the Protestant ethic *exalts* this dualism as the price of human redemption, both Marx and Milton condemn it as the price of an alienation that must be overcome. Unaware of the monistic and Arminian basis of the mature Milton's theology, Weber thus overlooked the fact that *Paradise Lost* actually places this alienating form of the Protestant ethic in the mouth of demons, and removes it from the mouth of the reeducated Adam. Instead, along with Eden, Adam must renounce simplistic divisions between sheep and goats, and with them, optimistic projections that the sheep will soon inherit the earth.[6]

Hence if Christopher Hill, Andrew Milner, and Jackie DiSalvo have correctly emphasized Milton's attachment to such bourgeois virtues as "frugality or thrift, industry, [and] selective rather than indiscriminate alms-giving,"[7] they are wrong in assuming that this vague collection of values wholly identifies his thought with that of a larger body of Calvinist thinkers who regarded these virtues as a sign of their sanctification in this world and their justification in the next. Precisely *because* of the radical dichotomies inserted between works and grace, Calvin's doctrine of predestination required that its adherents possess an at once absolute and purely internal sense of their own salvation, one that thereby refocused their energies upon externally demonstrating their capacity for "functional, voluntary, self-regulating behavior."[8] Yet according to Dennis Danielson, Arminians like Milton opposed the Calvinists' "Five Heads of Doctrine" (particularly the fifth, "the perseverance of the saints through God's preserving grace") precisely because they felt they conduced to an "overconfidence that could lead to moral laxity and irresponsibility," either in the form of an optimistic antinomianism,[9] or, as Keith Stavely adds, in the form of a self-justifying work ethic that provided a conveniently "circular proof of their own salvation." And in fact, because of the internal weaknesses that alarmed the Arminians, and despite the reformers' nominally traditional suspicion of economic activity, the Reformed church ultimately fell back on works as signs that could be regarded as "sanctified, sanctifying, and significant of justification." As Stavely further remarks, by hustling in by the back door what had been "debarred . . . any entrance whatsoever by the front door," the reformers tacitly left both wide open to the forces of market capitalism.[10]

Thus besides permitting the believers to regard their industry as evidence of their position among the elect, the reformers' attitude toward the sanctified nature of their callings actually encouraged them to accumulate ever-increasing amounts of surplus value. As Stephen Foster remarks, "Precisely *because* men labored for God and *not* for gold (or status or honor), they had to continue working in their callings constantly: material needs or even the desire for riches might be satisfied at some finite point, God never."[11] As this remark suggests, since this ethic claimed no role in earning a divine approval supposedly meted out in advance, it placed its adherents in the ironic position of endlessly needing to demonstrate their "divine right" by refashioning the external world in the image of a God that was ultimately an image of themselves.[12] Hence a relentlessly self-justifying and acquisitive Protestant ethic came into being which, particularly after it was secularized and validated on a national scale, but even earlier,[13] conduced toward meliorism, the "belief that the world naturally tends to get better and, especially, that this tendency can be furthered by human effort" (*Webster's New World Dictionary*).

Like his philosophical monism, both Milton's metaphysical theory and his literary practice deviate strikingly from the mainstream mentality described by Weber and his followers. Thus when critics cite the conclusion of *Paradise Lost* as a testament to the triumph of a sober but still jubilant "worldly asceticism," they ignore not only the antipredestinarian, Arminian basis of Milton's theology, but also his poetic attempt to discredit all schemas for assured worldly sanctification, particularly the self-satisfied ethic associated with meliorism. As Danielson forcefully argues, the whole notion of Adam's fall as a fortunate or necessary step toward an ever-ascending freedom and glory not only proves utterly incompatible with a close reading of *Paradise Lost*, but dismissive of its closely reasoned theodicy. By ignoring Milton's "free will defense" of God, Lovejoy, like Weber, at once erroneously links Milton to the opposing theology of the *felix culpa* held by Calvinists, and overlooks the importance of Michael's correction of Adam's premature jubilation.[14] Further, by replacing Adam's false expectation of an automatic, predestined restoration with that of a painful and partial recovery of an internalized Eden, Michael actually destroys a primary article of Calvinist conviction: that since individuals are either saved or damned, their earthly condition may be "read" as concrete evidence of their eternal fate. Hence, the partially reeducated Adam's first response to his vision of Christ—"O goodness infinite, goodness immense! / That all this good of evil shall produce, / And evil turn to good." (XII, 469–71)–is reversed only one hundred lines later, when he accepts a more sober and strenuous understanding of the conditions of human freedom and redemption, rewards which for Milton are not only paradoxically immaterial, interchangeable, and achievable, but as a synthesis of all three, very nearly inscrutable:

> Henceforth I learn, that to obey is best,
> And love and fear the only God, to walk
> As in his presence, ever to observe
> His providence, and on him sole depend,
>
> . . . .
> that suffering for Truth's sake
> Is fortitude to highest victory,
> And to the faithful Death the Gate of Life
>
> (XII, 561–64, 569–71)[15]

In uttering these words, Adam not only shows that he understands what he had earlier overlooked, the *un*fortunate fate of the faithful remnant whom his fall will expose to the "th'unfaithful herd / The enemies of truth" (481–82), but also demonstrates his distance from the ethics of the "quintessential self-made man."[16] Both by acknowledging the efforts of these faithful yet frequently unsuccessful Christian soldiers, and by accepting that the "sign" of his fortitude will be seen only in "Death the Gate of Life," Adam thus models an ethic that forcefully de- rather than resecularizes the Protestant imperative of working in one's vocation. Directing human endeavor toward a course of self-sacrificing personal accountability rather than toward a program of self-aggrandizing accomplishment, Michael's reeducation has taught him that history offers a prospect in which "works of Faith / [will] Rarely be found," a lesson only too clear once he recognizes how self-serving his own hopes for instant regeneration actually are. Adam's painfully achieved insight thus humbles the melioristic impulse of the Protestant ethic by signaling his acceptance of the nonpreservation of the saints, who, like him, must acknowledge that "so shall the

World go on, / To good malignant, to bad men benign, . . . till the day /
Appear of respiration to the just" (537–40).

Yet despite its sobering realism, Michael's prophecy need *not* be
understood as a complete rejection of Milton's revolutionary aspirations,
but only as his own sadder-but-wiser attempt to ground legitimate hope
for human progress in accurate self-appraisal rather than in the infinitely
malleable and easily corruptible outlook associated with Protestant meliorism. Significantly, both the misleading rigor and the actual weakness of
this outlook are carefully probed from the very moment of Satan's rise to
power in hell, a *disastrous* rise engineered by one of Satan's most successful inventions, the doctrine of the demons' fortunate fall. Thus Satan's
opening speech to his sadder-but-scarcely-wiser crew circumvents the
uncomfortable facts of their altered state by bribing them with sanguine
assurances of ascent. He quickly dismisses the deplorable results of their
"not inglorious" strife (although "th' event was dire," I, 623–24) by propos-
ing a new myth of his "divine right" to rule, here linked to the myth of the
demons' divine right of progress. Although this political maneuver owes
something to his typical incapacity for either sincerity or self-knowledge,
it owes more to his quite practical need to fabricate a doctrine which will
seem to mitigate without truly addressing the actual cause or effect of
their fall. With extraordinary political and semi-prophetic intuition, Satan
then proposes the doctrine most amenable to leading his rebel host further astray, the idea that their fall *inevitably* presages their return to
glory:

> For who can yet believe, though after loss,
> That all these puissant Legions, whose exile
> Hath emptied Heav'n, shall fail to re-ascend
> Self-rais'd, and repossess thir native seat?   (I, 631–34)

These claims, like the Calvinist doctrine of election which they resemble,
are not simple falsehoods, but dangerous half-truths. Although Satan and
his host will never regain their "native seat," they *will* "re-ascend / Self-
rais'd." Thus because the freedom to accept or reject the idea of an inherent right to rise belongs to fallen men as well as to the fallen host of hell,
the ends, means, and especially the *cost* of his melioristic philosophy must
be thoroughly discredited from its very source, the site of Satan's throne.

From this beginning, satanic meliorism and Miltonic pragmatism
throughout the poem are presented as two conflicting attitudes toward the
human condition.[17] Like a good Calvinist who regards himself as already
fated to be either "doomed" or "saved," Satan can only play out his sense
of himself on the vast stage of the *theatrum mundi;* whether hero or

villain/victim, the supposed aloofness of the divine puppet-master allows the suffering sinner to cast himself in either role, or (as is so often true of Satan) to assume each alternatively.[18] The Miltonic hero has no such excuses. Not actor but coauthor of an improvised performance, he does not merely display but vitally transacts his role in the world as the vital arena of moral, spiritual, and social salvation.[19] Or course, neither view is without its price. The first offers at least the illusion of limitless subjectivity, as well as the imminent expectation of a triumphant round of applause—unless, like Satan, the actor is peremptorily hissed off the stage (X, 545–47). Even before this moment of truth, however, Satan's quest has already led him from the heights of romantic self-assertion to the depths of unbounded objectification, a denial of legitimate otherness in favor of the demands of the illegitimate self.[20] In contrast, the Miltonic subject pays its price first: an acceptance of transcendental loss, assisted only by a vague and "wand'ring" form of revelation (XI, 335–54). While this acceptance initially evokes the shedding of some "natural tears," eventually it yields a higher and less dependent form of selfhood, one capable of encountering the limitless horizon wherein "The World was all before them, where to choose / Thir place of rest, and Providence thir guide" (XII, 646–47).

The wrong alternative, the mistaken route of meliorism originated by a "Satan who offers short cuts,"[21] is framed by Pandaemonium, the gilded monument to a form of enterprise that magically transforms the demons' worldly dungeon "in an hour." Standing as an eternal warning to all those "who boast in mortal things" that they "are easily outdone / By Spirits reprobate" (I, 693–97), not only its technical marvels but its work ethic are exposed as empty achievements by their ironic association with the work of bees, a traditional topos of benign social organization here gone wrong (I, 768–75). The pointed misapplication of this simile then allows the poet to link their misuse of external forms of endeavor and signs of success both with the false freedoms enjoyed by the demonic council and with the false family romance of the satanic trio, father/Fiend, mother/ Sin, and brother/Death. Underlying as well as undermining these products of Satan's social engineering is his other intellectual offspring, the ideology of the secular myth of progress. Like Sin and Death themselves, this last will prove a self-consuming progeny: by causing the proud who covet Caesar's crown to rely upon Mammon's gold and Belial's luxury, the il / lustrious idols of empire (I, 536–39) will ultimately appropriate and conquer both his subjects and himself. Beneath the flattering self-images that leader/fathers mirror to their subject/slaves is a series of illegitimate alliances grounded in narcissistically corrupt desire, a desire that palliates even as it advances their inevitable decay (II, 764–67, James i, 14–15). Thus, to an even greater degree than mere icons of progress like Pandaemonium, Satan's self-aggrandizing program of substituting "free-dom of enterprise" for truly strenuous spiritual endeavor lulls and finally engulfs its victims with a sense of false security and spurious achievement. Like Mammon's exhortation to "Hard liberty before the easy yoke" (II, 256), it paves the way for mining and other inventions that only dig the demons deeper into the bowels of their gilded pit.

Clearly, then, the fact that Mammon's heavily applauded plan for self-restoration, Beelzebub's imperialistic amendment, and even the re-jected proposals of Moloch and Belial are alike permeated and perverted by Satan's melioristic ideology can hardly be coincidental. Chief among the "wandr'ing mazes" in which the demons are lost (II, 561), his version of the *felix culpa* brings about a woe to demonkind that is ultimately coterminous with the woe to mankind that such demagogic designs for an "automatic" escape from history inevitably produce. Like Sin springing full-grown from the head of Satan, although this doctrine's "attractive graces" (II, 755–63) are opposed to authentic optimism and freedom, its real uses are many. Insinuating it into the demons' midst through a combi-nation of rhetorical inflation and logical inversion, Satan first uses it to transform a bitter acknowledgment of defeat (I, 84–93) into a virtual assurance of victory (I, 118–24). Part false prophet, part falsifying politi-cian, this prototype of the historical Caesars and Anthonys (but literary descendent of their Shakespearean versions) skillfully rallies his troops by performing logically contradictory tasks: convincing his army not only that they remain undefeated, but also that their quite visible loss is actually a gain. With appropriate irony, Satan bases his "proof" of his victory on what he has lost, his immortal, god-given condition: "For since no deep within her gulf can hold / Immortal vigor, though opprest and fall'n, / I give not Heaven for lost" (II, 12–14). This leap of logic provides the groundwork for his later justification of the demonic doctrine of the fortu-nate fall. Not hesitating to soar where Michael warns Adam not to tread, he further claims that

> From this descent
> Celestial Virtues rising, will appear
> More glorious and more dread than from no fall,
> And trust themselves to fear no second fate.   (II, 14–17)

Yet the most insidious aspect of Satan's proclamation that a phoe-nixlike, unearned glory will spontaneously arise from the ashes of their "immortal vigor" (13) is not its illogic but its tendentiousness. While neither their *former* substance nor their fall can prove anything but their now-terminated connection to the divine source of light and life, Satan's unchallenged boasts *do* confirm the demons' unwavering commitment to the doctrine of inalienable privilege that first won them to his cause. Politically, their assent to this doctrine places Satan in the position of a Caesar who shrewdly co-opts the ideological opposition in advance. Nevertheless, to secure his position further, he must guard against the counter-revolutionary applications of his own dogma. Thus in order both to defuse potential challenges to his dubious conflation of free assent/ascent and to further the illusion of democratic debate, he must continually inflate the already corrupt doublespeak of his reign. If only in this ironic sense, his "election" *does* then proceed from "just right, and the fixt Laws of Heaven" (18), just as he claims: their common delusion and his greater vigilance have made these subjects "rightfully" his. Not only "in Counsel or in Fight" (20) has he won the title to his hellishly "safe unenvied Throne / Yielded with full consent" (23–24), but won it through his ability to conceal in council the actual aftermath of their fight. His half-truths thus reveal/conceal the potentially damaging fact that since their consent has *always* been conditional upon his ability to maintain their status—first by resisting the "eclipse" of their "magnific Titles" that he leads them to think will follow from the Son's anointing (V, 772–77), and now by promising to reverse the consequences of their "second fate"—it will continue to remain conditional upon his ability to supply at least the illusion of ascent.

Because of Satan's awareness of this precarious aspect of his rule, both his military strategies and the propaganda with which he and Beelzebub surround them are carefully crafted to obscure its inherent weakness. Both demons understand the vapidity of his claim that while the war in heaven yielded an enviable glory, his right to rule is wholly unenviable now that leadership yields only the "greatest share / Of endless pain." In fact, Satan's confident assertion, that "where there is then no good / For which to strive, no strife can grow up there / From Faction; for none sure will claim in Hell / Precedence, none, whose portion is so small / Of present pain, that with ambitious mind / Will covet more" (II, 29–35), is as self-contradictory as it is hypocritical. Not only did *all* their pains begin with their first blows against God (VI, 327, 452–64), but like any defeat incurred by a usurper or tyrant, his failure to produce a promised victory might well overturn his rule. Hence when he recalls these events it is only to blur and recast them in the half-light of meretricious hope, rousing them to the tyrant's tune of military pomp and nationalistic glory by proclaiming his "divine right" and their "manifest destiny." Yet the price of these attractive anodynes is ruinously high: an easeful death ushering in oblivion, not millennium; and a deathful ease bringing comfort paid for with complicity.[22] Even their purported unity and fellowship are but meager myths glossing over the secret conclaves of deepest Pandaemonium, bitter euphemisms for a self-imposed state of inequality in which, ironically, only *morally* are they all one.

Hence from this rhetorical starting point, the same brilliant sophistry that here allows Satan to pose as the idol of liberté, egalité, and fraternité, inevitably *requires* him to become the golden calf of the myth of progress. As he "logically" concludes,

> With this advantage then
> To union, and firm Faith, and firm accord,
> More then can be in Heav'n, we now return
> To claim our just inheritance of old,
> Surer to prosper then prosperity
> Could have assur'd us.   (II, 35–40)

By conflating an ironically "authentic" faith and freedom with the advance of a "surer prosperity," Satan skillfully distracts the "ambitious minds" of potential rivals by redirecting them toward less strenuous but still nominally heroic paths. Hence in one sense, at least, his propaganda accurately reflects his real political aims: both promote a "firm Faith" whose real "accord" consists in a mutually agreed upon distortion of the facts. Even the most superficial reflection would reveal that Satan's "just inheritance" is an egregious euphemism for just punishment, and that his promises of "prosperity" depend upon a reductive definition of the word: it can no longer mean "increasing in fortune or happiness," but merely *increasing*. Yet, once they accept these linguistic substitutions, Satan can "honestly" assure them that they will prosper better *without* prosperity—that is, without divine favor. By thus twisting etymologies, Satan not only fosters an empty work ethic, but a mentality that is indeed "its own place," the rhetorical placeholder of hell. Hence his conversion of the meaning of *union, faith,* and *harmony* to connote unquestioning servitude to him illustrates the true reversion implicit in his hell: the parodic displacement of the real communion modeled by the Father and Son, of dialogue in which harmony is based upon difference.[23]

From this examination of the logical corruption behind Satan's later devolution, Book II expands its focus to include the effects of satan-speak among his followers. These effects are greater both in proportion to their victims' literalistic investment in them and in the degree of mental or moral sloth behind that investment. Nevertheless, in every case satanic meliorism produces one consistent result: a nihilism as evident in their futile epics bemoaning the injustices of fate (II, 550–52) as in their political oratory. The oratorical sign of their common condition is evinced first and most strikingly in Moloch, the initial speaker in the demonic council and the one most inclined to violent and extreme remedies. Nevertheless, Moloch's motive in advocating a renewal of "open War" (51) stems not merely from his character, but in large part from his belief in the satanically inspired doctrine of manifest destiny, the belief that "descent and fall / To us is adverse" (76–77). If the pun on *adverse* is *inadvertent* on the part of the angel, it is scarcely so on the part of the poet. Moloch is above all adverse *to* "descent and fall," but only his nihilistic self-delusion can convince him that it is not equally adverse *for* him.

Thus in the long run, Moloch's simplification of an already reductive case is not only a potential source of embarrassment to Satan, but a possible hindrance to his purposes. Only by means of an indirect retaliation can the latter hope to rally and consolidate his forces. To accomplish this aim, he needs to assure his cohort that "ascent is easy" (81), while postponing any test of this highly questionable proposition. Thus because an active confrontation with their Foe is, as Moloch admits, an "event [to be] fear'd" indeed (82), Satan knows he cannot retain his rule by facing, but only by *appearing* to face a force whose final decrees cannot easily be disguised with misleading assurances. This program is particularly jeopardized by Moloch's stoical definition of success: he prefers to die forever rather "Than miserable to have eternal being" (98), to face his final destiny rather than to await an uncertain reward or punishment. Ironically, because his straightforward assessment has more in common with the newly fallen Adam's honest fears than with Satan's tortuous circumlocutions, it too obviously displays the flaw at the heart of the demons' self-congratulatory escapism. Moloch immediately grasps what both the unrestored Adam and his fellow captives must ultimately acknowledge: that without repentance, their only "positive" course is a despairing one, a gamble leading either to pyrrhic victory or to total oblivion (II, 95–105; X, 845–56).[24]

Thus if baldly nihilistic, impolitic, and inopportune, Moloch's guess that their semi-deferred engagement with God must ultimately be resolved one way or the other is close enough to the truth that it must be immediately repressed by the more optimistic of the demons. This is, of course, no mean feat, since even in abeyance, the Almighty's power over them is hardly nonexistent. Not only does it clearly debar them from light and its attendant joys, as here, but it will later force them to perform a humiliating repetition of their own and mankind's Fall (X, 515–21). In this respect, Moloch's perception that neutrality is impossible as well as undesirable only underscores the even more fantastic conceits that Satan's doctrine of the fortunate fall typically produces in his peers. These delusions are especially embodied in the character of the next speaker, Belial, the unrepentant advocate of the deathful ease that will lead them all to gradual destruction. Applying Satan's ideology in a manner diametrically opposed to Moloch, he recommends making the best of what is at least not the worst of all possible worlds, "for his thoughts were low; / To vice industrious, but to Nobler deeds / Timorous and slothful" (115–17). Yet precisely because Belial promotes an unheroic form of meliorism remote from that envisioned by either Satan or Moloch, his remarks shed light on the inherent fatalism of the philosophy even when divorced from Moloch's militarism or Satan's imperialism. For much the same reason, his approach eloquently illuminates its universally degrading consequences.

In contrast with Adam's final resolve to endure despite the hardships of his "second fate," Belial's solution is paradoxically less pragmatic and less truly optimistic. Despite and even because of the stoical sentiments in which his epicurean fantasies are couched, his avowed disbelief in God's continuing opposition only thinly conceals his own failure of will and lack of integrity. His commitment to a policy of neutrality thus rests upon two related errors: a disbelief in divine justice, and a disbelief in the need for individuals to come to terms with it. By this means, his vision of a "necessary" or spontaneous rather than a just basis for ascent is linked to a dream of irresponsibility, a puerile fantasy less realistic but not ultimately more nihilistic than Moloch's. Yet while Belial errs in thinking that an unassailed Almighty might forget to exact full justice, his cowardice at least makes him fully cognizant of Moloch's chief oversight, the fact that since God *remains* almighty and unassailable,

> our great Enemy
> All incorruptible would on his Throne
> Sit unpolluted, and th' Ethereal mould
> Incapable of stain would soon expel
> Her mischief.   (II, 137–41)

This undeniable truth, one that the reader will actually see enacted when God's "immortal Elements . . . purge off" our grand parents from Eden (XI, 50–53), results in a deadlock between the two positions. If Moloch's program is impracticable, Belial's is illogical. Nor is this parallelism surprising given that both demons make the error of conflating two incompatible objectives: a reascent to heaven, and a continuing rejection of its dictates. The parallel extends to their mental attitude, which in either case resembles the futile prospect Belial complains of in Moloch: "our final hope / Is flat despair" (142–43).

Both demons thus propose programs either too obviously fatalistic or too self-deluding to be palatable to the others. Moloch's fanatic aggression proves as objectionable as Belial's blithe passivity, which stems from his cringing insistence that

> since fate inevitable
> Subdues us, and Omnipotent Decree,
> The Victors will. To Suffer, as to do,
> Our strength is equal, nor the Law unjust
> That so ordains.   (II, 197–201)

In thinking to illuminate the hidden power, Belial thus reveals only the hidden weakness of classical stoicism, the same philosophy scornfully rejected by the Redeemer of *Paradise Regain'd*.[25] The reasons for that rejection are even clearer here, where Belial's banal equation of individual fortitude with eternal Law parodies the complex coordinates of Christian integrity. By placing its hope in inevitable historical cycles, it actually seeks *only* to suffer, not to do. Here as elsewhere, the demonic tendency to objectify the more mysterious ways of God's "second fate" causes sound inferences to yield empty conclusions. Hence Belial's groundless hope that the Almighty may "remit his anger" and "not mind us not offending" degenerates into circuitous, vapid doggerel:

> these raging fires
> Will slack'n, if his breath stir not thir flames.
> Our purer essence then will overcome
> Thir noxious vapor, or enur'd not feel,
> Or chang'd at length, and to the place conform'd
> In temper and in nature, will receive
> Familiar the fierce heat, and void of pain;
> This horror will grow mild, this darkness light,
> Besides what hope the never-ending flight
> Of future days may bring, what chance, what change,
> Worth waiting, since our present lot appears
> For happy though but ill, for ill not worst,
> If we procure not to ourselves more woe.   (II, 213–25)

In Belial's mouth, stoical meliorism then becomes its own parody, its vague trust in automatic ascent achieving only his own downward spiral into an ever-greater accommodation of evil, as long as evil can be redefined as good. Belial's social philosophy thus presents a horrific fusion of the emotional decadence of a *Brave New World* with the linguistic duplicity of a *1984*, a prospect not entirely lost on his audience, who regard his proposal as mere "words cloth'd in reasons garb / [that] Counsell'd ignoble ease, and peaceful sloth, / Not peace" (226–28). All too accurately, his words reflect his complete alienation from a divine ray which only in his imagination will ever make "this darkness light." Thus as if to underscore the point that there can be no recuperation apart from divine mercy and individual acceptance of "the better fortitude / Of Patience and Heroic Martyrdom" (IX, 31–32), the next demon's counsel falls between the horns of the dilemma created by the arguments of the preceding speakers without actually extricating itself from the pitfalls of either position. Although Mammon not only spots but even "corrects" the more glaring errors in Belial's logic, his proposal is no real improvement. In the place of "ignoble ease," he proposes a more energetic and worldly wise but equally futile form of meliorism—an active rather than passive plan of self-incrimination. Yet at least superficially, Mammon's program is not only more appealing but far more practicable; so practicable, in fact, that it is destined to supply an important ingredient in Satan's general design. Shrewdly isolating the common weakness in the positions of both previous speakers, Mammon points out that both rely upon an unrealistic assessment of Chance, a fickle force that can hardly insure their recovery (II, 229–37). Thus because his "better" logic is that of a secular Calvinist, one who proposes to "seek / Our own good from our selves, . . . to none accountable" (II, 252–55), he usefully illustrates the most subtle danger of all self-made meliorisms: their false assessment of worldly pleasures as opposed to godly pains. As Adam's corrected understanding later attests, only those of contrite heart and "sorrow unfeign'd" can know the authentic joy and hope of repentance, and only they can see that in their Judge's face, "When angry most he seem'd and most severe, / What else but favor, grace, and mercy shone?" (X, 1095–96).

Mammon's role in the debate is thus central because he at once improves upon and shares the delusions of the previous speakers. Rejecting the "servile Pomp" of heaven (II, 257), he nevertheless hopes not merely imaginatively but materially to replicate and even to overgo its splendors. Like the god of worldly ambitions that he is, he improves upon Belial's pseudo-Stoicism by cloaking its self-aggrandizing aims in a pseudo-Christian work ethic. He thus claims that their "greatness will appear"

> when great things of small,
> Useful or hurtful, prosperous of adverse
> We can create, and in what place soe'er
> Thrive under evil, and work ease out of pain
> Through labor and endurance.   (II, 257–62)

This noble rhetoric, already suspect in the mouth of Mammon, the chief contractor of Pandaemonium, will later be fully discredited as the exact inversion of the reeducated Adam's goal, always "with good / Still overcoming evil, and by small / Accomplishing great things," thereby *subverting* "worldly strong, and worldly wise / By simply meek" (XII, 565–69), *not working* "ease out of pain." Thus Adam's own expulsion and curse (X, 201–06), combined with the circumstances of his renewed resolution, expose the inherent weakness of Mammon's progressivism: its mistaken assumption that creatures may live well or even thrive in alienation from God by taking advantage of the divine "calling" to rise inherent in God's "one first matter" (V, 472). As Raphael explains to Adam, an internal condition is placed upon this matter's natural tendency to return to God, the condition that both he and it refuse to be "deprav'd from good" (V, 471).

By extrapolation, then, Mammon's meliorisim is tenable only on the basis of a neoclassical or Calvinist dualism, a divorcement of spiritual from material works which the poet everywhere rejects. Because in *Paradise Lost* the workings of the spirit represent incomplete, alterable *tendencies* that cannot fully signify final *realities* (except in time),[26] any work ethic that separates worldly pleasures from divine grace will be as distorted as one that conflates them. Both must be regarded as modified Manichaeisms: supposedly beneficial but actually detrimental divisions of the spiritual and material forms of the Good.[27] Yet like other heresies, this one's inherent lack of viability seems not to inhibit but actually to enhance its power; and as a result its ethical and political consequences prove as real as those of other forms of delusion. Not only has it already produced a splendid Pandaemonium, but it will continue to produce all the other edifices of human pomp and tyranny from Babel to the present. Although these will, Babel-like, ultimately fall, their destruction is neither especially imminent nor especially progressive. Instead, the outline of history developed in the poem's conclusion shows a human saga of erratic progress and regress, an ongoing nightmare with many intermittent escapes but only a single permanent one, the day of "respiration to the just."

Thus like the later doctrine of the *felix culpa*, the demonic creed that time will inevitably "remove / The sensible of pain" (II, 277–78) represents a dangerous form of half-truth. Like the naive fideism extolled by the chorus of *Samson Agonistes*, these doctrines place their faith in a guaranteed *temporal* recovery based solely on the "miracles" of individual triumph over external circumstance.[28] Further, by expecting the restoration of lost glory without an authentic personal struggle for reconciliation either with God's laws or their correct application to his material universe, they demean the Son's prior act of atonement (III, 227–65) even while taking advantage of its temporal dispensation. Like the demons who "hail the Horrors" of hell and welcome their newfound "freedom," the adherents of these doctrines conveniently forget the extent to which redemption bestows greater glory *only* upon God and his Son, not upon their opposers, for whom it creates pains innumerable, nor even upon those who accept free grace without being able fully to merit *or* fulfill its provisions.[29] Thus eventually, because all must suffer and die, and because even the faithful remnant cannot expect more immediate results from the atonement than a form of hardship tempered with goodwill (XII, 477–78), in the very best of circumstances victory can be gained only at the hard price of *two* "heroic martyrdom[s]," their own and the Son's.[30]

While the most successful demagogues always seem to grasp this painful truth, they use it only to further their own destructive ambitions. Unlike the naive and slothful Belial, they understand their situation in order to control others, and to retain their power have struck the devil's bargain: to sacrifice the true ascent accorded the few for the approval and consent of the many. Hence unlike the more naive meliorists who precede them in the council of demons, Beelzebub and Satan do not so much subscribe to the sanguine platitudes of their doctrine of the fortunate fall as find it useful in extending their reign in hell and on earth. They know that like Belial and Mammon, most of the demons will prefer comfortable platitudes to the truly strenuous requirements of "hard liberty." If by now they cannot repent, their fate is the same as that of human philosophers who will not;[31] their common dream of prospering in terms of a purely evanescent prosperity makes them easy prey for tyrants and demagogues. Beelzebub's next task is thus a relatively simple one. Calling attention to the fatal flaw in even Mammon's scheme—its failure to account for the opposing forces of the Almighty—Beelzebub corrects this flaw by offering them a substitute Savior. Because without *some* god on its side—chance, fate, or Satan—the fallen myth of progress collapses, and because the former two have been examined and found wanting, Beelzebub's maneuver thus rounds out the reader's understanding of the inevitably idolatrous basis of the myth from its beginning. At the same time, his warning that no "peace will be giv'n / To us enslav'd, but custody severe" (II, 332–33), reminds us of the reality behind the myth, that on this earth the warfare between the "unfaithful herd" and the lovers of truth will never cease.

Of course, like Satan himself, Beelzebub is adept at drawing his audience's attention to harsh realities in order to placate them with false solutions. To the slothful herd who desire no "dangerous expedition" (342) but "some easier enterprise" (345), the luxury of believing that they are not "hatching vain Empires" (378) will turn out to depend upon a final remission of their sovereignty into Satan's hands, the final goal of the father of lies in league with the lord of the flies (378–80). The council thus reaches its appropriate climax in an acceptance speech whose repeated double entendres raise the self-parodic element of Satan's performance to a deafening crescendo. Yet once again, the double meanings contained in his promises disclose as much as they conceal about the actual fate awaiting all those who put faith in a fortunate fall. Since "like to what ye are" the demons have "great things resolv'd," Satan predicts that their "resolve"

> Will once more lift us up, in spite of Fate,
> Nearer our ancient Seat; perhaps in view
> Of those bright confines, whence with neighboring Arms
> And opportune excursion we may chance
> Re-enter Heav'n; or else in some mild Zone
> Dwell not unvisited of Heav'n's fair Light
> Secure, and at the bright'ning Orient beam
> Purge off this gloom; the soft delicious Air,
> To heal the scar of these corrosive Fires
> Shall breathe her balm.   (II, 391–402)

This glorious misalliance of realistic aspiration and utter fabrication allows us to see Satan himself as the fullest flower and finest satire of the meliorist impulse. Characteristically substituting the euphemism *fate* for any more direct and dangerous allusion to the Almighty, he ultimately traps himself in his own circumlocutions in a way that unintentionally prophesies their results. As he promises, his imperialistic expedition will allow them to enter the more "soft delicious Air" of a milder zone, a place, in fact, "nearer our ancient Seat." Yet not only will this "ascent" merely succeed in making earth more hellish, but in the process Satan will himself discover that his psychic pains intensify even as they follow him *everywhere* (IV, 75). For this and a number of related reasons, instead of healing he can only further degrade the scarred substance of those to whom "all good . . . becomes / Bane" (IX, 122–23). When these qualifications are taken into consideration, Satan's myth of progress not only loses considerable attraction, but becomes a "second fate" actually to be feared—a fall both more agonizingly fatal than the first, and of far greater duration then the quick end Moloch had envisioned.

Thus Satan's pose as the redeemer who makes a self-sacrificing journey through "the coasts of dark destruction" in order to win "deliverance for us all" (II, 465–66) is exposed as a hollow substitute both for Christ's redemption, and for the individual *struggle* necessary to avail oneself of it. Those who place their faith in this kind of progress reap not only the hollow reward they sow, but pains far greater than those accompanying godly repentance and faith. In contrast, true victory demands both an initial acknowledgment of sin and a lifelong confrontation with its many forms, ranging from the external "enemies of truth" to the secret enemy within, the easeful, sensual self. Yet in the end, the benefits of this struggle incomparably outweigh its costs: both in this world and the one to follow, false hope produces slavery and death, while true hope yields freedom and life. Finally, then, the darkest aspect of our "second fate" is that defeat will always be most probable when most palatable, when posed as some false assurance or false messiah offering easy victory at the price of easy slavery. On the other hand, its bright side is equally assured, if not always equally visible: divine mercy and justice will still assist the "wandering steps and slow" of imperfect but faithful humans, who will thereby continue to advance in freedom and grace (III, 185–97). Thus our sad "second fate" may be overcome—not by accepting the premature bliss of the *felix culpa* or any of its melioristic progeny, but by acknowledging that the consequences of Adam's most unfortunate fall preclude the over-confident projections based upon "our just inheritance of old" (II, 38) to which Satan and his fellows cling.

As these observations are meant to suggest, there is a vast difference between regarding the fall as fortunate and in regarding it as affording a trial in which mankind may potentially be vindicated. Many who continue to regard it as fortunate—including Christopher Hill—overlook the difference between Adam's, Samson's, or any other individual's opportunity *"when the time comes, . . .* to cooperate to bring [God's kingdom] about" (italics mine), and actually being present when the time is right.[32] They also forget that since Milton neither experienced nor, in all probability, expected to experience that time, he seems expressly to have designed his epic to confront its absence. The logical demands of this absence include the formulation of an ethic divorced from any immediate expectation of personal reward—either the expectation of witnessing the divine vindication of the saints, or the concrete signs of this vindication. By rejecting these scarcely disinterested forms of commitment, which always implicitly regard Adam's fall as fortunate *for some*, his progeny can prove their faithfulness by viewing their own, along with the history of all mankind, as an open-ended struggle whose short-term results remain open to conjecture. While God's goodness *will* ultimately produce a new heaven and a new earth, the names of its occupants like the circumstances and time of its approach remain, from the human perspective, utterly unknowable.

Further, as Adam learns, his most humble commitment to renewed love and obedience will no more prevent him from suffering the needless pains of familial fratricide, than will the truth of the "faithful few" guarantee their freedom from every form of bondage (XII, 524–37). Even their most concrete spiritual rewards will produce a spirit of ceaseless moral and political reform rather than the spirit of meliorism or capitalism. Finally, Milton's variation on the Protestant work ethic, a Samson-like form of exemplary individualism that *if* it achieves social renewal, usually does so at the price of personal sacrifice and even failure, differs so strongly from any calling to accumulate tangible signs of moral or material excellence as to discredit it in advance. For Milton, to affirm "the perseverance of the saints through God's preserving grace" would be to deny the circumstances of Eve's seduction by such signs, the justice of Adam's exile, and the painful yet real regeneration of both.

A brief demonstration of how even a subtle conflation of the Miltonic and the Weberian work ethics must strain seriously against the poem should further clarify these points. By developing the parallels between the internalized form of social regulation described in Michel Foucault's *Discipline and Punish* and the postlapsarian conditions of Adam and Eve, Laura Knoppers concludes that their newfound "paradise within" acts as an ethical corollary to the spirit of accumulation, even though it lacks the same emphasis on actual material production. Thus whatever its divergences from the Calvinist model, she concludes that the Miltonic work ethic ultimately recuperates it. However, to make this case, Knoppers must argue two positions which strongly conflict with the findings outlined above: (1) that the fall is fortunate, and (2) that its "fortunate" aspect consists in repressing Eve's (satanic) obsession with the "image of her own beauty and desiring knowledge as power." In this way, Eve learns the value of self-regulation according to the Protestant model, where advancement depends on assimilating *another's* standards of what it means to work in one's own vocation.[33] This assessment not only implies that the conclusion of *Paradise Lost* replaces the internal, immaterial dialogue between man and God with external constraints, but that this substitution valorizes the consequences of sin in much the same way as Satan's "enterprising" ideology.

Just as problematic, however, is Knoppers's largely traditional and un-Miltonic interpretation of Eve's fall. Although Christian theologians, poets, and painters had typically regarded female narcissism as the source of Eve's error, Book I of *Paradise Lost* assigns the "cause of all our woe" first to the deception of "the original serpent," then expands it in Book X to include not merely Adam's own effeminacy (as opposed to femininity per se), but also the more generally *human* desire for the satanic idols of unearned ascent.[34] Further, far from succumbing to narcissism, in spite and perhaps because of the ominous warning implicit in her dream,[35] Eve easily and absolutely rejects Satan's first attempt to exalt herself or the forbidden fruit with "over-praising" (IX, 562–65, 615–16). Nor does knowledge itself prove to be her downfall, but only a carefully constructed misrepresentation of its uses. Significantly, this misrepresentation reveals the poet's awareness of the temptations inherent in the core attitudes of the Protestant ethic. Satan's successful temptation of Eve actually follows the same course as his success-ful seduction of his fallen legions: both are deceived with variants of the myth of progress. He assures her that because creatures have an unquali-fied right to profit from and control their domain, the fruit will promote effortless empirical advance (IX, 679–82, 716–28); that she may attain recuperation and grace independent of the works (or abstinences) that God has been misinterpreted as requiring (IX, 685–97); and, last but not least, that the example of the self-promoted serpent affords a tangible guarantee of the *benign* effects of a fall which can only prove fortunate (IX, 705–15). Hence unlike his own daughter, Sin, his narcissistic "other half," Eve is not seduced by flattery, but by pseudooptimistic assurances that she can ignore or reinterpret the words and promises of God. When she falls, it is thus as an all-too-familiar victim of the standard satanic hoax, the belief that "from this descent / Celestial Virtues rising, will appear / More glorious . . . than from no fall."

In this scene as in the description of Satan's equivocal announcement that the defeated demons are now "surer to prosper than prosperity / Could have assur'd us" (II, 39–40), there can be little doubt that the poet means to expose the dangers with which Stavely finds him concerned, those aroused by false idols of progress who will fortunately allow the chosen few "to bring the world into fuller conformity with God's will."[36] Those who ignore God in order to follow these *ignes fatui* here succeed only in bringing about an ironic inversion of the state of affairs that they envision. Further, by portray-ing the demons as for the most part hardworking and even, in a sinister sense, heroic ("for neither do the Spirits damn'd / Lose all thir virtue"), Milton provides a means of distinguishing their acts from those of the faithful angels that corrects the primary oversight of the Protestant ethic: its inability to separate true virtue from "specious deeds . . . , which glory excites, / Or close ambition varnisht o'er with zeal" (II, 482–85). Although the difference between the saved and the damned is reflected in *some* outer appearances and inner sensibilities, throughout the poem their primary difference is shown to consist in the willingness of the former to *continue* to struggle with the burdens and to refuse the temptations inherent in their

freedom. Hence, the immediate rewards received for continuing this struggle are wholly distinct from the blessings awaiting the Calvinist saints.
Allowing for temporal failure as well as success, just as it allows for lapses in
humility, love, and faith, this ethic frees the heroic individual from the need
actually to produce *any* material sign of his salvation, so long as he achieves
a final peace with God.

From this perspective, not only Adam's redemption but the seemingly more glorious vindication of Samson indicate the extent to which the
Weberian ethic is not affirmed but overturned by Milton's critique of the
melioristic conviction that for the elect ultimately "all is best." Like that of
the demons who rejoice with Satan, the choral observers of Samson's
victory here voice only an ironic half-truth (1745). More wrong than right,
they are ignorant of the fact that like Enoch's, this victory accumulates no
symbolic capital negotiable in this world.37 In their lifetimes, both heroes
experience more hatred and failure than renown, their escapes from or
through death serving chiefly to show "what reward / Awaits the good, the
rest what punishment" (XI, 708–10). Samson's "glory" in fact exceeds
Enoch's only by combining repentance with faith, by achieving *through*
both personal and social failure the fulfillment of his name, "here for the
second time." This feat is in turn possible only once he has freed himself
from the false "dependency" hung in his hair (59), from the merely external signs of election. In fact because his self-liberation carries with it the
continual possibility of defeat that ends only at "Death the Gate of Life,"
Samson's "special vocation" cannot be separated from the general vocation
of trial to which all are subject. Hence it is not, as John Guillory claims,
the recuperation or "*return* of election, the return of being chosen rather
than choosing,"38 but actually its opposite: a special but unpredestined
opportunity which guarantees Samson's worldly success no more than it
does the perserverance of the other "saints."39 Because, as Mary Ann
Radzinowicz points out, "The words *deliverer* and *deliverance* sound
throughout the play in two senses: delivered from or liberated, and delivered up or enslaved," neither Samson's own nor the fate of his tribe is ever
assured. As he himself realizes (460–71), God may reserve his vindication
for another time, place, and hero; and in fact, because his tribe does not
"fight the good fight of the faith," it "vanished from history as Samson
might have vanished had he been merely mighty."40

Thus much like Knoppers, Guillory can recuperate Samson for Weber's view of Calvinist election only by ascribing to Milton positions that
his text(s) reject: (1) by ascribing authority to the unreliable and frequently self-contradictory Chorus; (2) by conflating Samson's strength
with his success; and (3) by inserting a false distinction between the

parable of the talents and that of the workers in the vineyard. Very few critics of Milton's tragedy, revisionist or otherwise, would agree that it supports either of the first two positions; simply put, only the *Chorus* regards Samson as one of the elect who "may be figured as visibility itself," the antithesis of obscurity; and only they regard the fulfillment of his vocation as an act of maintaining "vocational rigidity" or "fixity" (Guillory, pp. 157–58). Whether or not the chorus sees it, the essence of Samson's achievement is *interior change*, a struggle to come to terms with the conditions of his existence that either succeeds or fails in the eyes of a God who remains offstage.[41] Thus in regard to Guillory's third point, Samson's "one talent which is death to hide" is actually opposed to physical strength, just as it is opposed to the chorus who Calvinistically lament its loss. As *both* parables in Matthew indicate, all that God really requires is a reasonable attempt to use whatever light he allots in the varying time he allots it. Further, because all his talents are ultimately the same, portions of the same truth that prosper better in some hands and in some times than in others, the amount of return on the investment is *not* a criterion of reward, but only one's *using* it, as the "evil servant" and the early workers in the vineyard fail to see. Thus Samson is hardly in danger of being condemned for having "no vocation," as conventional Puritans like William Perkins might fear, but merely for neglecting whatever light remains to him, especially the purely "inward light" that if it fails to turn *"a profit"* (Guillory, pp. 158–59), despite the choral obtuseness, indeed "puts forth . . . [a] visual beam" (162–63). In fact, this "beam" seems to have saved Samson *before* his reported triumph, a suggestion underscored by the scene's striking deviation from the account in Judges. According to the messenger, he does *not* pray aloud for miraculous vindication, but silently puts himself in the hands of his God, "as one who pray'd, / or some great matter in his mind revolv'd" (1637–38). The moment thus affords no visual or verbal sign indicating the clear meaning of his achievement, one that exists only in the report of the messenger and in the perspective of the faithful, who must (and do) make of it what they will.

Finally, then, Guillory presents a much better reading of the logic of Calvinism than of the dialectic of *Samson Agonistes*.[42] As Radzinowicz has shown, both parables in Matthew were consistently central to Milton's understanding of the concepts of talent and election, and both were synthetically understood by him. In his sonnets as in his major poems, he uses them to formulate a gradual but fundamental theological revision whereby "the ethics of purity through election is modulated into an ethics of purification through trial in free choice." Yet at this later "ethical stance, [from which] Milton never deviated," mainstream Calvinism never arrived. Due to this factor as well as to the poet's mature rejection of "facile optimism about the inevitability of human progress and . . . the easy resolution of contradictory impulses or inconsistent aims,"[43] it becomes flatly impossible to reconcile an authentic Miltonic ethic either with Weber's Protestant ethic or with the melioristic impulses which accompany its secularization. In this sense, even Grossman's emphasis on the purely proleptic rewards which the early Milton hopes his poetic production to accrue in his "Divine Taskmaster's eye" overstates his long-term view of a proper work ethic. At least by 1652, if not earlier, while continuing to regard vigorous effort as essential to the redemption of his God-given "talents," the poet clearly regards his final vindication as independent from a fame that could permit the expropriation of his work by a "peculiarly divine corporate manager."[44] Blind, discouraged, and writing for an audience that he can only hope is "fit . . . though few" (VII, 31), in Sonnet XIX as in *Paradise Lost*, Milton consistently argues that the faithful individual must uproot the idea of God as a petty Protestant accountant, replacing it with the conception of a Being who blesses not only repentant Eves, humbled Adams, and struggling Samsons, but also all those who can no longer gloriously strive, and so must merely "stand and wait."

Memphis State University

NOTES

1. See Arthur O. Lovejoy, "Milton and the Paradox of the Fortunate Fall," *ELH* IV (1937), 161–79.

2. Max Weber, *The Protestant Ethic and the Spirit of Capitalism*, trans. Talcott Parsons (New York, 1958); see especially pp. 87–88. Critics who apply the basic schema of Weber's influential essay (which first appeared in 1904–1905) include Jackie DiSalvo, *War of Titans: Blake's Critique of Milton and the Politics of Religion* (Pittsburgh, 1983); Andrew Milner, *John Milton and the English Revolution* (London, 1981); and Herman Rapaport, *Milton and the Postmodern* (Lincoln, Nebr., 1981).

3. Marshall Grossman, "The Fruits of One's Labor in Miltonic Practice and Marxian Theory," *ELH* LIX (1992), 77–195, quoted p. 83.

4. Grossman, "The Fruits of One's Labor in Miltonic Practice and Marxian Theory," pp. 92, 98.

5 See André Bleikasten, "*Light in August:* The Closed Society and Its Subjects," in *New Essays on "Light in August,"* ed. Michael Millgate (Cambridge, 1987), pp. 81–102, quoted p. 96. Although Bleikasten is commenting on a much later critique of the Protestant ethic, his work provides a convenient synopsis of the consequences in question here.

6. Based on his own examination of Satan's tactics, Keith W. F. Stavely also views Milton's rejection of the imminent arrival of the New Jerusalem as a rejection of the chief

rationalization behind the acquisitive, "reifying" impulse of the Protestant ethic. See *Puritan Legacies: "Paradise Lost" and the New England Tradition, 1630–1890* (Ithaca, N.Y., 1987), pp. 62–97.

7. Christopher Hill, *Milton and the English Revolution* (London, 1977) pp. 263–65. For Milner and DiSalvo, see note 2.

8. See David Little, *Religion, Order, and Law: A Study in Pre-Revolutionary England* (New York, 1969) p. 75. According to Little, this social evolution occurs within Calvinism since by "eagerly harmoniz[ing] their own specific gifts with the gifts of others, for the good of all. . . . They are the wave of the future, the new elite" (p. 74). Eventually, then, once the Christian has externally demonstrated his capacity for disciplined works, "In the new elite, he has become a law unto himself" (p. 125). Little's study remains one of the best brief discussions of the validity of Weber's hypothesis for mainline Calvinism.

9. See Dennis Danielson, *Milton's Good God: A Study in Literary Theodicy* (Cambridge, 1982), pp. 70–75. Although Danielson emphasizes the importance of Milton's opposition to the Westminster Confession (p. 81), he overlooks some important *practical* implications that the fifth article of the Arminians (which the Calvinists oppose with their fifth article, quoted above and by Danielson, p. 71) has upon the ethics of *Paradise Lost;* see especially p. 75.

10. For a more comprehensive treatment of post-Weberian scholarship on the connections between Protestantism and capitalism, see Stavely, *Puritan Legacies*, pp. 62–71; quoted, pp. 64–65.

11. Stephen Foster, *Their Solitary Way: The Puritan Social Ethic in the First Century of Settlement in New England* (New Haven, 1971), p. 105.

12. Although partially indebted to Stavely, this formulation also modifies an inherent contradiction in his thesis. In fact, the Protestant ethic did *not* minimize "the need to ground . . . justification in external reality" (p. 67), but in order to mitigate the uncertainties inherent in predestinatory theology, *maximizes* this need. Hence although Milton's Arminian theology follows some similar (and not, as Stavely argues, always radically different) assumptions, its focus on moral attainment not only idealizes but fundamentally reverses the appetitive direction of the Protestant ethic.

13. For the argument that "Milton seems like Coppe, Nayler, and others who experienced the revolutionary years to have passed so 'tumultuously through the secularization process that would take [his] culture several centuries to experience, [that he] bypassed the stage of capitalist ideology altogether,' " see Stavely, *Puritan Legacies*, pp. 70–71.

14. See Danielson, *Milton's Good God*, pp. 202–27.

15. This and all other references to Milton's poems are taken from *John Milton: Complete Poems and Major Prose*, ed. Merritt Y. Hughes (New York, 1957).

16. Stavely, *Puritan Legacies*, p. 78. Although I fail to see how Satan's expedition could quite so *specifically* represent "the journey made by Anglo-American culture as it moved from the sixteenth to the late nineteenth century," certainly his voyage demonstrates the materialistic consequences of the wrong attitudes toward historical progress.

17. For an excellent examination of Milton's skeptical pragmatism, see Donald L. Guss, "Enlightment as Process: Milton and Habermas," *PMLA* CVI, (1991), 1156–69.

18. Here I am assuming that the poem suggests a continuity between traditional religious and secularized or progressivist optimism, both of which are seen as forms of either transcendental or sociopolitical escapism with satanic overtones. For an important examination of the changing meaning of the *theatrum mundi* in the late Renaissance, see Jean-Christophe Agnew, *Worlds Apart: The Market and the Theatre in Anglo-American Thought 1550–1750* (Cambridge, 1986).

19. For this aspect of *Paradise Lost*, see Marshall Grossman, *"Authors to Themselves": Milton and the Revelation of History* (Cambridge, 1987).

20. See Stavely's similar comments on Satan in *Puritan Legacies*, p. 92.

21. See Christopher Hill's discussion of Samson's strenuous recovery, in *Milton and the English Revolution*, p. 386.

22. This pattern is nowhere more evident than in the passage cited in Book VI, where Nisroch's complaints and veiled threats concerning that he will "owe" (VI, 469) to him who can deliver him from pain are quelled by twin forms of "dev'lish machination," Satan's cannon and bombastic political rhetoric.

23. For an illuminating analysis of this exchange, see Michael Lieb, "Milton's 'Dramatick Constitution': The Celestial Dialogue in *Paradise Lost*, Book III," in *Milton Studies* XXIII, ed. James D. Simmonds (Pittsburgh, 1987), pp. 215–40.

24. Of course, although Adam can hardly contemplate an actual assault upon heaven, he does similarly challenge and curse his creation, preferring death to his present terrors (X, 849–53).

25. Hence although Malcolm Kelsall convincingly argues that the hero of *Paradise Regained* is a historically and biblically informed *type* of stoic individual, *contra* Christ's, Belial's stoicism is shallow, corrupt, and misinformed. See Kelsall on "The Historicity of *Paradise Regained*," in *Milton Studies* XII, ed. James D. Simmonds (Pittsburgh, 1978), pp. 235–51.

26.   For Time, though in Eternity, appli'd
To motion, measures all things durable
By present, past, and future. (V, 580–82)

27. For a fuller exposition of this thesis, see R. A. Shoaf *Milton, Poet of Duality: A Study of Semiosis in the Poetry and the Prose* (New Haven, 1985).

28. See Joan S. Bennett's illuminating discussion of the unreliability of the chorus and the fallacy of the *felix culpa* ("All is best'") in *Samson Agonistes*, in *Reviving Liberty: Radical Christian Humanism in Milton's Great Poems* (Cambridge, Mass., 1989), pp. 137–60; especially p. 138.

29. Of course, in spite of these similarities, there are many differences; for Calvinists, the temporal recuperation of the *felix culpa* occurs through justification; for Catholics, through the sacrament; and for secular Calvinists, like Milton's demons, through a blend of material and social distinction. Nevertheless, all afford only illusory and insubstantial rewards.

30. Thus although "heroic martyrdom" may take many forms, moral as well as physical, in *Milton's Good God* Danielson sums up its short-term meaning: that the "better fortitude" of Adam and Eve represents "a heroically significant 'painful achievement,'" and not the result merely of divine fiat" (p. 90).

31. Keith Stavely takes this argument still further, persuasively arguing that the Arminian basis of the poem holds out the possibility of repentance to the devil himself; see Keith W. F. Stavely, "Satan and Arminianism in *Paradise Lost*," in *Milton Studies* XXV, ed. James D. Simmonds (Pittsburgh, 1989), pp. 125–39.

32. Hill, *Milton and the English Revolution*, p. 386.

33. Laura Lunger Knoppers, "Rewriting the Protestant Ethic: Discipline and Love in *Paradise Lost*," *ELH* LVIII (1991) 545–59; see especially pp. 554–57.

34. See Diane McColley, *Milton's Eve* (Urbana, Ill., 1983), and Diana Benet, "Abdiel and the Son in the Separation Scene," in *Milton Studies* XVIII, ed. James D. Simmonds (Pittsburgh, 1983), pp. 129–43.

35. For a fuller consideration of this aspect of Eve's dream, see my article entitled

"Ithuriel's Spear: Purity, Danger, and Allegory at the Gates of Eden," *SEL XXXIII* (Winter, 1993) 167–90.

36. See Stavely, *Puritan Legacies*, p. 66.

37. See John Guillory for the opposing argument, that "Like Samson, Milton makes a return, with interest, upon his father's investment: 'to himself and Father's house eternal fame' "; "The Father's House: *Samson Agonistes* in Its Historical Moment," in *Remembering Milton: Essays on the Texts and Traditions*, ed. Mary Nyquist and Margaret W. Ferguson (London, 1987) p. 172.

38. Guillory, "Father's House," p. 156.

39. Of course, this does not mean that there is no political or spiritual lesson to be learned from his life, but simply that Samson himself "would have lived a happier life had he not sinned"; thus his recovery is still exemplary, but only to those capable of learning from it. See Burton J. Weber, "The Worldly End of Samson," in *Milton Studies XXVI*, ed. James D. Simmonds (Pittsburgh, 1990), pp. 306–08.

40. Mary Ann Radzinowicz, *Toward "Samson Agonistes": The Growth of Milton's Mind* (Princeton, 1978), pp. 93, 108. Since as Radzinowicz further argues, "God may not act through Samson, but God will act" (p. 96), Samson's earthly success is only indirectly related to his spiritual survival.

41. Even the most ironic readings of the tragedy, such as those of Irene Samuel and Stanley Fish, both of which would deny Samson spiritual success, also deny both that the chorus accurately defines him, and that he achieves any validation of his predestined place among the elect. See Fish, "Spectacle and Evidence in *Samson Agonistes*," *Critical Inquiry* XV (1989), 556–86, and Samuel, "*Samson Agonistes* as Tragedy," in *Calm of Mind*, ed. Joseph A. Wittreich, Jr. (Cleveland, 1971), pp. 235–57.

42. Thus according to Little in *Religion, Order, and Law*, unlike Milton's Samson, Perkins exhibits the classic Calvinist "tendency to equate prosperity with the sign of God's blessing—that is, as the mark of, or reward for, voluntary industriousness. If one does a job well, he can, in general, be sure of prosperity, for that kind of activity or obedience is precisely the direction of the will of God" (pp. 119–20). From this perspective alone, Guillory's equation of Perkins's position with Milton's seems wholly arbitrary.

43. Radzinowicz, *Toward "Samson Agonistes"*, pp. 133, xx, respectively; her discussion of the parables appears on p. 141.

44. Grossman, "The Fruits of One's Labors in Miltonic Practice and Marxian Theory," p. 81.

"GOD IS ALSO IN SLEEP": DREAMS
SATANIC AND DIVINE IN *PARADISE LOST*

Kristin Pruitt McColgan

They that sow in tears shall reap in joy.
He that goeth forth and weepeth, bearing precious seed, shall
doubtless come again with rejoicing, bringing his sheaves with him.
(Psalm cxxvi, 5–6)

AFTER MICHAEL INSTRUCTS ADAM aboutthefuture in Books
XI and XII of *Paradise Lost*, the archangel charges him to waken Eve
and "at season fit / Let her with thee partake what thou has heard" (XII,
597–98).[1] Adam, however, "found her wak't" (608) and eager to share her
revelation: "God is also in sleep, and Dreams advise" (611). This statement,
emphatically placed near the end of Book XII, brings to closure an important theme of Milton's poem, that both God and Satan work through
dreams. As such, it is linked to Adam's dreams recounted to Raphael in
Book VIII and to Satan's attempt, in Book IV, to "forge [in Eve] / Illusions as
he list, Phantasms and Dreams" (802–03), which together suggest that
dreams may represent either divinely sanctioned relationship with an
"*other* self"[2] (VIII, 450; italics mine) or satanic exaltation of oneself.

I propose to examine the verbal and thematic echoes, parallels, and
reversals in these dreams in view of Milton's avowed intention to "assert
Eternal Providence" (I, 25). My reasons for devoting considerably more
attention to Eve's dreams are twofold. First, Adam's dreams, because of
their divine source, have not elicited much critical disagreement. Eve's
first dream, because of its satanic inspiration, has stimulated much controversy. Second, the effect of the Satan-inspired dream on Eve has been too
often exaggerated, whereas the effect of her God-inspired dream has been
frequently ignored.[3] What has not been sufficiently emphasized is that
Milton positions Eve's account of her second dream close to the end of
Paradise Lost where it constitutes the poem's final spoken words. This
placement seems calculated to redress the imbalance created by Satan's
earlier attempt to seduce Eve through dream and by Adam's reports of his
two dreams, both unquestionably of divine origin. Moreover, in his han-

135

dling of the dream episode in Book XII, Milton not only leaves the reader with a positive final view of Eve as character but also underscores the creative potential of her postlapsarian relationship with Adam in the enactment of "Eternal Providence."

Adam's and Eve's dreams conform to the *OED* definition of "a vision during sleep," a vision, according to the same source, being "an appearance of a prophetic or mystical character, or having the nature of a revelation, supernaturally presented to the mind either in sleep or in an abnormal state." Since, as William B. Hunter has pointed out, the highest level of dream experience is accorded to Adam,[4] I will begin by examining his account to Raphael, which clearly distinguishes the hallmarks of divine revelation, its foundation in reality and its emphasis on relationship. Set against Adam's dreams, the parallels and reversals of the dream Satan inspires in Eve become apparent. He audaciously borrows from what he has heard and observed in Paradise and from what he experienced in heaven, imprinting his version with characteristic perversity and appeals to self-aggrandizement. Eve's first dream, then, is a mystical (of "mysterious origin" and "character" [*OED*]) expression of Satan's wish-fulfillment, an illusion that anticipates the Fall but in no way necessitates its occurrence. Her dream described in Book XII, which Milton carefully contrasts with her earlier demonic dream and links to Adam's dream of her creation, is divinely inspired prophecy of the role of Providence in human history.[5]

Adam's account to Raphael of "how human Life began" (VIII, 250) is the first illustration, chronologically, of God's presence in sleep. Adam recalls that, after unsuccessfully seeking to identify his Creator, "gentle sleep / First found me" (287–88), and although the possibility of uncreation, of "passing to my former state / Insensible . . . forthwith to dissolve" (290–91), occurs to him, "suddenly stood at my Head a dream, / Whose inward apparition gently mov'd / My fancy to believe I yet had being, / And liv'd" (292–95). From its beginning, this dream, inspired by an actual presence, is one of creation, initiating confidence in Adam of his "being." The "shape Divine" (295) that appears to Adam in his dreamlike state explains that he has come at Adam's summons to be his "Guide" (298) and thereafter leads his newly created being "by the hand . . . rais'd, / . . . as in Air" (300–301) up "To the Garden of bliss" (299). There, Adam is greeted by a limited, domestic prospect, "A Circuit wide, enclos'd, with goodliest Trees / Planted, with Walks, and Bowers" (304–05). Beholding his "Mansion" (296), he declares that "what I saw / Of Earth before scarce pleasant seem'd" (305–06). While Adam is struck with "sudden appetite" (308) at the sight of the fair, abundant fruit "that hung to the Eye / Tempting" (307–08) on each tree, he awakens before plucking and eating and discovers "all *real*" (310; italics mine), and further wandering and confusion are forestalled when the Guide appears before Adam. This God-inspired dream, then, serves as a prologue to divine instruction about "The rigid interdiction . . . / . . . though in [Adam's] choice / Not to incur" (334–36) and to dialogue, which involves exercise of his reason.

Adam's second dream, which follows his "celestial Colloquy sublime" (VIII, 455) regarding his need for a mate ("but with mee / I see not who partakes" [363–64]), occurs when, "Dazzl'd and spent, [he] sunk down" (457) into a beneficent sleep. "[T]he shape" (463) he sees by means of "internal sight" (461) is the same "before whom awake [Adam] stood" (464), and the subsequent vision of Eve's creation leads him to new heights of feeling, for she is "so lovely fair, / That what seem'd fair in all the World, seem'd now / Mean, or in her summ'd up" (471–73). There is again the sense that "what I saw / Of Earth before scarce pleasant seem'd" as Adam observes the forming of one who is to share his "Mansion," a sight far fairer than the "fairest Fruit" (307) of Paradise. But the euphoria accompanying Adam's view of Eve's birth from his side vanishes along with Eve, and Adam wakes "out of hope" (481), only to discover the reality of divine benevolence: The "Heav'nly Maker" (485) leads Eve, "Such as [Adam] saw her in [his] dream" (482), to him. Once again, he "found / Before [his] Eyes all real," since discovery and restoration, not loss, are the substance of visions inspired by God.

That Eve also understands the preeminence of relationship with another is demonstrated in her creation account. Viewing her own image in the pool, she is warned by a voice that "What there thou seest fair Creature is thyself" (IV, 468), and, following this self-discovery, she is told to follow the voice to him "Whose image thou art" (472) and thereby to fulfill her role as "Mother of human Race" (475). When, however, Eve first sees Adam he seems "less fair" (478) than the image of self reflected in the pond; but his "pleaded reason" (VIII, 510) and his "gentle hand" that "Seiz'd [hers]" cause Eve to yield, "and from that time see / How beauty is excell'd by manly grace / And wisdom, which alone is truly fair" (IV, 488–91). As Adam tells Raphael, "To the Nuptial Bow'r / I led her blushing like the Morn" (VIII, 510–11). The loving Maker thus encourages the couple, Adam through dream, Eve though disembodied voice, to partake of the "fair," "sweet" fruit of relationship, "Heav'n's last best gift" (V, 19), an alternative to the destructive appetite for self proffered by Satan in Eve's dream in Book IV.

Eve's recognition that "*God* is also in sleep" (italics mine) in Book XII marks her first implied reference to the Satan-inspired vision since she woke from "unquiet rest" (V, 11) with both relief and bewilderment and described the cause of her distress to Adam:

> My Glory, my Perfection, glad I see
> Thy face, and Morn return'd, for I this Night
> such night till this I never pass'd, have dream'd,
> If dream'd
>
> . . . .
>
> of offense and trouble.   (29–32; 34).

Much of the critical attention devoted to this episode has focused on Eve's contribution to the dream and on whether, at this point in the poem, she is already fallen, falls, or is fallible but innocent. E. M. W. Tillyard, expressing the once standard view, sees Eve's reaction to the dream as evidence that she has "passed from a state of innocence to one of sin," and Irene Samuel believes that "however much [the dream] was *in*duced by Satan, it was *pro*duced by Eve's own mind."[6] While Northrop Frye acknowledges that "The occasion of her dream was Satan whispering in her ear," he sees its content as "a Freudian wish-fulfillment dream."[7] On the other hand, John S. Diekhoff challenges those who "read the account . . . as a revelation of [Eve's] unconscious," and his argument that "It was Satan, not Eve, who had fallen" anticipates my own.[8]

Both the pattern and the content of the vision demonstrate how skillfully Satan produces the drama of self on the stage of Eve's imagination, writing the script, directing the action, playing the lead, even using "more pleasing light" of evening (V, 42) to contribute to effect.[9] Unlike the heavenly Guide who comes in response to Adam's call, an unsolicited Satan first mimics the "gentle voice" (37) of Eve's spouse. As she tells Adam, "I thought it thine" (37), and for this reason, she responds immediately: "I rose as at thy call, but found thee not; / To find thee I directed then my walk" (48–49). Searching for her "other self," her spouse, Eve explains that "methought, alone I pass'd through ways / That brought me on a sudden to the Tree / Of interdicted Knowledge" (50–52). Whereas Adam was led by God's hand to Paradise and Eve was led by God's voice to Adam, Satan does not take Eve by the hand in her dream, touch being so important to relationship, but rather she seems to wander, guideless, away from her spouse in an effort to find him. Satan's strategy of allowing Eve to make her own way to the Tree of Knowledge creates the illusion of free will and simultaneously achieves his purpose: only if Adam is absent from the dream sequence can Satan appropriate his position and recommend self-exaltation as superior to relationship. In Adam's dream, "Each tree / Load'n with fairest Fruit" (VIII, 306–07) stimulates appetite; Eve's attention is focused on *the* tree, which, in the moonlit evening, seemed "Much fairer to my Fancy than by day" (V, 53).

Predictably, much as the Creator had appeared in Adam's dream as "shape Divine," so also Satan assumes the guise of a heavenly angel, "One shap'd and wing'd" (55), who

> on that Tree . . . also gaz'd;
> And O fair Plant, said he, with fruit surcharg'd,
> Deigns none to ease thy load and taste thy sweet,
> Nor God, nor Man; is Knowledge so despis'd? (57–60)[10]

Seeking to inspire Eve with the same self-love that characterized his own rebellion, Satan exalts her status from "Nature's desire" (45) to "fair Angelic Eve" (74) and escalates from praise of the "fair Plant . . . with fruit surcharg'd" to worship of the "Fruit Divine" (67). He urges her to "Partake thou also" (75), that she may "Ascend to Heav'n, by merit thine" (80), moving her from horror at the sight of the "bold" angel's eating of the fruit (66) to the conclusion that she herself is destined to eat. As she tells Adam, the angel

> to me held,
> Even to my mouth of that same fruit held part
> Which he had pluckt; the pleasant savory smell
> So quick'n'd appetite, that I, methought,
> Could not but taste. (82–86)

Here is a parody of relationship, a kind of perverse joining of Satan and Eve, through eating of "that same fruit," in which touch is conspicuously absent. By subtly equating "fair Angelic Eve," the "fair Plant," and the "Fruit Divine, / Sweet of thyself, but much more sweet thus cropt" (67–68), Satan suggests both the motivation of character and the denouement of his plot. Eating the fruit is tantamount to a "quick'n'd appetite" for "fair," "sweet" self, and its result a rise and fall so often associated with tragedy, in which the protagonist attempts to exceed human limitations. As Eve tells Adam,

> Forthwith up to the Clouds
> With him I flew, and underneath beheld
> The Earth outstretcht immense, a prospect wide
> And various. (86–89)

Subsequently, her Guide disappears and "I, methought, sunk down, / And fell asleep; but O how glad I wak'd / To find this but a dream!" (91–93).

Adam, in his first dream, appears to leave the ground as he is led to Paradise, but his view is "enclos'd," not the dizzying, unearthly "prospect wide" that his spouse observes. And whereas in his second dream Adam "sunk down" into "sleep . . . call'd / By Nature as in aid" (VIII, 458–59), Eve's sinking into "unquiet rest" is a conclusion to her "high exaltation" (V, 90).

Inverse parallels exist not only between Adam's dreams and Eve's satanic vision but also between that vision and Eve's creation story of obedience rewarded, which Satan has heard her recount to Adam. In typical fashion, the fallen archangel reverses the order and meaning of events in that drama in which Eve learns of her self, responds to her Maker, and is "invisibly led" to a relationship with her mate, making it a drama of uncreation (a rise followed by a fall). In Satan's version, Eve is separated from her "other self" through deception, "invisibly led" to the Tree of Knowledge, and encouraged to substitute disobedience (eating of the fruit) and self-exaltation ("Angelic Eve") for obedience to her role as "Mother of human race" and the gift of relationship, visually imaged in hand-holding.

Details in the dream suggest the warped mind and motives of one who "always appropriates, or tries to appropriate, things to himself that are conjoined with God."[11] For example, in his speech, Satan lyrically captures the beauty of the evening and eloquently flatters the woman into whose ear he whispers:

> *Why sleep'st thou Eve?* now is the pleasant time,
> The *cool,* the silent, save where *silence* yields
> To the night-warbling Bird, that now *awake*
> Tunes *sweetest* his love-labor'd *song:* now *reigns*
> Full Orb'd the Moon, and with more pleasing light
> Shadowy sets off the face of things; in vain,
> If none regard; *Heav'n wakes with all his eyes,*
> Whom to behold but thee, Nature's desire,
> *In whose sight all things joy,* with ravishment
> Attracted by thy beauty still to gaze.   (V, 38–47; italics mine)

But on another level, the use of a rhetorical question, "Whom to behold but thee," manipulatively closes off inquiry and perversely echoes Eve's sincere query to Adam the night before about the stars and moon.[12] And even more insidiously, the passage parodies the poem's first chronological event, when the Father pronounces and extols a perfect unity of relationship of all beings created by the Son with the Son, relationship which Satan, seduced by self, seeks to undermine. As recounted by Raphael, the legions ("eyes") of Heaven wake "on such day / As Heav'n's great Year brings forth" (V, 582–83) and gather to hear the divine decree:

> This day I have begot whom I declare
> My only Son
>   . . . .
>   whom ye now *behold*
> At my right hand; your Head I him appoint;
>   . . . .
> Under his great Vice-gerent *Reign* abide
> United as one individual Soul
> For ever *happy:* him who disobeys
> Mee disobeys.   (603–604; 605–606; 609–612; italics mine)

After the heavenly host participate "In *song* and dance about the sacred Hill" (619), the visible and audible manifestation of "harmony Divine" (625), and "*sweet* repast" (630), "communion *sweet*" (637), the "grateful Twilight . . . / . . . and roseate Dews dispos'd / All but the unsleeping *eyes* of God to rest" (645–47). The angels, "among the Trees of Life, / . . . slept / Fann'd with *cool* Winds, save those who in thir course / Melodious Hymns about the sovran Throne / Alternate all night long: but not so *wak'd* / Satan" (652; 654–58; italics mine). Because he "could not bear / Through *pride* that sight, and thought himself impair'd" (664–65) by the exaltation of the Son, "in whose sight all things [should] joy," Satan, at the hour "Friendliest to sleep and *silence*" (668), awakens Beelzebub to plot rebellion: "*Sleep'st thou*, Companion dear, what sleep can close / Thy eye-lids?" (673–74; italics mine). In his first attempt to seduce humankind, then, Satan borrows and perverts elements of setting, language, and action from the very scene that initiated his fall. What Barbara Kiefer Lewalski says about his "serenade" to Eve in dream, that it "solicits clandestine encounters and forbidden acts,"[13] certainly applies to Satan's behavior after the heavenly convocation, and his successful seduction of his "Companion dear" in heaven clearly is the precedent for his attempt to "[inspire] venom" and thereby "taint" Eve by "ingend'ring *pride*" (IV, 804, 809; italics mine). The fallen angel's transformation of the sacred into the secular in Eve's dream, wherein the "Melodious Hymns" of heaven have become the "love-labor'd Song" of the nightingale and the exaltation of the Son is recast as "courtly service and worship of a lady,"[14] bears an unmistakable satanic signature.

Other descriptions in the dream, such as "the Tree / Of interdicted knowledge," "Ascend to Heav'n, by merit thine," and "fairer to my Fancy than by day," also point to their infernal author. When, in Book IV, Adam speaks to Eve of the "easy prohibition" (433), when he counsels that they "at [the Creator's] hand / Have nothing merited" (417–18), Eve agrees: "what thou hast said is just and right" (443). There is no evidence that "The angel who eats the fruit in the dream does what she herself wants to do," that Eve harbors "a restiveness" as a result of the prohibition.[15] But Satan, overhearing this conversation, immediately takes offense: "Knowledge forbidd'n? / Suspicious, reasonless" (515–16). It is he who sees the tree as "invented with design / To keep [humankind] low whom Knowledge might exalt / Equal with Gods" (524–26), he whose sense of injured merit had led to his rebellion, he who finds "shades of night" (1015), guises of angels, and bodies of serpents "fairer" for obscuring his evil purposes.

Although Eve uses the term dream to characterize her ordeal, she distinguishes it from her typical dreams, grounded in emotions and experience, of her spouse and their labors in and plans for the garden (V, 32–33). True, there is much in the sequence that is "familiar": a tree, moonlight, Adam's voice, angels. But the source is Satan, who supernaturally implants a vision in Eve's mind in sleep. This dream, then, is not an indication of what Eve is but rather of what Satan has become; it does not reflect Eve's anxiety, resentment, or wish-fulfillment but the fallen angel's, who creates a scenario in which exaltation and disobedience are characteristically joined. Because the script is Satan's, not Eve's who helplessly plays the role in which she has been cast, and because she recognizes that the angelic presence in her vision is the source "of offense and trouble," this effort to corrupt her is, as Charles W. Durham argues, unsuccessful.[16] Her innocence is further supported by her relief as a result of seeing Adam and finding this "but a dream." She is clearly horrified by the dream's suggestion of her participation in a relationship with anyone but her spouse, and her sense of having done so accounts for the "glowing Cheek" (V, 10) that contrasts dramatically with her prenuptial "blushing like the Morn." Understandably, Eve feels violated, contaminated, but ironically, because Satan controls the drama, allowing Eve no free will, no "*choice* / Not to incur" (italics mine), this is not a genuine temptation, and she is still "innocent" (V, 209).

Nonetheless, Eve's dream foreshadows her fall, when the freely chosen appetite for self will lead to Death's opportunity "To stuff this Maw" (X, 601), to the dust and ashes of human mortality. But despite Satan's claim of victory achieved, as he tells the assembled host in hell, "the more to increase / Your wonder, with an Apple" (X, 486–87), he and his serpentine followers immediately thereafter chew "bitter Ashes" (566) "instead of Fruit" (565), proleptic of their final defeat through the providential agency of the Son, "Fruit Divine." Similarly, Michael's history lesson presents a vivid picture of "the world destroy'd" by sin and death, a vision ultimately overcome by his narrative of the "world restor'd" (XII, 3). And fallen Eve, the first victim of Satan's successful attempt to corrupt, has the last spoken words in Milton's poem, words that testify to the presence of God in sleep and faithfully, confidently, proclaim restoration.

Before leading Adam to the "top / Of Speculation" (XII, 588–89), Michael suggests a parallel between Eve's final dream and an earlier dream of creation: "let Eve (for I have drencht her eyes) / Here sleep below while thou to foresight wak'st, / As once thou slep'st, while Shee to life was form'd" (XI, 367–69). Subsequently, the reader witnesses Adam's emotional falls and rises, in response to Michael's history lesson, that culminate "in peace of thought" (XII, 558). Not surprisingly, Eve's prophetic vision is intended to bring her to a similar state. As Michael tells Adam before they return to Eve, "Her also I with gentle Dreams have calm'd / Portending good" (595–96), suggesting that Adam reveal to his spouse "The great deliverance by her Seed to come / . . . on all Mankind" (600–601).

It is significant that Eve's report of this dream identifies God, not Michael, as its ultimate source, an idea confirmed by its effect on her, by its contrast to the satanically inspired dream, and by the fact that she clearly *knows* about "The great deliverance by her Seed to come." As she describes her experience,

> Whence thou return'st, and whither went'st, I know;
> For God is also in sleep, and Dreams advise,
> Which he hath sent propitious, some great good
> Presaging, since with sorrow and heart's distress
> Wearied I fell asleep: but now lead on;
> In mee is no delay; with thee to go,
> Is to stay here; without thee here to stay,
> Is to go hence unwilling; thou to mee
> Art all things under Heav'n, all places thou,
> Who for my wilful crime art banisht hence.
> This further consolation yet secure
> I carry hence; though all by mee is lost,
> Such favor I unworthy am voutsaf't,
> By mee the Promis'd Seed shall all restore.   (610–23)

In Book V, Eve woke from "unquiet rest"; here, she recalls falling asleep "with sorrow and heart's distress / Wearied" and wakes to greet Adam "with words not sad" (XII, 609). Satan's dream led Eve away from Adam; this leads her to acknowledge the healing power of relationship: "with thee to go, / Is to stay here [in Paradise]." Satan recommended self-exaltation on the basis of "merit"; God promises "favor" to the "unworthy." Satan exposed Eve to the "damp horror" of his "deed so bold" (V, 65–66); God, through "gentle Dreams," protects her from the grisly horrors, the grim realities, that punctuate Adam's lesson from the archangel. That Eve learns about the "Promis'd Seed" directly from God, rather than through report from Adam as Michael had suggested, indicates how important it was to Milton for Eve to possess this knowledge before she leaves Paradise. Just as Milton took care to demonstrate that both Adam and Eve were "Sufficient to have stood, though free to fall" (III, 99) at the time of the satanic temptation in Book IX, so, too, the poet here shows a "sufficient" Eve, prepared to enter the fallen world with a sense of her special place and crucial meaning in the unfolding of Providence.

In these fourteen lines, Eve both demonstrates her comprehension of paradox and describes reaching the spiritual destination that Adam, after much wandering and considerable error, finally achieved as a result of Michael's instructions. Joan Malory Webber suggests that "Although both attend to lectures, Eve is more responsive to dreams: the work of reeducating her after the Fall thus is much less laborious than that of teaching Adam, who has to have everything explained to him. These are aspects of the traditional opposition between the minds of men and those of women."[17] Catherine I. Cox makes a similar distinction: "Eve's dream, implying a passive and intuitive way to truth and grace, complements Adam's more active, intellectual experience on the mountain. Thus the events of Books XI and XII, by distinguishing the virtues of ways of knowing particular to each sex, rejoin the male and female figures for the providential dance."[18] In addition to highlighting the traditional male/female "ways of knowing" that lead Adam and Eve to the same *place*, this passage is designed to leave the reader with a positive final view of Eve, in particular her eloquent brevity and her insight, and is reminiscent of her simple, straightforward admission of guilt in the judgment scene ("The Serpent me beguil'd and I did eat" [X, 162]) following Adam's rationalizations and accusations.

That the fourteen lines of Eve's final speech constitute an embedded sonnet reinforces their meaning. In the Petrarchan form, the octave often identifies the problem or situation which the sestet resolves. Milton follows this pattern, although his presentation breaks naturally into two five-line "quatrains" before the displaced volta and concluding quatrain, thereby offering three variations on the theme of love, the traditional subject matter of the sonnet. But Eve's presentation breaks from tradition in transforming an originally secular form into a vehicle for expressing the sacred truth imparted to her. Lines 1–5 state, in a general way, the benevolence of God in providing consolation through prophetic dreams, the half-line "but now lead on" serving as transition into the next section. Lines 6–10 bring the theme into the realm "under Heaven," suggesting the consolations of human love. Adam, banished from Paradise "for [Eve's] wilful crime," becomes her Paradise, "all things . . . all places." These lines echo the sentiment expressed in Eve's love lyric (IV, 641–56), which has, according to Lewalski, "a subject, structure, and texture akin to those aspects of the Petrarchan sonnet" and in which "Eve proclaims Adam the epitome of the Edenic condition for her."[19] Lines 11–14 bring together human and divine in the ultimate expression of selfless love, when "God with man unites" (XII, 382) in Christ, "the Promis'd Seed." Through consummation of their relationship, whereby two become one, Adam and Eve will initiate the cycle of love to restore humankind. Overall, the more complex treatment of the theme of love in this sonnet emphasizes Eve's considerable development between her second speech in *Paradise Lost* and her last.

About the specific content of her dreams, Eve is silent. Weidhorn assumes that Eve's final dream is of Adam observing and hearing about the unfolding of history and argues that this picture of Eve in a dream beholding Adam foreseeing the future "is symbolic of the traditional hierarchy of the Great Chain of Being."[20] But, as Diane Kelsey McColley points out, "The images of [Eve's] vision are not vouchsafed to us," and she believes that "Her dream is one of those passages that the poet leaves open for the progression of truth within the reader."[21] Still, given the poet's biblical knowledge and the dense texture of scriptural allusion in Books XI and XII, Milton almost invites the reader to speculate. Perhaps Eve, like Adam, was enlightened by a movement from "shadowy Types to Truth" (XII, 303), a vision of female counterparts to "Types" like Enoch, Noah, Abraham, and Moses who lead toward fulfillment in the "Truth," the antitype, the Messiah. Lines 614–18 are an echo of Michael's words to Eve after she learns of the expulsion from Paradise, "Thy going is not lonely, with thee goes / Thy Husband, him to follow thou art bound; / Where he abides, think there thy native soil" (XI, 290–92), but the lines also anticipate Ruth, an Old Testament model of love, loyalty, and faith in God's Providence: "Intreat me not to leave thee, or to return from following after thee: for whither thou goest, I will go; and where thou lodgest, I will lodge: thy people shall be my people, and thy God my God" (Ruth i, 16). A woman like Ruth, then, could serve for Eve as a faith-strengthening example in much the same way the patriarch Abraham, called by God through vision, serves for Adam: "with what Faith / He leaves his Gods, his Friends, and native Soil" (128–29). Despite

Naomi's belief that Ruth, in leaving Moab, "[her] Gods, [her] Friends, and native Soil," will be sacrificing her opportunity to remarry, Ruth chooses an uncertain future that connects her with the lineage of David and Christ. As the women tell Naomi after her daughter-in-law has borne a son: "he shall be unto thee a *restorer* of thy life" (Ruth iv, 15; italics mine). Moreover, in recognizing that "though all by mee is lost, / Such favor I unworthy am voutsaf't," Eve is also associated with Mary, who was told by Gabriel that she "has found favour with God" (Luke i, 30) and identified by Elisabeth as "Blessed . . . among women, and blessed is the fruit of thy womb" (Luke i, 42). Eve's humility in the face of God's miraculous intervention in human history anticipates Mary's response that God "hath regarded the low estate of his handmaiden. . . . [H]e that is mighty hath done to me great things" (Luke i, 48–49). These biblical echoes suggest that "second Eve" (X, 183) could represent to "Mother of human Race" the ideal expression of womanhood and maternity, the humble vehicle for fruition of "Love, / By name to come call'd Charity, the soul / Of all the rest" (XII, 583–85).

Of course, the pain of childbearing announced in the Son's judgment (X, 193–95) and a world suffused with sin and death await Eve outside the gates of Paradise. But whatever their content, Eve's final visions strengthen her to meet the future and "advise" her to live with Adam "in one Faith unanimous though sad . . . yet much more cheer'd / With meditation on the happy end" (603–05), the end Satan attempted to undermine by rebellion and seduction, when the faithful will be "United as one individual Soul / For ever happy," when the just will reap the "fruits Joy and eternal Bliss" (XII, 551), when "God shall be All in All" (III, 341), the supreme relationship. Psalm cxxvi captures the tonal and thematic modulations of the final book of *Paradise Lost*. Eve's dreams, like Michael's narrative to Adam of the Messiah whose "God-like act / Annuls thy doom, the death thou shouldst have di'd, / In sin for ever lost from life" (XII, 427–29), are the restorative balm for "heart's distress," and the couple might well proclaim, as does the psalmist, that "The Lord hath done great things for us; whereof we are glad" (3). For though they "sow in tears," they have been promised a harvest of "joy." Adam and Eve, sinful humanity on the threshold of "the World . . . before them" (646), embody the paradox at the heart of Milton's poem: as they go forth, after "Some natural tears they dropp'd, but wip'd them soon" (XII, 645), they do so "hand in hand" (648), bearing the "precious seed" of relationship and redemption.

Thus Eve's final dreams in *Paradise Lost*, which "assert Eternal Providence," foretell that "though *all* . . . is *lost* . . . the Promis'd Seed shall

all restore" (italics mine). Her words proclaim a poetically just, divinely authored revision of the satanic script of loss through self-exaltation, for while "Man's First Disobedience, and the Fruit / Of that Forbidden Tree . . . / Brought Death into the World, and *all* our woe, / With *loss* of Eden" (I, 1–4), Eve's dreams, "some *great* good / Presaging," herald the creation of "one *greater* Man / [who will] *Restore* us, and regain the blissful Seat" (I, 4–5; italics mine).²² From the opening lines of his epic to its last spoken words, Milton demonstrates that "Who seeks / To lessen [God], against his purpose serves / To manifest the more [his] might: his evil / [God] usest, and from thence creat'st more good" (VII, 613–16). Ultimately, then, "the great deliverance by [Eve's] Seed to come," advised through God's presence in sleep, confirms that the satanic dream of self is an illusory, self-negating one, and far from writing the script, directing the action, and playing the lead, Satan is the foil to "one greater Man," indeed, is a character secondary to all "greater men and women"²³ in the drama of "Eternal Providence."

Christian Brothers University

NOTES

I would like to thank Charles W. Durham and John T. Shawcross for their invaluable insights offered during the writing and revising of this essay.

1. *John Milton: Complete Poems and Major Prose*, ed. Merritt Y. Hughes (New York, 1957). All references to Milton's poetry will be to this edition.
2. The Almighty characterizes Eve to Adam in this way. As I have argued in "The Way to Pardon: 'Self' and 'Other' in *Paradise Lost*," *ANQ* V (1992), 7–15, the distinction between *self* and *other* is an important one throughout Milton's poem.
3. Although both Michael (XII, 595) and Eve (XII, 611) speak of dreams in the plural, both are referring to a single experience.
4. William B. Hunter, "Prophetic Dreams and Visions in *Paradise Lost*," reprinted in *The Descent of Urania: Studies in Milton, 1946–1988* (Lewisburg, Pa., 1989), pp. 21–30, discusses the rabbinical and Neoplatonic traditions available to Milton in presenting divine revelations in *Paradise Lost* and states that, "according to Maimonides, the prophetic power could descend upon man during sleep," and, in the highest form, God seems to speak to the prophet (p. 25).
5. In a note, Alastair Fowler, ed., *Paradise Lost* (London, 1971), p. 640, cites Macrobius's definition of a prophetic vision "as a dream that 'actually comes true.' "
6. E.M.W. Tillyard, *Studies in Milton* (London, 1951), p. 12; Irene Samuel, *Purgatorio* and the Dream of Eve," *JEGP* LXIII (1964), 445. Others who see in the dream and Eve's response evidence of her fallen nature include Millicent Bell, "The Fallacy of the Fall in *Paradise Lost*," *PMLA* LXVIII (1953), 867; Arnold Stein, *Answerable Style: Essays on*

"*Paradise Lost*" (Minneapolis, 1953), p. 88; and Fredson Bowers, "Adam, Eve, and the Fall in *Paradise Lost*," *PMLA* LXXXIV (1969), 269.

7. Northrop Frye, *The Return to Eden: Five Essays on Milton's Epics* (Toronto, 1965), p. 75. See also C. A. Patrides, *Milton and the Christian Tradition* (Oxford, 1966), p. 106; and Shari A. Zimmerman, "Milton's *Paradise Lost*: Eve's Struggle for Identity," *American Imago* XXXVIII (1981), 255–56.

8. John S. Diekhoff, "Eve's Dream and the Paradox of Fallible Perfection," *MQ* IV (1970), 5; 7. Others who have argued for Eve's innocence include Wayne Shumaker, "The Fallacy of the Fall in *Paradise Lost*," *PMLA* LXX (1955), 1185–87, 1195–1202; H.V.S. Ogden, "The Crisis of *Paradise Lost* Reconsidered," *PQ* XXXVI (1957), 1–19; Stanley Fish, *Surprised by Sin: The Reader in "Paradise Lost"* (New York, 1967), p. 226; Barbara Kiefer Lewalski, "Innocence and Experience in Milton's Eden," in *New Essays on "Paradise Lost*," ed. Thomas Kranidas (Berkeley and Los Angeles, 1969), p. 87; Dan Collins, "The Buoyant Mind in Milton's Eden," *Milton Studies* V, ed. James D. Simmonds (Pittsburgh, 1973), pp. 229–48; and Diane Kelsey McColley, *Milton's Eve* (Urbana, Ill., 1983), pp. 89–90.

9. William G. Riggs, *The Christian Poet in "Paradise Lost"* (Berkeley and Los Angeles, 1972), p. 94, argues that "By insisting on the similarities between the dreams of Adam and Eve, Milton seems concerned to show us that the difference between the two inspired visions is not so much one of quality as one of source." According to William B. Hunter, in "Eve's Demonic Dream," reprinted in *The Descent of Urania: Studies in Milton, 1946–1988* (Lewisburg, Pa., 1989), p. 46, "contemporary dream and demon lore" helped to shape Milton's portrayal of Eve's dream.

10. John T. Shawcross, in "The 'Gaze' and *Paradise Lost*," an unpublished talk, points out the negative connotations of "the gaze."

11. John T. Shawcross, *John Milton: The Self and the World* (Lexington, Ky., 1993), p. 27.

12. In *With Mortal Voice: The Creation of "Paradise Lost"* (Lexington, Ky., 1982), p. 70, John T. Shawcross discusses the significance of these lines in some detail, suggesting that "In Satan's use of the stars as eyes, the metaphoric meaning of their existence is perverted" and "they become elements to vent man's vanity."

13. Barbara Kiefer Lewalski, *"Paradise Lost" and the Rhetoric of Literary Forms* (Princeton, 1985), p. 200.

14. Ibid., p. 200.

15. Manfred Weidhorn, *Dreams in Seventeenth-Century Literature* (The Hague, 1970), p. 49.

16. Charles W. Durham, " 'If Dreamed': Eve's Satanic Vision in *Paradise Lost*," unpublished talk.

17. Joan Malory Webber, "The Politics of Poetry: Feminism and *Paradise Lost*," in *Milton Studies* XIV, ed. James D. Simmonds (Pittsburgh, 1980), p. 16.

18. Catherine I. Cox, "Dance and the Narration of Providence in *Paradise Lost*," in *Milton Studies* XXVI, ed. James D. Simmonds (Pittsburgh, 1990), p. 187.

19. Lewalski, *"Paradise Lost" and Rhetoric*, pp. 188; 187.

20. Weidhorn, *Dreams*, p. 155.

21. McColley, *Milton's Eve*, p. 214.

22. Ruth Mohl, *Studies in Spenser, Milton and the Theory of Monarchy* (New York, 1949), pp. 69–70, underscores the importance of Milton's use of the phrase "one greater Man," suggesting that "Milton's purpose in writing *Paradise Lost* was . . . to present the theme of 'the making of the greater man'–not simply the greater Man, Christ . . . , and not the chosen few, predestined to be saved, but the better human being everywhere."

23. Mohl, *Studies in Spenser*, p. 93.

MILTON'S EARTHY GROSSNESS: MUSIC AND THE CONDITION OF THE POET IN *L'ALLEGRO* AND *IL PENSEROSO*

Marc Berley

After the heavenly tune, which none can hear
Of human mold with gross unpurged ear.

—*Arcades, 72–73*

IN *ON TIME* MILTON USES THE PHRASE "Earthy grossness" to designate the conditional inability of humankind either to hear or to sing divine harmonies. Milton, variously described as a divine poet, a prophet, and a priest, has two tasks: to hear "the heavenly tune" and then to echo it on earth. When he writes in *Arcades* about the time "after the heavenly tune, which none can hear / Of human mold with gross unpurged ear," Milton questions his ability to hear divine music.[1] In fact, conditional statements concerning this ability recur in most of his poetry, but most directly in early poems, such as *L'Allegro* and *Il Penseroso*, where they indicate Milton's awareness of his "Earthy grossness." This awareness, a central element in Milton's poetic career, has not been fully recognized in critical accounts of the poetry.

Drawing from sources such as Plato and Boethius, Milton developed a Pythagorean-Platonic theory of music that, following others, he made Christian.[2] In *De Musica*, derived mostly from Pythagorean sources, Boethius distinguished three types of music: *musica mundana, musica humana, and musica instrumentalis*. The first is music of the spheres; the second, of man; the third, of instruments.[3] The relation between *musica mundana* and *musica humana* is the relation between macrocosm and microcosm; *musica instrumentalis* is the human production, the mediating term for the attempt to restore the relation between earth and heaven. This division underlies Milton's theory of music and, as we will see, of his poetry as well.

Critics who attempt to identify the divine music about which Milton writes are usually divided into two schools: they claim (1) that Milton was writing about music he merely contemplated or (2) that Milton was writing about music he actually heard.[4] Critics pay too little attention to Milton's ear, for the ear and not the music presents Milton with his dilemma, a fact that renders the distinction between hearing and contemplating specious. Milton knew the music was sounding and he knew he could not hear; the subject of the poems about music is not so much music as the ear that would hear it.

When Milton wrote about music—about harmony—he therefore distinguished between two kinds: earthly music (*musica instrumentalis*), which suffers from "grossness" after the fall, and heavenly harmony (*musica mundana*), which before the fall was truly echoed on earth. According to Milton, we all have a "gross unpurged ear" (the symptom of "disproportioned sin") and are all, therefore, discordant souls (discordant *musica humana*), unable to echo *musica mundana*, unable to join in the harmony of the spheres. *Musica instrumentalis* is a musical harmony according to contemporary technical laws produced by "gross" ears, not a spiritual harmony (in the Pythagorean-Platonic and Christian sense), nor a measure that accords with the eternal laws of divine harmony.[5] It therefore troubled Milton that poetry is a form of *musica instrumentalis*. For these reasons, Milton concerns himself with the potential retuning of the microcosm to the harmony of the macrocosm. He writes not about a divine music that causes or is a result of ascent but about a purgation that would allow him to ascend. Milton does not consider music a cause of ecstasy, purgation, or regeneration; rather he argues repeatedly that purgation and regeneration must come first. According to Milton, hearing "the heavenly tune" is a sign that one has a chaste ear; and having a chaste ear is a sign that purgation and regeneration have already occurred. It is a good Miltonic tautology, an expression of the Protestant problem of election.

At a Solemn Music, a poem about the difference between earthly music and heavenly harmony, is perhaps Milton's most concise statement of his desire to hear once again the divine harmony. The poem is comprised of two sentences; the first, twenty-four lines, contains three commands:

> *Wed* your divine sounds, and mixt power *employ*
> Dead things with inbreath'd sense able to pierce,
> And to our high-rais'd fantasy *present*
> That undisturbed Song of pure concent.   (3–6)

But the sentence is divided by a semicolon at line 16; the description of the harmony then ends with:

> the Cherubic host in thousand choirs
> Hymns devout and holy Psalms
> Singing everlastingly. (14–16)

Then and only then does the wish behind the commands become clear:

> That we on Earth with undiscording voice
> May rightly answer that melodious noise;
> As once we did, till disproportion'd sin
> Jarr'd against nature's chime, and with harsh din
> Broke the fair music that all creatures made
> To their great Lord, whose love their motion sway'd
> In perfect Diapason, whilst they stood
> In first obedience and their state of good. (17–24)

The lost ability (lost with original sin) to hear and to answer "that melodious noise" is followed by a consideration of the problem of restoring it. This poem, typical of Milton's early works about divine music, expresses the poet's state of "Earthy grossness" by devising a grammar of "gross" poetry. The grammatical and expository transition from commands to clauses of purpose ("That we on Earth . . . May") and finally to exhortations expresses not only the poet's present condition but also the conditional status of the redemption of his soul and thereby the purging of his ear and voice:

> O may we soon again renew that Song,
> And keep in tune with Heav'n, till God ere long
> To his celestial consort us unite,
> To live with him, and sing in endless morn of light. (25–28)

Milton expresses his condition of "grossness" by means of grammatical enactment. The second sentence of the poem further advances the movement of the first; the exhortation (subjunctive) makes all successive clauses conditional. Surely we would live with him, Milton suggests, but we are waiting "till God ere long" brings us to him.

Both *L'Allegro* and *Il Penseroso* end with passages about divine music. They are often read by critics as descriptions of two different sorts of music—one mirthful, one melancholy—that evoke two different responses from one who hears them, but they are rather companion accounts in which the poet is asking for nothing other than the reattuning of the human soul, asking for an end to "Earthy grossness," and for the ability to enjoy (as did Adam and Eve before the fall) what James Hutton has called the "harmonious structure of the universe reflected in the human soul."[6] Other critics have tended to write about these passages and therefore the poems as examples of Neoplatonic ascent or ecstasy; this tendency inclines them to pay little or no attention to the importance of the conditional couplets with which both poems end.[7]

In a famous passage from *L'Allegro*, we find Milton is telling us about himself; he is asking for the retuning of the human soul:

> And ever against eating Cares,
> Lap me in soft *Lydian* Airs,
> Married to immortal verse,
> Such as the meeting soul may pierce
> In notes, with many a winding bout
> Of linked sweetness long drawn out,
> With wanton heed, and giddy cunning,
> The melting voice through mazes running;
> Untwisting all the chains that tie
> The hidden soul of harmony.[8]   (135–44)

It is important to notice here the conditional nature of this statement, particularly the conditional phrase "Such as . . . may pierce." For it is only the renovated soul that may be pierced, since it alone may be reattuned to the harmony of the spheres. The plea for "Untwisting all the chains that tie / The hidden soul of harmony" is close to the view recounted by Simmias in Plato's *Phaedo:*

You might say the same thing about tuning the strings of a musical instrument, that the attunement is something invisible and incorporeal and splendid and divine and is located in the tuned instrument, while the instrument itself and its strings are material and corporeal and composite and earthly and closely related to what is mortal. Now suppose that the instrument is broken, or its strings cut or snapped. . . . You would say that the attunement must still exist somewhere just as it was, and that the wood and strings will rot away before anything happens to it.[9]

The "hidden soul of harmony"—untied from the body's "grossness"— would be *musica humana* in harmony with *music mundana*, and *musica instrumentalis*—as it was in Paradise, as it is in Book IV of *Paradise Lost*—would then be a perfect echo of divine harmony, the product of a *musica humana* in harmony with *musica mundana*. Milton does not describe a Platonic or Neoplatonic ascent but rather asks to be rid of the "muddy vesture of decay," to be purged that he *might* ascend. The two events would be coterminous but are as yet unfulfilled. We see the same kind of request also in *Il Penseroso:*

> And as I wake, sweet music breathe
> Above, about, or underneath,
> Sent by some spirit to mortals good,
> Or th'unseen Genius of the wood.   (151–54)

The music is sent only "to mortals good." Edward S. LeComte has re-marked that "'sweet' and 'sweetness' are words that this poet reserves, almost always, for music, for paradise, and for the originally perfect affec-tion between Adam and Eve."[10] Both *L'Allegro* and *Il Penseroso* remind us of the sweetness of heavenly harmony and love in earthly paradise only to remind us more strongly of the bitter discord (brought on by the fall) in man's present condition.

Announcing the condition of discord, *Il Penseroso* begins with a depic-tion of the limits of the human senses:

> Hail divinest Melancholy,
> Whose Saintly visage is too bright
> To hit the Sense of human sight;
> And therefore to our weaker view,
> O'erlaid with black, staid Wisdom's hue.   (12–16)

Likening metaphors of hearing and seeing when discussing the subject of fallen human senses, which we see in many other of Milton's poems, has its roots in Cicero's discussion of the harmony of the spheres.[11] A consequence of the poet's "weaker view" and "gross unpurged ear," all seeing and hearing are conditional. As in *At a Solemn Music,* in which the poet commands, "Wed your divine sounds, and mixt power employ / Dead things with inbreath'd sense able to pierce," the subject of the companion poems is the present inability of the soul to be pierced by music: in *L'Allegro,* "that may pierce" and in *Il Penseroso,* "as may pierce."

Dr. Samuel Johnson was apparently the first to notice that more is conditional in the companion poems than their final couplets: "Both his characters delight in musick; but he seems to think that cheerful notes would have obtained from Pluto a compleat dismission of Eurydice, of *whom solemn* sounds only procured a conditional release."[12] Indeed, the poems are similar in their propensity to express things conditionally. *L'Al-legro* and *Il Penseroso* share with *At a Solemn Music* (and other early poems about music) a common grammatical structure—a command fol-lowed by a purpose or result (subjunctive) clause. In *L'Allegro*—

> That *Orpheus'* self may leave his head
> From golden slumber on a bed
> Of heapt *Elysian* flow'rs, and hear
> Such strains as would have won the ear
> Of *Pluto,* to have quite set free
> His half-regain'd *Eurydice*—   (145–50)

Milton employs a subjunctive ("may leave"), a past contrary to fact ("as would have won"), and another past contrary to fact dependent on the first ("to have quite set free"). The "quite" provides nice emphasis when we read "half-regain'd." The companion passage from *Il Penseroso* reminds us that this is half the story:

> But, O sad Virgin, that thy power
> Might raise *Musaeus* from his bower,
> Or bid the soul of *Orpheus* sing
> Such notes as, warbled to the string,
> Drew Iron tears down Pluto's cheek,
> And made Hell grant what Love did seek.   (103–08)

What "love did seek" was only "half-regain'd" not because poetry failed but because the poet, lacking the fortitude not to turn back, failed to do what would have secured the return of Eurydice. Orpheus did not obey the god's command, and so Pluto did not grant what would be something like Christian grace. Thus the poet bids "the soul of *Orpheus* sing," but this is an Orpheus who has, like Adam, disobeyed a god. The power of his music was subjected to a greater law, which, when disobeyed, rendered it ineffective. The example of Orpheus is an inversion of Milton's case: there is nothing wrong with Orpheus' ears but with his song, "such strains as would have won the ear" of Pluto. Milton must, paradoxically, reach the ear of God, receive grace, and hear the divine harmonies, all before he can write the kind of poetry that would be "such notes as . . . Drew Iron tears." When Milton bids Orpheus sing "such notes . . . " he asks that poetry succeed where the will of the poet failed. This is the weak command of a strongly Christian poet. He is not commanding but asking.

Throughout the long history of criticism of the poems, too many critics have ignored what Milton painstakingly shows us in the urgent command, the plaintive exhortation, and the conditional clauses—the grammatical enactment of waiting. The history of reading these passages as actual ascent, ecstasy, or purgation results from the mistake of ignoring "as may."[13] Seemingly, ascent is precisely what the young Milton desires to achieve in *Il Penseroso* and elsewhere, to experience an inner, religious, spiritual vision, to hear with his ears and to see with his eyes the universal harmony of the spheres. But the desire is immediately unful-fillable. For this reason, both poems begin with commands that eventually (and subtly) shift into hortatory subjunctives and finally into the condi-tional couplets that conclude both poems. The structure of the poems constitutes the grammatical enactment of asking and waiting for grace. In *Il Penseroso* the shift becomes noticeable at line 147: "me Goddess bring" (132), "Hide me" (141), "And let" (147), "But let" (155), and finally:

> There let the pealing Organ blow
> To the full voic'd Choir below,
> In Service high and Anthems clear,
> As may with sweetness, through mine ear,
> Dissolve me into ecstasies,
> And bring all Heav'n before mine eyes. (161–66)

Il Penseroso does not *experience* the "ecstasies"; he exhorts ("There let") that he may (*"as may"*) be pierced ("through mine ear") and dissolved into "ecstasies." Nor is heaven brought before his eyes. Indeed, there is poi-gnant ambiguity in "And bring." Is it another imperative? Or does it depend on "as may," a contingency of the optative? The ambiguity empha-sizes that the occurrences are conditional.

Not only is nothing achieved and nothing chosen, not only are the demands of the conditional couplets not satisfied—but that is the point of the poem. *Il Penseroso* expresses the poet's condition and his attitude toward it: his relation to divine harmony, his wait for Christ, for redemp-tion, when time will bring back the golden age. Just as he contrasts his urgent *now* and God's eternity in *At a Solemn Music*, so too in the compan-ion poems does Milton express his condition as both man and poet by making a command that secures only the condition of waiting.

Milton expresses this condition within each poem in the grammatical structure built by the sequence of conditional couplets that unites the poems. In addition to the two conditional couplets with which the poems conclude, there is, of course, a third. It occurs early in *L'Allegro:*

> And if I give thee honor due,
> Mirth, admit me of thy crew. (37–38)

In this, the first conditional couplet to appear in the companion poems, the poet places the burden of giving on himself. The second conditional couplet concludes *L'Allegro:*

> These delights if thou canst give,
> Mirth, with thee I mean to live. (151–52)

Here the reversal of the earlier couplet marks strongly the poet's movement from a plaintive stance to a demanding one. But the three couplets work as a triad, the third couplet drawing to a close the rhetorical development of the companion poems:

> These pleasures *Melancholy* give,
> And I with thee will choose to live.   (175–76)

If we read the three conditional couplets as a development—and I think we must—we notice the variations of grammatical form that suggest a parallel development in the attitude of the poet. Within the development there are two shifts: from giving (in the first couplet) to receiving (in the second). But the most important shift in attitude (from the second couplet to the third) is expressed by a change from one type of conditional statement to another. The first two are present simple conditionals; both the protases and apodases are in the present tense: the first, "if I give" (present), "admit" (imperative); the second, "if thou canst give" (present), "I mean" (present). The third, unlike the first two, is an odd sort of mixed conditional: "give" (imperative), "and I will choose" (future). The mixed conditional has the force of expediency (imperative) in the protasis and uncertainty (future) in the apodasis. Moreover, Milton does not write "and I will live" but rather "I will choose to live." He urgently commands ("give"), yet the completion of this command is the condition not for immediate action or choice but only for the postponement of choice; only then (in the future) he "will choose." The urgent uncertainty confirms now what the poet seems earlier reluctant to acknowledge: there is currently no possibility of fulfilling the conditions but only of stating them.[14]

Together, by means of their grammatical structure, the poems enact the condition of the poet: waiting—until grace purges his "grossness" and brings the music and light of heaven to his ears and eyes. Before the music may be heard there must be grace, remission of sin, and renovation. But all is uncertain, as Milton writes in the *Christian Doctrine*, quoting from and interpreting Exodus xxxiii, 19: "*I will be gracious to whom I will be gracious,* that is, not to enter more largely into the causes of this graciousness at present, Romans ix, 18. *he hath mercy on whom he will have mercy,* by that method, namely, which he had appointed in Christ."[15] At that time, there will be "the remission of sins, even in his human nature," Milton writes, quoting Isaiah xxxv, 4–6: "*behold, your God will come with vengeance, even God with a recompense, he will come and save you: then the eyes of the blind shall be opened.*" And there will be "renovation," writes Milton, quoting 2 Corinthians v, 17–18: "*behold, all things are*

*become new, and all things are of God, who hath reconciled himself to us
by Jesus Christ.*"[16]

Arthur Barker has shown that the three movements of *Lycidas* begin
with "invocation[s] of pastoral muses" and end with "perfectly controlled"
Christian "crescendos."[17] In the companion poems we see a similar movement in the triad of conditional couplets. As in *At a Solemn Music*, a poem
in which Milton writes not about the *nunc stans* of the Nativity ode but
about himself as a poet and his earthly *now*, Milton here expresses *his*
condition in the movement of the conditional couplets, and in a way that
demonstrates his acceptance of it. With the movement from urgency to
uncertainty in the final couplet, Milton completes his grammatical enactment of waiting, to which we must contrast the *nunc stans*.[18] In the
Nativity ode, Milton writes about the time for which all are waiting, the
time when the golden age will be brought back: "And then at last our bliss
/ Full and perfect is" when, as Edward Tayler has written, "instead of the
expected future ("will be"), the poet writes in a kind of eternal present, for
as Joseph Fletcher says, 'God . . . needeth not the distinctions of Time'—
the notion stated most memorably by Sir Thomas Browne: 'in eternity
there is no distinction of Tenses.' "[19] But the poet lives in time, not in
eternity; and poetry is subject to the laws of time. Time, the awful part of
"grossness," is the punishment for original sin. With nothing available to
the poet but tenses, Milton therefore chooses them differently when
writing about God and when writing about himself. For in God's eternal
time, Christ has already come, whereas Milton must wait, must express
himself only in the temporal terms we know on earth. Only by ridding
himself of time, Milton writes in *On Time*, will he rid himself of his
"Earthy grossness":

> When once our heav'nly-guided soul shall climb,
> Then all this Earthy grossness quit,
> Attir'd with Stars, we shall for ever sit
>> Triumphing over Death, and Chance, and thee
>> O Time.   (19–23)

Our "heav'nly-guided soul shall climb," and ascent shall be made possible, by a realignment of macrocosm and microcosm; by a retuning of
musica mundana with *musica humana* into harmony—by grace—our
imperfect, impure soul shall be made new. Milton describes the good
end of time with a tellingly odd temporal clause ("when once") and
promises "we shall for ever." The soul is truly unable to be *pierced*, in
Milton's terms, until it is purged, renovated, until it is drawn home,
where it "shall for ever sit / Triumphing over Death, and Chance, and

thee / O Time," that is, when the poet, having triumphed over the muddy decay of earth, may sing about himself as he would sing about heaven. This will be a long wait, Milton knows, a wait requiring much patience. Milton will wait "Till old experience do attain / To something like Prophetic strain" (173–74).

Eager to receive his poetic fate, Milton concludes in *Sonnet VII:* "All is, if I have grace to use it so, / As ever in my great task-Master's eye." The sense conveys resignation while the syntax, which enacts the temporal uncertainty it expresses, reveals anxiousness. Milton expresses his condition—all is conditional ("if I have grace to use it so"). In the companion poems he expresses this tension between anxiousness and patience by means of the series of conditional invitations that plays upon the tradition of pastoral invitation and reply that emerges with Marlowe and Raleigh. Milton seems to have adopted not Marlowe's invitation but Raleigh's mock acceptance, which is acceptance on the grounds that a whole list of counterfactual conditions be satisfied. Raleigh answers Marlowe's promises of future delights—"Come live with me, and be my love / And we will all the pleasures prove"—by turning Marlowe's "will" into a counterfactual "could" and conditional "might":

> But could youth last, and love still breede,
> Had joyes no date, nor age no neede,
> Then these delights my minde might move
> To live with thee, and be thy love.[20]

Milton seems to have picked this up; he built into the progression of the three conditional couplets of the companion poems something like Marlowe's promise and Raleigh's mocking reply. In the final couplet of the companion poems—"These pleasures *Melancholy* give / And I with thee will choose to live"—the series of invitations culminates in its own reply (a rejection) to itself by ending with the indefinite postponement of choice. Milton effectively rejects both the pagan goddess and the pastoral (the Marlovian) invitation, suggesting instead that he has begun his wait for Christian grace.

In the companion poems (and other poems about music), Milton doubts not the power of music to draw him home but the power of his ear to hear it and be drawn. Milton suggests that until one receives grace and undergoes renovation music can neither pierce one's "earthy grossness" nor draw the soul out of the body. Does all this mean that music (*musica instrumentalis*) draws one only to awareness of the impenetrable, "gross" decaying house of clay, or can it still draw one up to God? The companion poems and *At a Solemn Music* provide the same answer:

> O may we soon again renew that Song,
> And keep in tune with Heav'n, till God ere long
> To his celestial consort us unite,
> To live with him, and sing in endless morn of light.   (25–28)

According to Milton, music itself does not have the Orphic power to draw one home; rather we must first be drawn home to God in order to hear, and then to sing the divine harmony. Music does, however, make us aware of one's condition.

Milton makes commands, and directs them not to his unchaste soul but to the heaven he longs to hear, the heaven that could make him chaste, and not boldly; he rather softens the commands, changes them to exhortations, that heaven might stoop to him. For the hope is, as the final lines of *Comus* state: "Or if Vertue feeble were, / Heav'n itself would stoop to her" (1022–23). In the companion and other early poems Milton transforms his soft commands to heaven into hard conditional statements to himself: for surely he would live with him, but he knows he must wait "till God ere long" brings us to him.

Writing about the companion poems, Isabel MacCaffrey has suggested that "in a sense . . . these poems represent Milton's first effort to render Paradise in his poetry."[21] But the companion poems are neither the first nor the last of Milton's efforts to express the reason why the poet cannot "render Paradise." By the poet's own admission, Milton's was a poetic career in which, both early and late, too much was conditional (dependent on grace) to allow a continuous process of maturation from early premeditation to later success. Critics have seemed nevertheless not to notice what Milton understood too well. Milton's poetic career was dominated by the intense concern that divine poetry could not be a human endeavor, that a postlapsarian poet could not write the sort of divine poetry we all agree the young Milton wanted to write and many critics have suggested the "mature" Milton finally did write. In the early poems we read the epic of the poet trying to purge his "grossness"; in the later poetry we read about the poet—still "gross"—who has nevertheless learned to devise a strategy that allows him to sing his song anyway, but not without telling us about the problem of singing it. We ought to revise the dichotomous casting of Milton's career as the young poet (putatively immature), the writer of occasional verse, and the mature poet, the great poet of grand themes who wrote epics. The condition of "grossness" may after all make maturity irrelevant, since, as Milton tells us in *On Time*, a Christian poet may truly mature only by receiving grace.

Columbia University

NOTES

Many thanks to Margaret W. Ferguson, Anne Lake Prescott, Edward W. Tayler, and Richard Wollman for their comments.

1. All quotations are from *John Milton: Complete Poems and Major Prose,* ed. Merritt Y. Hughes (New York, 1957).

2. See Sigmond Spaeth, *Milton's Knowledge of Music* (1913; rpt. Ann Arbor, 1963); James Hutton, "Some English Poems in Praise of Music," *EM* II (1951), 1–63; Leo Spitzer, *Classical and Christian Ideas of World Harmony,* ed. Ann Granville Hatcher (Baltimore, 1963); Marjorie Hope Nicolson, *The Breaking of the Circle* (Evanston, 1950); and Ernest Brennecke, Jr., *John Milton the Elder and His Music* (New York, 1938).

3. John Caldwell, in "The *De Institutione Arithmetica* and *De Institutione Musica,*" in *Boethius,* ed. Margaret Gibson (Oxford, 1981), p. 145, explains: "The line of demarcation between the latter two was often misunderstood by later writers, who (perhaps because the instances given of instrumental music do not include the voice) understood human music as vocal. But the description of it by Boethius makes it clear that it is to be understood as a metaphor of the parts of the soul and of the body, and of their relation to each other."

4. See Gerard H. Cox, "Unbinding 'The Hidden Soul of Harmony': *L'Allegro, Il Penseroso,* and the Hermetic Tradition," in *Milton Studies* XVIII, ed. James D. Simmonds (Pittsburgh, 1983), pp. 45–62; Norman B. Council, "*L'Allegro, Il Penseroso* and 'The Cycle of Universal Knowledge,'" in *Milton Studies* IX, ed. James D. Simmonds (Pittsburgh, 1976), pp. 203–20; and Christopher Grose, "The Lydian Airs of 'L'Allegro' and 'Il Penseroso,'" *JEGP* LXXXIII (1984), 183–99.

5. Cladwell, *Boethius,* p. 152. *Musica instrumentalis* is both voice and instrumental music. Caldwell writes: "Vocal music and speech, however, together with an intermediate category appropriate to epic recitation, are dealt with . . . with the clear implication that all three fall within the category of 'musica instrumentalis.'"

6. Hutton, "Some English Poems in Praise of Music," p. 10.

7. See Kester Svendsen, "Milton's *L'Allegro* and *Il Penseroso,*" *The Explicator* VIII (1950), item 49; and Rosemond Tuve, "Structural Figures of 'L'Allegro' and 'Il Penseroso,'" in *Images and Themes in Five Poems by Milton* (Cambridge, Mass., 1957).

8. Much criticism has followed either the letter or the spirit of Merritt Hughes's note about the Lydian mode, in *John Milton: Complete Poems and Major Prose,* p. 71. Hughes, however, misstates Hutton, who writes, in "Some Poems in Praise of Music," p. 46: "the commentators inform us that Milton dissents from Plato's condemnations of the Lydian mode; but that is beside the point." The important thing, Hutton argues, is the claim about piercing put forth by Cassiodorus. In paying too much attention to the Lydian mode and too little to piercing and the condition of grossness, critics often miss the point.

9. *Phaedo,* trans. Hugh Tredennick, *The Collected Dialogues,* ed. Edith Hamilton and Huntington Cairns (Princeton, 1961), p. 68.

10. Edward S. LeComte, *Yet Once More* (New York, 1953), p. 16.

11. *De Republica,* trans. Clinton Walker Keyes (Cambridge, 1988), p. 273: "'But this mighty music, produced by the revolution of the whole universe at the highest speed, cannot be perceived by human ears, any more than you can look straight at the sun, your sense of sight being overpowered by its radiance.'"

12. *Lives of the English Poets,* ed. G. B. Hill, 3 vols., (Oxford, 1905). Others have remarked the hypothetical nature of the delights and pleasures, but none with attention to music and the ear that may or may not hear it. Thomas M. Greene, "Four Studies in Milton:

The Meeting Soul in Milton's Companion Poems," *ELR* XIV (1984), 159–74, is the only critic who has written of the conditional elements with any view to the impossibility of fulfilling them, although he does so very briefly and with an emphasis different from mine. Whereas I am interested in the way poems express conditionally the ability of music to pierce the human soul, Greene is interested in the way the conditionals make it "not easy to gauge the reality of what does or might or might not happen."

13. Rosemund Tuve writes, for example, in *Images and Themes in Five Poems by Milton*, p. 32: "The poem ends firmly, with a climactic last representative of those who taste Melancholy's pleasures in the pursuit of wisdom; for certainly the hermit who spells out the secrets of the physical universe in his solitary cell is no concession to religiosity but the very type of the withdrawn seer who experiences the last pleasure: to know things in their causes and see into the hidden harmonies of the cosmos." See also Greene, "Four Studies in Milton," p. 169: "the 'ecstacies' which dissolve il penseroso as he hears the full-voice choir"; Kester Svendsen, "Milton's L'Allegro and Il Penseroso": "For the pensive man in his ecstasy experiences what Milton said in the nativity hymn could happen through the 'holy Song' of the spheres and the angels"; and D. C. Allen, *The Harmonious Vision* (Baltimore, 1954), p. 10: " 'Il Penseroso' is 'more accomplished' and 'more mature' than 'L'Allegro'. . . . 'Il Penseroso' is the poem of a poet that has found his way."

14. Stanley Fish, "What It's Like to Read *L'Allegro* and *Il Penseroso*," in *Milton Studies* VII, ed. Albert C. Labriola and Michael Lieb (Pittsburgh, 1975), pp. 77–99, has written unpersuasively that "the poems *mean* the experience they give; and because they so mean, the conditionals with which they end are false. . . . These conditionals are false because the conditions they specify have already been met."

15. *John Milton: Complete Poems and Major Prose*, p. 919.

16. Ibid., pp. 958–59.

17. Arthur Barker, "The Pattern of Milton's Nativity Ode," in *UTO* X (1941), 171–72.

18. See Edward W. Tayler, *Milton's Poetry: Its Development in Time* (Pittsburgh, 1979), pp. 32–33, on the poetic *nunc stans* and Milton's awareness of writing *sub specie aeternitatis*, of which the grammatical enactment of waiting is, in striking contrast, not an example. It rather expresses "what do I do now?" Milton here is waiting for Christ. He is, like other Christians, a man in human history waiting for grace.

19. Ibid., p. 36.

20. Christopher Marlowe, *Complete Plays and Poems*, ed. E. D. Pendry (1909; rpt. London, 1983); Robert Ny, ed., *Sir Walter Raleigh's Verse* (London, 1972).

21. MacCaffrey, quoted by Douglas Bush, *A Variorum Commentary: The Minor Poems*, ed. A.S.P. Woodhouse and Douglas Bush (New York, 1970), p. 267.

RHYME AND DISORDER IN
SAMSON AGONISTES

Keith N. Hull

W HAT DID MILTON REALLY MEAN by his apparent denuncia-
tion of rhyme in the prefatory paragraph to *Paradise Lost?* John
Shawcross speculates that the poet "petulantly countered reader antago-
nism [to blank verse]" and Dryden's defense of rhyme in *An Essay of
Dramatick Poesy.* William Riley Parker, in making his case for *Samson
Agonistes*'s early composition, took Milton seriously indeed, reading into
The Verse a denunciation so heartfelt that the poet never again rhymed. J.
Max Patrick interprets the paragraph as "a public confession . . . of some-
thing close to stupidity" in giving in to "precedent and custom" and to
Baroque virtuosity. Robert Beum more temperately excuses Milton for a
momentary passionate rejection born of his new enthusiasm for blank
verse and his dislike of Royalist literary fashion. Michael Cohen sees *The
Verse* as Milton's statement that he would not be "subject to the tyranny of
a particular rhyme scheme" with its "jingling sound."[1]

In interpreting Milton's comments, however, critics seem to overlook his intention in *Paradise Lost* of pursuing "Things unattempted yet in
Prose or Rhyme" (I, 16).[2] While one may read this passage as a further
disparagement of rhymed verse, a claim that it is not up to the poet's great
task, another interpretation is possible. Given Milton's elegant, rhymed
short poems and the rhymed lines in *Paradise Lost* and *Samson
Agonistes*—which seems to have settled down again as a late poem—a
complete rejection of rhyme in *The Verse* seems unlikely. Rather, Milton
makes it poetry's usual definitive characteristic, distinguishing it from
prose. The phrase, then, may imply real respect for rhyme. Milton forcefully rejects "the jingling sound of like endings," but he is discussing
rhyme "as a thing of itself." Again, considering Milton's rhyming before
and after his comment, perhaps *The Verse* disparages only rhyme written
in response to his old nemesis, custom, and used only as a decorative
feature serving no meaningful purpose. If so, Milton's apparent detraction
actually opens the possibility of rhyming for other purposes.

In *Samson Agonistes* Milton had serious reasons to rhyme. Readers may or may not find musical delight in the poem's odd rhyming, but they will find purposeful, challenging technique that reinterprets the Samson story while driving Milton's Christian thinking to its most radical lengths. Does Samson act on his own? Does he respond to divine influence? To what extent? Might he be entirely controlled by God? The poem's rhyme offers an analog to Samson's relation to God, constituting a powerful indicator of how to answer these troublesome questions. Ambivalent rhyme corresponds to the deliberate ambivalence of God's role—or nonrole—in *Samson*.

Milton's God is order and orderer. The universe of *Paradise Lost* is harmonious and predictable—the sun will rise and the stars wheel across the sky; man and angel need but fulfill their functions to be happy and achieve eventual oneness with God when heaven and earth achieve a new, more complex, more meaningful order. Satan causes difficulties, altering the final unification which will eventually exclude fallen men and angels, but God can accommodate the countercurrent. The ultimate stable state, the great unity, will be as orderly as that composed of God only, but more complex. Among Milton's devices conveying such order are two that are especially significant here. First, God simply tells us that all this is true (III, 290–341). Second, harmony of verse, imagery, metaphor, action, character imply God's order. In *Paradise Lost* technique embodies a major theme.

In *Samson Agonistes*, we find, in the first case, a radical contrast. God is never clearly present—we do not see him, he does not speak. Even his past utterances filter through the memories and interpretations of those who have heard him; in understanding *Samson*'s events, characters and readers are on their own, making the second principle from *Paradise Lost* significant. Rhyme is a powerful ordering device that can establish, emphasize, and control a poem's thematic structure while conveying unity, continuity, and closure. These functions derive from like sounds which establish predictable patterns we delight in hearing propagated and completed. Yet rhyme also contains potential for delightful surprise. As a poem reveals its rhyme structure, it exploits our ignorance of what will happen next. What word will complete the rhyme? What pattern will eventually emerge?[3]

Once the pattern is clear, we also delight in seeing it broken; good rhymes should be mostly unanticipated. In other words, rhyme not only establishes order, it also imperils order through constant potential for the unexpected. Ordinarily, we feel secure with the emerging order, but *Samson* adds the peril of any rhyme's being accidental or haphazard, since the overwhelming majority of the poem is unrhymed; there is no apparent generic or thematic reason for its appearance, implying that disorder and God's order both exist and may be indistinguishable from each other. This implication reveals much meaning in *Samson* where rhymes and rhyming structures constitute a continuum ranging from order to disorder, or intention to accident, analogous to the degree of God's presence or absence in *Samson*'s events.

Assuming that God somehow influences Samson during the poem seems valid. God has affected Samson's past life. Manoa talked twice with God's angel, who "ordain'd [Samson's] nurture holy" (361–62). Samson himself participated in the miracle of water springing from dry ground (581–83). The youthful Samson felt God in him when the "Spirit . . . first rusht on [him] / In the camp of *Dan*" (1435–36), and he married the woman at Timna "from intimate impulse" that "motion'd was of God" (222–23). In the poem, Samson agrees to accompany the Public Officer after twice refusing because he begins "to feel / Some rousing motions . . . which dispose / To something extraordinary [his] thoughts" (1381–83). At the end, the Messenger describes him in an attitude that might indicate divine impulse: "with head a while inclin'd, / And eyes fast fixt he stood, as one who pray'd" (1636–38).

In *Samson*'s structure, we find other evidence for God's influence as seen in the poem's orderliness. Whatever else happens, Samson moves from lassitude to activity, and presumably something occurs with his visitors to cause this change, an apparently orderly process. Manoa forces Samson to deal with his most difficult problem: his relationship with God now that Samson has betrayed him. Dalila confronts Samson with the preceding phase, when he enslaved himself and his apparent greatest problem was his marriage. Harapha recapitulates an earlier phase still, when Samson's problem was how to deal militarily with his enemies.

These issues progress from the present to the past, from the most complex to the simplest to resolve, from the greatest spiritual importance to the least. Samson's visitors take him backward through his life, tracing his development into an enslaved, troubled sinner, experiencing disturbing ranges of emotion, thought, and discourse that force him to revisit traumatic events until he subsumes them in a broader, deeper wisdom— Jackie DiSalvo even argues for the poem's suggesting a "pyschoanalytic process."[4] So systematic a cure for Samson's spiritual ills powerfully suggests God's ordering influence.

Another order-based argument for God's presence in Samson's life is the Chorus's belief that he is there. Their final speech tells us:

All is best, though we oft doubt,
What th'unsearchable dispose
Of highest wisdom brings about,
And ever best found in the close.   (1745–48)

The Chorus perceives God working actively. "Dispose" is "ordering," as John Shawcross notes.[5] "Brings about" makes God the virtual designer of Samson's life, and "close" says they perceive its ordered, satisfying closure. "True experience" of this pattern begets "peace and consolation" as well as calm of mind, Milton's problematic interpretation of catharsis. By both lines of argument, Samson's life is divinely ordered, even if the order is only retrospectively perceptible. Among others, Parker has expressed many of these ideas, stating flatly that the Chorus's speech is "the final interpretation."[6] Mary Ann Radzinowicz approaches this issue through *De Doctrina Christiana,* stating we see God's nature and our relationship with him in the "patterns of God's ways with man."[7]

Approaching the issue of God's active role from another angle argues for the reverse interpretation: order in *Samson Agonistes* is doubtful and, if there, may not reflect God's presence at all. Radzinowicz makes the crucial observation that God is not "on stage," (p. 282) and that there is "no use of divine persons" (p. 184). In fact, *Samson* is the only major Milton poem devoid of supernatural beings. These observations, plus the fact that Samson's "intimate impulse[s]" are so intimate that only he experiences them, raise doubt about their validity.

His first marriage exemplifies how doubtful his impulses are. Was Samson inspired by God? Some critics think not. Helen Damico, comparing Samson's impulse to that which led Jesus into the wilderness in *Paradise Regained,* notes that the son responded to "a force outside the self," while "Samson feels his surge within himself . . . , [so] his 'motions' are neither explicitly nor implicitly defined as originating with God."[8] Damico notes too that Samson's plan to deliver Israel seems unclear if the Timnian bride is involved; citing the marriage's illegality, she concludes that Samson's impulses probably have nothing to do with God. The logical extension of this doubt is to question Samson's "motions" occurring just before he exits with the Public Officer to commit another forbidden act. As Stanley Fish says, "the reader who remembers the history of Samson's 'rousing motions' may be wary of labelling the new motions 'of God.' "[9]

Then too, Samson's final action is too ambiguous in its nature and results to delineate a clear case for divine inspiration. Refusing to see Samson's final act as a triumph, Irene Samuel is especially stern. Gathering evidence from throughout the poet's work, she shows how forcefully opposed to violence Milton was and how unlikely he was to conclude a major poem with a violent act we should approve. Samuel also cites evidence within Samson to bolster her point. Assuming, like Damico and Fish, that Samson's inspiration is suspect, she raises the important point about whether readers should rejoice with Manoa and the Chorus over Samson's "death-dealing." Considering the Public Officer's reasonable, even kindly, behavior, Harapha's comic blustering, and Dalila's limitations, Samuel asks what kind of victory destroys such people, especially when the Israelites cooperate in their own oppression, and have already refused once to exploit Samson's feats.[10] Samuel's skepticism is reasonable; for most of the poem—maybe never—Samson has no conscious plan for himself, and if his actions are bad what about their alleged divine inspiration? Once that becomes doubtful, so does God's role in Samson's life. Acts that seem to reflect God's order become gratuitous, haphazard, accidental. What does *Samson* mean then?

This balance between two interpretations finds a technical counterpart in *Samson's* rhyme which reveals substantial order in some places, is absent in others, and constitutes a continuum between the two that keeps the issue of God's presence or absence before the reader. Manoa's lament at Samson's fallen condition and his own ironic misfortune illustrates the order-disorder continuum:

> O miserable change! is this the man,
> That invincible *Samson*, far renown'd,
> The dread of *Israel's* foes, who with a strength
> Equivalent to Angels' walk'd thir streets,
> None offering fight; who single combatant
> Duell'd thir Armies rank't in proud array,
> Himself an Army, now unequal match
> To save himself against a coward arm'd
> At one spear's length. O ever failing trust
> In mortal strength! and oh, what not in man
> Deceivable and vain! Nay, what thing good
> Pray'd for, but often proves our woe, our bane?
> I pray'd for Children, and thought barrenness
> In wedlock a reproach; I gain'd a Son,
> And such a Son as all Men hail'd me happy;
> Who would be now a Father in my stead?
> O wherefore did God grant me my request,
> And as a blessing with such pomp adorn'd?
> Why are his gifts desirable, to tempt
> Our earnest Prayers, then, giv'n with solemn hand
> As Graces, draw a Scorpion's tail behind?   (340–60)

Nothing about this passage prepares readers for rhyme except some rhyme earlier in the poem, scattered to offer no guidance about when it might recur. Unless we count the repetition of "Reason" in lines 322–23, the last clear rhyme is "free . . . purity" in lines 317 and 319. No title or rhyme system anticipates what happens in lines 348–51. Readers who expect line-end rhymes would miss the rhyme concentrated here—three separate instances in four lines within an otherwise unrhymed speech.

Once seen, "length . . . strength," "O . . . oh . . . woe," and "vain . . . bane" reveal surprising order. "Length," "strength," "vain," and "bane" insistently close grammatical units, and the rhymes emphasize key words. Oddly, these seemingly unconventional rhymes fulfill conventional functions, closure and emphasis; so, with rhyme as a guide, we can read these lines in other combinations to reveal other kinds of order and emphasis:

> At one spear's length?
> O
> Ever failing trust in mortal strength!
> And, oh,
> What not in man deceivable and vain!
> Nay, what good thing pray'd for, but often proves our woe,
> Our bane?

In trying alternative orderings, we are unimpeded by meter or line length, which are also relatively unrestrained in *Samson Agonistes*. Hence we find the discipline of rhyme functioning with freedom from other devices to give readers different ordering principles and emphasizing order more or less.

Furthermore, rhyme singles out some lines—why do they differ from others? Answering, we discover yet another ordering principle within Manoa's speech. In the passage above, the rhymed lines offer a general comment on humankind. Rhyme again serves traditional purposes, closing Manoa's pronouncement with a stressed, perfect rhyme that also accents the parallelism of the second question, about good becoming bane, with the first, about what in man is not deceivable and vain. Equally significant, however, is the untraditional appearance of the rhyme's first half at midline. Following the pattern of the other two rhymes, "vain" meets our expectations created by the rhyme scheme—if "scheme" describes such an unconventional grouping—while "bane" violates our expectations, appearing at the (un)conventional place, the line's end.

Thus Manoa's observations receive emphasis through a traditional device—rhyme—used in an untraditional way, appearing amidst a seemingly unrhymed speech. Yet the traditional device itself is, in context, unconventional to the point of making the usual line-end rhyme appear unusual. Manoa's speech is conventional wisdom, though it has a personal immediacy. On the one hand, rhyme emphasizes the proverbial; on the other, its unexpected aspects support the speech's applicability to unexpected, personal circumstances. As this passage exploits, alters, and questions our expectations about rhyme, so it exploits, alters, and questions Manoa's concepts of man, goodness, and received wisdom.

Reading through Manoa's speech, we discover the rhyme's order, simultaneously discovering its disorder. The rhymes are not where we would expect them. A pattern of couplets ("length . . . strength . . . vain . . . bane") that end grammatical units is interrupted by a tercet ("O . . . oh . . . woe") that not only rhymes at line middles but at the beginning and amidst the grammatical units in which the rhyming words appear—if "O . . . oh" is a rhyme. These instances are harbingers of disorder that appear just when we think we know what to expect; rhyme points in opposite directions, one orderly, safe, and reassuring, the other disorderly, dangerous, and disturbing. Are these apparent groupings rhymes or accidents? As we will see, even E. J. Dobson's work on Milton's pronunciation helps little in deciding where on the rhyme/no rhyme, intention/accident, order/disorder continuum we find ourselves.

The Chorus's speech in reaction to Dalila's visit exemplifies these difficulties (1010–60). The passage begins after Dalila's last speech, in which she rhymes only twice in thirty-six lines. Lines 971–74 close with a couplet on the general "double-mouth'd" quality of fame which, "On both his wings, one black, the other white, / Bears greatest names in his wild aery flight." The couplet closes the general passage firmly before Dalila addresses her specific black-and-white fame. Such meager rhyme is hardly preparation for *Samson*'s most extensively rhymed passage; indeed, the Chorus and Samson have just spoken twice each with no rhyme. Possibly in response to Italian practice noted by F. T. Prince, the Chorus's long speech fulfills the general pattern throughout *Samson* of rhyme's occurring most frequently in choral speeches[11] and often, but not always, in what Robert Beum considers "universal" passages, addressing humankind's condition (pp. 180–81). The Chorus's reflections abruptly seem to confront us with strong order:

> It is not virtue, wisdom, valor, wit,
> Strength, comeliness of shape, or amplest merit
> That woman's love can win or long inherit;
> But what it is, hard is to say,

Harder to hit,
(Which way soever men refer it)
Much like thy riddle, *Samson*, in one day
Or seven, though one should musing sit.   (1010–17)

Beum feels this passage "runs on two rhymes for eight lines," with an AAABAABA structure, a sensible reading (180–81). I first read an ABBCABCA rhyme scheme but revised it to ABBCAACA, at first rhyming "refer it" with "merit . . . inherit." Unsure of that reading, I rhymed "it" with "wit . . . hit . . . sit." This reading in turn called my attention to the odd rhyme of "But what it . . . / . . . Harder to hit," which parallels the other line middle-line end rhymes in *Samson*. Are these instances really rhyme? How much order is here? If so, is one reader's perception of it as valid as another's?

My last reading might be farfetched, but I disagree with Beum about rhymes for "refer it." "It" matches the other "-it" words, but the last syllables of "merit" and "inherit" are unstressed, as is "it" after "refer it." Even factoring in Milton's own likely pronunciation does not unqualifiedly solve the problems of what rhymes with what, however. Dobson reads "refer it" as a perfect rhyme with "merit" and "inherit" pronounced as in Modern English, still allowing a "wit . . . hit . . . it . . . sit" rhyme. [12]

Beum and I represent two distinct possibilities, while J. Max Patrick offers a paradoxical third, reading this passage AA'A'BA(A')BA, indicating by A, A' and (A') the similarities and subtle differences among the sounds of "valor, wit," "merit," and "refer it" (p. 111). Again, Milton's readers encounter a dilemma. Patrick's reading acknowledges one rhyme for "wit," "merit," and "refer it" while acknowledging three different sounds with his A/A'/(A') distinctions. Three sounds are one—but not quite; three symbols are A, but two are not A.

These different readings are thematically significant, representing distinct approaches to the question of order in *Samson*. Beum sees clear rhyming order. Patrick accepts orderliness in the passage, though the order he perceives is more complex than Beum's, and he, too, displays uneasiness over his reading: "These rimes almost disappear. The first endword, *wit*, is overwhelmed in the cumulative force of the list [of traits that will not win a woman's love]. And since the accent falls on the first syllable of *merit*, its last syllable hardly rimes at all with *wit*" (pp. 111–12). Patrick continues, raising difficulties with the passage's rhyme but coming only to the conclusion that Milton created here a tour de force, responding to a "fantastic challenge."

What Patrick does not fully perceive is that readers who agree with him on the rhyme's structure must balance opposite views of what the rhyme means. To Beum it means order; rhyme unifies the passage, implying throughout that reason, control, predictability, and wisdom prevail. Again the Chorus is generalizing, sagely or naively, ascribing Samson's problem with Dalila to woman's shifty nature, a simple, apparently satisfying explanation expressed in controlled rhyme. Patrick's view, however, reveals more complex order—there are three rhymes, not two; some are not exact rhymes, and metrics and line length cloud the issue of whether or not two words rhyme. Does "Harder to hit" really rhyme with "men refer it"? If we see three rhymes instead of two, there does seem to be more complex order in the passage. Conversely when we read apparent rhymes that cast doubt on themselves, as with "wit . . . merit" or "inherit . . . refer it" we read a tendency in the verse away from the order that rhyme ordinarily implies and an analog of the poem's movement away from the order that God imposes on Samson's life. Moreover, even if we settle on one description of the rhyme there is still no rhyme scheme, no clear system to AAABAABA, ABBCABCA, or AA'A'BA(A')BA. Rhyme leads us to expect order but gives us doubtful order at one level, chaos at another.

The next verse paragraph reinforces this tendency toward disorder. Where the first seems to have clear rhymes reflecting its clear wisdom, the second paragraph teeters between rhyme and no rhyme. Switching from the generalities of the first sentence to Samson's specific problem, the Chorus begins:

> If any of these or all, the *Timnian* bride
> Had not so soon preferr'd
> Thy Paranymph, worthless to thee compar'd,
> Successor in thy bed,
> Nor both so loosely disallied
> Thir nuptials, nor this last so treacherously
> Had shorn the fatal harvest of thy head.   (1018–24)

The rhyme here can be read AXXBAXB; "bride . . . disallied" and "bed . . . head" certainly rhyme. Yet, the three lines between the first two A . . . A rhyming lines violate expectations that usually see no more than two lines between rhymes. This three-line leap occurs in *Samson Agonistes* previously in lines 63–67 and 606–10, so readers have encountered it already—if they noticed it at all. That Milton considered such a three-line interval legitimate is clear; four sonnets—II, VI, VII, and XII—split rhymes between lines nine and thirteen. The choral passage has none of a sonnet's structural strength, however, and the split asks if there is rhyme here or accident. The question weakens rhyme's ordering effect, especially considering that a one-syllable word rhymes with a three-syllable word ("bride . . . disallied"). Or should we see a two- or three-syllable word plus a one-syllable word as the rhyme's first half ("Timnian bride")?

Accepting the rhyme "preferr'd . . . compar'd"—Dobson is equivocal (pp. 169, 174)—strengthens the sense of this passage's being rhymed, and the rhyme then becomes ABBCAXC. In the abstract this scheme instills greater order in the passage, but, seen another way, the BB couplet does not quite rhyme, especially if we consider the disparate line lengths and meters: "Had not so soon preferr'd / Thy paranymph, worthless to thee compar'd." Do such unlike lines really rhyme? Again, from one viewpoint, yes, but from another, what seems a couplet is a disordering device using an imperfect rhyme to suggest the disunity and haphazardness that the line length and uncertain metrics also seemingly display.

We see another device at work in these lines:

> Successor in thy bed,
> Nor both so loosely disallied
> Thir nuptials, nor this last so treacherously
> Had shorn the fatal harvest of thy head.

Here again we have a wide disparity in line length, though the rhyme and meter are clear and consistent. The interpositions of the one possible unrhymed line in the passage and the one line that has to look back over three others for its match, however, have a disordering effect that violates the order implied in rhyme and meter. The suggestion of rhyme only amplifies disorder.

The next sentence in the verse paragraph further weakens the sense of order rhyme implies:

> Is it for that outward ornament
> Was lavish't on thir Sex, that inward gifts
> Were left for haste unfinish't, judgment scant,
> Capacity not rais'd to apprehend
> Or value what is best
> In choice, but oftest to affect the wrong?
> Or was too much self-love mixt,
> Of constancy no root infixt,
> That either they love nothing, or not long?   (1025–33)

Here the drift away from order becomes stronger at first. After the certain rhyme of "thy bed . . . thy head" we get the uncertain slant rhyme, possibly feminine as well, of "ornament . . . scant" and the even less certain rhyme of these words with "apprehend." In these four lines, in fact, the most certain rhyme is "ornament . . . judgement"—if we admit such order. "Gifts" has no possible rhyme, and "best" only looks forward five lines to its repetition in the next verse paragraph. Indeed, if "ornament . . . scant . . . apprehend," "best . . . best," and "ornament . . . judgment scant" are rhyming pairs, they are on the most challenging fringe of what we would allow as rhyme.

The next paragraph seems at first to be almost completely unrhymed:

> Whate'er it be, to wisest men and best
> Seeming at first all heavenly under virgin veil,
> Soft, modest, meek, demure,
> Once join'd, the contrary she proves, a thorn
> Intestine, far within defensive arms
> A cleaving mischief, in his way to virtue
> Adverse and turbulent, or by her charms.   (1034–40)

After six unrhymed lines preceded by many intricately rhymed lines, we again find rhyme when "charms" refers back to "arms." There is a short passage of strong, perfect rhymes before the paragraph suddenly renounces rhyme again, concluding with three unrhymed lines:

> a thorn
> Intestine, far within defensive arms
> A cleaving mischief, in his way to virtue
> Adverse and turbulent, or by her charms
> Draws him awry enslav'd
> With dotage, and his sense deprav'd
> To folly and shameful deeds which ruin ends.
> What Pilot so expert but needs must wreck
> Embark'd with such a Steers-mate at the Helm?   (1037–45)

"Ends" may look forward to the beginning of the next paragraph to rhyme with "finds," but that pair only suggests rhyme, even if there is no reason why rhymes can not reach across paragraph divisions. Too, the question in the last two lines seems a perfect opportunity for using rhyme to emphasize the Chorus's pungent summary of the dangers of women, but there is no rhyme. These drifts into and out of rhyme are disorienting, especially when Milton undermines the ordering effects of what rhyme there is. From "demure" to "ruin ends," enclosing the only rhymed lines in the paragraph, there are no end stops, so the few rhymes become part of the musical flow. More, we see Milton again rhyming lines of unequal length ("enslaved . . . deprav'd").

So, does the Chorus speak with truth and wisdom here or with a foolish, narrow view of women? Beum, who perceives order in the rhyme, not surprisingly associates it with wisdom: "Thus the function of rhyme in the Chorus is twofold. It identifies that body in its wiser, more passionate, more universal aspect; and at the same time it underscores the wisdom, passion, and universality of its language" (p. 180). Cohen, who agrees that rhyme "lends to a statement a certain epigrammatic quality, a universality," nevertheless also thinks rhymed choral passages can reflect unfavorably on the Chorus: "The impression such lines create is that the chorus recites its inappropriate and unhelpful advice as if from a text" (p. 5).

Like the A rhyme that is not an A rhyme the Chorus, with rhyme's help, is wise and foolish. It sees God's ordering truth and an illusion fronting chaos. God is in *Samson Agonistes* yet is not. The rhymes in the next paragraph aptly reflect such ambivalence:

> Favor'd of Heav'n who finds
> One virtuous, rarely found,
> That in domestic good combines:
> Happy that house! his way to peace is smooth:
> But virtue which breaks through all opposition,
> And all temptation can remove,
> Most shines and most is acceptable above.   (1046–52)

To the ear "finds" almost rhymes with "combines," "smooth" less certainly with "remove," which then rhymes with "above" only to the eye. In seven lines there are three rhyming pairs and two unrhymed lines, mathematical magic worked by "remove"'s rhyming with two words, "smooth" and "above," that do not rhyme with each other. Such complexity has a precedent in Milton's poetry. Dobson notes that Psalm vii contains "two alternative ways of rhyming *vanity* . . . combined in a single sequence [he . . . vanity . . . lie]" (p. 162). Yet, for all the intense rhyming, there is no clear rhyme here except "remove . . . above," and that by tradition only (Dobson, p. 156). At one extreme this passage doesn't rhyme at all; passing through several possibilities, we see at the other extreme that it rhymes intricately, using an array of rhyming devices. We even see that six of the seven lines are end-stopped, including every line that completes a rhyme.

The Chorus ends with a powerfully rhymed, "universal" passage:

> Therefore God's universal law
> Gave to the man despotic power

> Over his female in due awe,
> Nor from that right to part an hour,
> Smile she or lour:
> So shall he least confusion draw
> On his whole life, not swayed
> By female usurpation, nor dismayed.
>   But had we best retire, I see a storm?   (1053–61)

These lines clearly rhyme ABABBACCX, the last line unrhymed to mark the change from the Chorus's meditation to further action with Harapha's arrival. The shift from definite rhyme to definite nonrhyme has narrative and conceptual significance, also marked by a paragraph shift. Still, only two lines scan identically: "Nor from that right to part an hour" and "So shall he least confusion draw," both reading easily as iambic tetrameter, yet they do not rhyme, and we have a device that can emphasize rhyme actually calling attention to nonrhymes. Of the other lines, no two are alike metrically, ranging from four stresses to the line in most cases to two lines with three and two stresses respectively. This prosodic free-for-all is accompanied by the wide disparity in metrics and line length in the couplet, "Nor from that right to part an hour, / Smile she or lour." In both cases, disordering devices cast doubt on the order implied by strong, clear rhymes.

Donald Wesling, writing of the contrast between modern free verse and comparatively rigid English neoclassical rhymes, says:

As a language habit, rhyme seems a derangement, seems to say something oñly about language, but there is always the possibility that it is also telling us something about ourselves. . . . When we perceive that language, like nature in the scientist's estimation, is only partially organized, we regain incentive for basic discoveries.

By boycotting puns and confining rhymes, English neoclassical poets wished to control this subversive likelihood of hidden perspectives within language and ourselves. (p. 98)

By such a standard, Milton is subversive in *Samson*, treading the line between rhyme and no rhyme, between reason and nonreason, offering "hidden perspectives" and subverting clear, linear interpretations. Yet, remarkably, in "universal" passages, Milton also upholds the rhyme-wisdom connection, and the reasonable, clear, orderly interpretation of events the Chorus prefers.

Such paradoxes disclose the poem's deepest meaning in *Samson*'s support and subversion of its own interpretation. Balachandra Rajan comes close to this view when he writes: "Like *Lycidas,* the play is a controlled turbulence in which an equilibrium is deliberately imperilled so that a richer, more inclusive equilibrium can be achieved through the process of disorientation."[13] While *Samson* may not reach a new equilibrium—Rajan, like Parker, feels that the Chorus's last speech represents the poem's final meaning (p. 145)—"controlled turbulence" excellently describes *Samson* and rhyme's role in creating the poem's meaning.

Critics see turbulence in other aspects of *Samson*. Meter has always been troublesome; indeed, meter is rhyme's partner in giving readers a sense of order and disorder analogous to God's presence or absence. Robert Bridges, attempting to analyze *Samson*'s rhythms, unintentionally defines that point at which the predictability of rhythm, like that of rhyme, verges into turbulence, suggesting the opposite of the order implied in regularity. Describing meter, Bridges might well be describing *Samson*'s rhyme or God's role in the poem: "Some knowledge of the structure or laws that govern free rhythms in poetry are indispensable to most persons before they will accept or reject a rhythm to which they are unaccustomed, according as they can or cannot perceive, or think they perceive, its structure."[14] Bridges then analyzes "the structure of [*Samson*'s] verse," trying to demonstrate that the poem's rhythms have structure without regularity, but missing the larger meaning of implied order and disorder.

On the other hand, Edward Weismiller is less intent than Bridges on systematizing *Samson*'s metrics, several times stressing how unsystematic Milton's metrics are, even while clinging to the idea of "basic meter." Milton, he says, adopted "any possible resource that would lend variety of movement to his syllabic line—even where that variety threatened for a moment his basic meter. . . . The introduction of [such resources] . . . into syllabic lines already irregular, lines of uneven and unpredetermined length, leaves such lines . . . in a state of nearly absolute uncertainty."[15] Wrestling with multitudinous metrical oddities and their possible precursors, Weismiller resolves his problems in a phrase that anticipates Rajan's "controlled turbulence": "Again we must assume that the strangeness is intended; but . . . it [is] a strangeness produced in the first place by a kind of controlled metrical-rhythmical disorientation" (p. 136).

Perhaps the most plausible approach to systematizing *Samson*'s prosody is John Shawcross's effort to demonstrate that Milton possibly imposed on the choruses a structured Latin quantitative versification based on vowel length rather than English syllabic versification based on stress. Shawcross's case is tentative, and his examination of a sample passage yields qualified results: "There are only a few false quantities introduced, . . . [and] there is a fair amount of symmetry between lines of like length."[16] If this surmise is valid, however, there is indeed order to *Samson's* choral metrics, and we find a prosodic principle which in effect matches *Samson's* rhyming principle—there is only sufficient order to suggest and question its own presence.

Stanley Fish carries the implications of such turbulence to an extreme, approaching Samson's life as something which the poem's characters, including Samson, try desperately to render sensible. Fish acknowledges the importance of context in judging Samson; however, he leaves God aside as unknowable, saying, "In the end, the only value we can put on Samson's action is the value he gives it in context. . . . *No other standard for evaluating it exists.*" ("Question," p. 260). For Fish, the final choral speech proves nothing; he sees no triumph other than what the Chorus willfully constructs for itself from an experience at odds with their interpretation of Samson's life.

In the same essay, however, Fish still expresses the reader's sense that, though no standard outside context exists, God is present: "Somehow the play immerses us in that pain [of Samson's life and death] without shaking our faith in something which is ultimately—but for the moment unhelpfully—more real; we are made to feel simultaneously that God is always with us and that in moments of crisis we are, for all intents and purposes, alone" (p. 263). The readers' turbulent situation, then, is charged with significant potential. In a second essay Fish sees *Samson* completing "a theory of personality that [Milton] had begun to construct in the *Areopagitica.*" Asserting that Milton by 1644 had come to believe that "inner certainty" was wrong for a true Christian, Fish continues:

In the *Areopagitica*, however, fixity of mind and judgement is stigmatized as the sign of spiritual sloth. Rather than being already complete, the true Christian self is imaged as "wayfaring," that is, as always being on the way and never having arrived. To think that you have already arrived is to have mistaken a stage in the "making" of your knowledge for its perfection; it is to have failed precisely by assuming that you have succeeded. . . . The alternative Milton urges in us is to embrace a life of "perpetuall progression . . . ," [Hughes, p. 739] in which we successfully revise our received opinions and rest only in the certainty that there can be no rest. In the context of such a life, constancy of mind is what one wants to avoid, while change, discontinuity, and endless transformation are what one avidly courts.[17]

Fish's principle is crucial to understanding *Samson* fully. For example, he judges Samson's actions as virtuous not because Samson eventually repents and fulfills God's mission but because he rejects the safety, the fixity, of slavery and thoughtless obedience to Hebrew Law rather than interpretation of it, preferring to act in "radical uncertainty." "Like Abraham," Fish continues, "Samson goes out, or rather, goes along . . . to he knows not what and with a mind constant only in its willingness to encounter possibilities" (p. 579).

Fish does not go far enough. He describes Samson as the dynamic Christian of *Areopagitica*, inadvertently identifying Samson's readers as Christian heroes. In the face of radical uncertainty about the poem, we nevertheless read it and struggle with making sense of it though there is no interpretation we reach that can not be reasonably undermined by evidence from the poem itself. We must encounter questions, answer them, and question the answers. If not simultaneously, then in a never-ending sequence of question and answer—to redirect Fish's own phrase—we must be readers agonistes, analogs to Samson as he wrestles with his life's purpose. As Joseph Wittreich says: "*Samson Agonistes* is . . . a tragedy of a special sort: one whose audience, but not 'hero,' has the potential for snatching spiritual victory out of natural defeat."[18] Milton's point is not to teach us doctrine. On the contrary, *Samson Agonistes* teaches us that doctrine is less important than "perpetuall progression." Rhyme indicates exactly this point. Our struggles in reading it are on a technical level the same struggles we face in understanding every level of the poem.

Samson's final speech makes a suitable conclusion for such a work, constituting not only the longest sustained rhyming passage, but also containing the poem's only rhyme scheme and the only passage using rhymes in their conventional, line-end places throughout. Only here do readers know what all the rhymes are and what structure they create— remarkably, a sonnet with a familiar, comfortable ABABCDCDEFEFEF pattern. The scheme appears conventional, yet it is a radical anomaly within the chaotically rhymed *Samson*, and so must have extraordinary meaning. So too have all the ironies inherent in making the customary and conventional anomalous.

The speech exploits sonnet conventions. The fourth and fourteenth lines close rhyming, grammatical, and conceptual structures emphatically: "dispose . . . close" and "intent . . . event . . . spent." The sense of finality is powerful, and perhaps responsible for the certainty so many readers feel that the Chorus sums up *Samson's* meaning. The most unusual rhyme in the speech is "returns . . . mourns," whose line-end position indicates a conventional if not a phonetic rhyme (Dobson, p. 175). Also, there is an octet, divided into two quatrains, and a sestet, so the general relationship of ideas to form matches the sonnet tradition, the theme turning in the eighth line from "all is best," as seen in Samson's case, to God's enemies and "servants." So powerfully organized and

executed a poem constitutes another substantial challenge to any interpretation that doubts God's presence in *Samson*. What could more emphatically indicate God's intentionality than declaring "His uncontrollable intent" in a sonnet?

However, *Samson* is nearly a completely unrhymed poem in which
rhyme is a troublesome indicator of accident as well as God's intention.
The small amount of rhyme even disallows the luxury of finding unity in
completely unrhymed verse. What is the meaning of the Chorus's suddenly breaking into a speech so polished and certain? Can we trust such
anomalous certainty and completeness born of technical reversal? Perhaps
the virtue of a sonnet here is that it is too finished, too certain, pat. We
have reason to doubt the Chorus's interpretation of Samson's life, and the
sonnet may be a way of stating it too positively. Earlier rhymed passages
indicate "universal" wisdom, but if the rhyme there makes such wisdom
easy, and perhaps ironically irrelevant, then the sonnet is a heightened
version of the same technique. Rather than having the last word, the
Chorus presents a last temptation to adopt a customary answer, rejecting
"turbulence" and "perpetual progression."

The passage is turbulent, however. Parker proclaims it only "reminiscent of a sonnet" ("Date," p. 148). Why "reminiscent"? Is it not a sonnet?
When we scan the *Samson* sonnet we rediscover the prosodic weirdness
that challenges the metrical regularity in Milton's avowed sonnets and
those of other Renaissance sonneteers—Ben Jonson might have hanged
Milton alongside John Donne for "not keeping of accent."[19] "With peace
and consolation hath dismist" and "Of true experience from this great
event" scan as iambic pentameter with no verbiage to fill out a foot and no
strained pronunciation. We can say the same about "And to his faithful
Champion hath in place" if we read "-ion" as one syllable, a natural pronunciation (Dobson, pp. 183–85).

With some possible variations, however, other lines read as four-
stress lines, the emphases sometimes falling awkwardly: for example,
"What th'unsearchable dispose" and "His uncontrollable intent." If we
impose an iambic pattern on these lines we twice stress "-able," so they
are best read without iambs. Even lines that scan smoothly with four
stresses are only partially iambic. "All is best, though we oft doubt" and
"Oft he seems to hide his face" begin with stressed syllables, but they are
not reversed iambs since there is only one unstressed syllable before the
next stress.

Perhaps the most mysterious line is "And ever best found in the
close." We can read this line with four iambic stresses if we want to stay as
faithful as possible to the regularity of those three metrical lines, but such

a reading stresses "in" and unstresses "found," which seems contrary to the principle of emphasizing key words. Another reading, "Aňd évĕr bĕst fóund iň thĕ clóse," makes the line a limerick opening. Surely a poet who abhorred "jingling sound" in rhyme would not tolerate such meter from a Chorus intoning the most profound truth—unless we are not to take the Chorus completely seriously. Paying attention to sense, I think the best reading is "Aňd evĕr bést fóund ĭn tĥe clóse." Unless we consider "found in" a reversed iamb, this reading abandons regular feet.

My point is not that the choral speech is not a sonnet. More unconventional sonnets than Milton's seem generically acceptable. The question of genre is fruitful though. It indicates Milton's significant use of convention to create Samson's first orderly rhyme sequence, at what seems the poem's most orderly, certain moment, simultaneously undermining order and certainty through nearly chaotic meter. Ironically, just as rhyme finally seems to indicate safe, familiar territory, three lines of regular meter reveal turbulence, radical uncertainty, and only enough order to make us question whether order is present at all.

University of Wyoming

NOTES

1. John T. Shawcross, "Milton and Blank Verse Precedents," *American Notes and Queries* III (1990), 160; William Riley Parker, "The Date of *Samson Agonistes*," *PQ* XXVIII (1949), 148–49; J. Max Patrick, "Milton's Revolution Against Rime, and Some of Its Implications," in *Milton and the Art of Sacred Song*, ed. J. Max Patrick and Roger Sundell (Madison, 1979), p. 108; Robert Beum, "The Rhyme in *Samson Agonistes*," *TSLL* IV (1962), 177; and Michael Cohen, "Rhyme in *Samson Agonistes*," *MQ* VIII (1974), 4.

2. All Milton citations are from *John Milton: Complete Poems and Major Prose*, ed. Merritt Y, Hughes (New York, 1957).

3. W. K. Wimsatt, Jr., and Monroe C. Beardsley, *The Verbal Icon: Studies in the Meaning of Poetry* (Lexington, 1954), pp. 163–64. Donald Wesling, *The Chances of Rhyme: Device and Modernity* (Berkeley and Los Angeles, 1980), pp. 71–72.

4. Jackie DiSalvo, "Intestine Thorn: Samson's Struggle with the Woman Within," in *Milton and the Idea of Woman*, ed. Julia M. Walker (Urbana and Chicago, 1988), pp. 211–12.

5. *The Complete Poetry of John Milton*, ed. John T. Shawcross (Garden City, 1971), p. 619.

6. William Riley Parker, *Milton's Debt to Greek Tragedy in "Samson Agonistes"* (New York, 1969) p. 52.

7. Mary Ann Radzinowicz, *Toward "Samson Agonistes"* (Princeton, 1978), p. 314.

8. Helen Damico, "Duality in Dramatic Vision: A Structural Analysis of *Samson Agonistes*," in *Milton Studies* XII, ed. James D. Simmonds (Pittsburgh, 1978), p. 105.

9. Stanley Fish, "Question and Answer in *Samson Agonistes*," *Critical Quarterly* XI (1969), 255.

10. Irene Samuel, "*Samson Agonistes* as Tragedy," in *Calm of Mind*, ed. Joseph Wittreich (Cleveland, 1971), pp. 249–52.

11. F. T. Prince, *The Italian Element in Milton's Verse* (Oxford, 1954), p. 156.

12. E. J. Dobson, "Milton's Pronunciation," in *Language and Style in Milton: A Symposium in Honor of the Tercentenary of "Paradise Lost*," ed. Ronald Emma and John T. Shawcross (New York, 1967), p. 169.

13. Balachandra Rajan, *The Lofty Rhyme: A Study of Milton's Major Poetry* (Coral Gables, 1970), p. 143.

14. Robert Bridges, *Milton's Prosody: With a Chapter on Accentual Verse* (Oxford, 1921), p. 51.

15. Edward Weismiller, "The 'Dry' and 'Rugged' Verse," in *The Lyric and Dramatic Milton*, ed. Joseph Summers (New York, 1965), pp. 119, 121.

16. John Shawcross, "The Prosody of Milton's Translation of Horace's Fifth Ode," *Tennessee Studies in Literature* XIII (1968), 83.

17. Stanley Fish, "Spectacle and Evidence in *Samson Agonistes*," *Critical Inquiry* XV (1989), 576.

18. Joseph Wittreich, *Interpreting "Samson Agonistes*," (Princeton, 1986), p. 101.

19. *Ben Jonson's Conversations with William Drummond of Hawthornden*, ed. R. F. Patterson (New York, 1974), p. 5.

UNIFYING MILTON'S EPICS:
CARLOTTA PETRINA'S ILLUSTRATIONS FOR
PARADISE REGAINED

Bruce Lawson

I T TOOK HALF A CENTURY, but Carlotta Petrina has begun to
receive attention as the first woman, the only North American, and the
only living artist, to publish a complete set of illustrations for *Paradise Lost*
and *Paradise Regained*.[1] Those who have noticed her work see her as a
clear-eyed interpreter of *Paradise Lost,* as a visual critic who is remarkably
sensitive to the theological structure and the scriptural and mythological
roots of Milton's text. Louis Martz praises her for catching the "Ovidian
implications" of *Paradise Lost;* Wendy Furman admires her as cognizant of
the epic's larger patterns—"the coming redemption seen in the apocalyptic
moment"; and Michael Lieb lauds her ability "to recreate the spirit of the
original within a 'modern' context."[2]

Petrina's twelve designs for *Paradise Lost* have been ably discussed at
some length by Lloyd F. Dickson in *Milton Studies* XXV, as "a thoroughly
christocentric interpretation . . . centering on the works of God the Father and his Son, with special focus on Christ's roles as mediator, soldier,
and savior."[3] Martz, Furman, and Lieb have written, respectively, about
the designs for Books IV, XII, and VI of *Paradise Lost* in relation to larger
Miltonic contexts and to designs by other artists. But Petrina's four illustrations for *Paradise Regained* (figs. 1–4) have received no attention.

I shall first review the comments on Petrina's *Paradise Lost* illustrations and follow with some biographical information on the artist and her
responses to what the Milton critics have written about her work. I shall
then examine in some detail the four illustrations for *Paradise Regained* in
relation to Milton's text, to its scriptural context, to certain visual
traditions—and to Petrina's illustrations for *Paradise Lost*.

My study reveals that Petrina's illustrations for *Paradise Regained*
establish close theological ties to those for *Paradise Lost* as she constructs
distinctive portraits of Christ in his changing but continuing roles as "Son
of God" and "Savior of men." Her illustrations show a clear and subtle
reading of the text of *Paradise Regained* that anticipates some of the

perspectives offered in recent verbal interpretations. She is always keenly aware of the narrative's biblical sources. Various visual traditions figure in her work, but she turns them to her own purposes. Finally, the connections she makes between the designs for *Paradise Lost* and those for *Paradise Regained* repeatedly suggest that she sees Milton's two epics as an entity.

It was in 1933 or 1934 that Petrina began work on the sixteen impressive full-page pencil drawings on parchment for *Paradise Lost* and *Paradise Regained*, to be published in 1936 in an edition of fifteen hundred copies by John Henry Nash for the Limited Editions Club.[4] Despite her knowledgeable interpretations and the attractiveness of the designs, Petrina's work on Milton received little notice at the time in either artistic or literary circles. Other illustrations by Petrina during the thirties and forties, those for *South Wind* by Norman Douglas and for *The Aeneid*, for example, were exhibited along with lithographs, prints, and drawings in one-woman shows in this country, France, and Italy—and received glowing reviews—but no gallery showed the Milton drawings.[5]

The first Miltonist to look closely at Petrina's vision of *Paradise Lost* was Martz in 1980, who comments on her sensitivity to Milton's use of classical myth. Martz reproduces her illustration for Book IV (fig. 7), showing the human pair with "two gentle fawns at play" beside the "smooth lake" in a flowering mythic garden. He observes that the artist "has caught the Ovidian implications of Milton's pastoral. The female figure making the advances could almost be the nymph Salmacis, and the passive, bemused male figure staring outward could almost be the unresponsive Hermaphroditus." Milton's "allusions to Ovidian myth," Martz asserts, "are far more than decorations, or acknowledgment of an epic predecessor":

they lie at the very heart of Milton's purpose: to show how this greatest of changes brought in all other forms of change and changing forms, and then to show how Ovid's sense of endless change may be converted into change that has a higher, a teleological design.[6]

Like Milton's allusions to Ovid, Petrina's graceful pictures are "far more than decorations," a point well established by Dickson in his discussion of the plates for *Paradise Lost*. Dickson characterizes them as "masterful" and indicative of her "thorough knowledge of the epic's biblical traditions and allusions" as well as her apprehension of the epic's theological structure.[7]

In his essay in 1988 (Labriola and Sichi, eds., pp. 21–58), Lieb too voices strong praise for the fidelity and the uniqueness of Petrina's illustrations for *Paradise Lost:* "the product of a penetrating mind and a sure hand, they are at once faithful to the spirit of Milton's epic and venturesome enough to offer an interpretation all their own."[8] Describing her illustration for Book VI of *Paradise Lost* (fig. 8) in relation to other pictures of the Messiah in the "Chariot of Paternal Deitie," Lieb writes:

With his cruciform aureole and his plated armor, he is the very representation of the *Christus Victor* portrayed in early medieval mosaics. At the same time, he is the product of a sensibility responsive to the devastating forces of modern warfare on a worldwide scale. The energies he embodies are those that were unleashed in the Great War and that were shortly to be set loose again in a form even more apocalyptic than the world had ever known.[9]

Lieb believes that Petrina "provides a 'reading' of the War in Heaven and its pivotal event that suggests her responsiveness to the currents of her time." He sees her design as "in some respects the most faithful we possess."[10]

Writing in *Coranto* (1990), Furman compares Petrina's expulsion scene for Book XII of *Paradise Lost* (fig. 9) to depictions by other artists. She remarks on its subtlety:

If the artist has reminded us how terrifying is the judgment of God, she has nonetheless attended to the coming redemption concealed in the apocalyptic moment. She shows us both how things appear to "men [and women] in the middest" and what they may mean from the *kairos* perspective of the End. . . . And the entire design—angels, flame, and sword—forms a tree rising behind, but also from, Adam and Eve. This tree suggests, of course, "that Forbidden Tree, whose mortal taste Brought Death into the World, and all our woe, / With loss of Eden"—but also the Tree upon which the Woman's Seed will die, redeeming, through tragedy, the tragedy of history.[11]

Furman adds that "however assailed by modern doubt" Carlotta Petrina may be, she "takes a stance as prophetic as Blake's: apocalypse her glass, she looks through it, albeit darkly, to a final, eschatological redemption."[12]

Are these Milton enthusiasts over-reading Petrina's illustrations for *Paradise Lost?* In 1992, at the age of ninety-one, Carlotta Petrina herself read for the first time the comments by Martz, Dickson, Lieb, and Furman. In a telephone interview, she was asked about her response to what these Milton critics had written. "I am deeply touched and pleased," she said. "You cannot imagine how exciting it is for an artist to know that her work is understood." She added that she has always been "a reader, a lover of Bible narrative, of Milton, and of Renaissance literature and art generally."[13]

Born in Kingston, New York, she studied art during the twenties in

New York City at the Art Students' League and at the Cooper Union Institute of Art and Science, and during the thirties, she studied and worked in New York, Paris, and Italy. She received two Guggenheim Fellowships, exhibited in a number of galleries, and taught several years at the Pratt Institute and for shorter periods at Hunter College and at Western College for Women at Macon, Georgia. She was "thrilled," she said, when she received the commission to illustrate Milton's epics. "I had always been fascinated by Milton and other literature of that era. As a youngster, I was torn between a career in literature or in art, and art won." In her early childhood, one of her grandmothers began reading Bible stories to her and continued for some years; from this experience she "came to know the Bible well as narrative rather than doctrine." She was "brought up" attending "high Episcopal services." As an adult, she converted to Catholicism in Italy, "partly because I loved the Latin mass."

In illustrating the epics, how did she decide what to draw? She read Milton. Then she sat down at her drawing board—and "it just came to me."

Reading Milton carefully, and making each drawing took a long time: "The publisher kept pressing me, but I would not be hurried." She made some of the drawings in Venice and Paris, while traveling and living there. Petrina acknowledges that many of her works over a period of seventy years, even the most recent oils on her easel and displayed in her studio, are strongly influenced by medieval and Renaissance artists, especially the Venetians, and by her long residence in Italy. "But," she adds, "anything an artist does is of its own era as well." She owes no debts to the hundred or more male illustrators of Milton who preceded her: she had never seen an illustrated edition of Milton.

What was the response in 1936 to her Milton illustrations? The publisher was pleased, she said, but everyone else simply took them for granted: "At the time, no-one really gave a damn. It is gratifying that after all these years, scholars are looking at my drawings, truly studying them."

At first glance, the four designs for *Paradise Regained* appear merely to portray a central dramatic moment from each of the four books—the baptism of Christ by John (fig. 1); the banquet scene with which Satan tempts Christ (fig. 2); Satan and Christ atop the mountain, as Satan presents the temptation to earthly power (fig. 3); and Christ being borne heavenward from the pinnacle as Satan falls (fig. 4). On closer study, however, we discover that Petrina develops evolving portraits of Christ that disclose important features of his nature and purpose. Ashraf H. A. Rushdy has pointed out that in *Paradise Regained* "there are various 'lives' of Jesus that play an important role in the poem," growing, he suggests, out of the disparate interpretations of various observers.[14] Petrina simi-

Figure 1. *Paradise Regained*, Book I

Figure 2. *Paradise Regained*, Book II

Figure 3. *Paradise Regained*, Book III

Figure 4. *Paradise Regained*, Book IV

Figure 5. *Paradise Lost*, Book I

Figure 6. *Paradise Lost*, Book III

Figure 7. *Paradise Lost*, Book IV

BOOK VI

Figure 8. *Paradise Lost*, Book VI

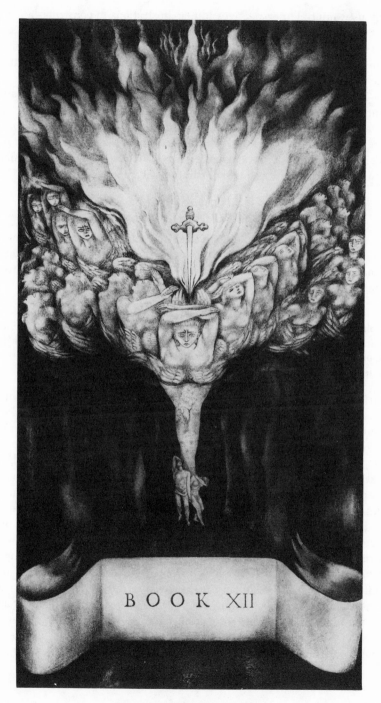

Figure 9. *Paradise Lost*, Book XII

larly uses multiple perspectives in her illustrations to construct her portrait of Christ. She pictures Jesus and events as through a lens that com-
presses all of redemptive history into four defining moments, and in so
doing presents the totality of Christ's redemptive act, extending from
Eden to the apocalypse.

As we look at the sequence for *Paradise Regained*, in order, we shall
examine a web of relationships with other Petrina designs and with New
Testament theology. In particular, her illustrations for Book III of *Paradise
Lost* (fig. 6), and for Book I of *Paradise Regained* (fig. 1), are basic to our
full understanding of the changing faces of Christ as Petrina envisions
them. I shall discuss these two illustrations at some length.

THE ILLUSTRATION FOR BOOK I:
THE BAPTISM OF CHRIST

The complexity of depicting Christ is described by James M. Pearce,
who observes that in *Paradise Regained*, Milton represents the union of
human and divine by showing Christ "in rapid succession, from shifting
points of view":

although Christ is at all times a unitary being, it is obvious that different scenes
emphasize different aspects of his constitution. Hence, Christ is depicted in the
poem by an argumentative pendulum, so to speak, which swings through the
regions of the divine, the human, the divine, a movement which also occurs on
the level of poetic detail. [15]

Petrina uses a similar strategy. Jesus is the God/man, simultaneously the
Son at the right hand of the Father offering himself as Redeemer, and the
Son of Man on earth, beginning by his Incarnation and baptism to enact
the offer of Redemption in flesh and in time. In the illustration for Book I
(fig. 1), Petrina portrays Christ at the moment after his baptism, and she
links the event with her portrayal of Christ in *Paradise Lost* III (fig. 6)
where the Son kneels beside the Father as the latter reveals his plan for
human salvation. In *Paradise Regained* I, Christ stands in the center of
the picture with his back to us, his head down and hands slightly outstretched in a posture of vulnerability and acceptance as he faces John.
Christ here is wearing the same loose garment that the Son is wearing in
Paradise Lost III, this time viewed from behind. The long hair of this
traditional image of the human Christ, as well as the shape of his arms, are
identical in the two illustrations. Petrina thus presents us with a front and
rear view of the same figure—the human Christ. In choosing to represent
the Son in the Heavenly Council in this form, Petrina is making an overtly
theological statement, since the Son in *Paradise Lost* III has not yet

experienced his kenosis and exists fully in his glory as part of the Godhead. The deliberateness of her interpretive move is underscored by the memorable contrasting representation of the Son in *Paradise Lost* VI (fig. 6), with its terrifying fierce-faced *Christus Victor*, winning the war in heaven, bearing down the page toward us in his "Chariot of Paternal Deitie" accompanied by a band of mounted warriors as he bombards the masses of fleeing and falling rebel angels with balls of fire from his hand: as Lieb describes him, a "truly awesome and terrifying figure."[16]

It is a much gentler figure that we see in the illustrations for *Paradise Lost* III and *Paradise Regained* I as Petrina presents the "Son of God" and "Savior of men" in their simultaneity, with Christ as the Son in heaven and the Son as Savior on earth. In *Paradise Lost* III, our eyes follow the Father's pointing finger and the Son's gaze downward to earth; then in *Paradise Regained* I, our stance and perspective have shifted spatially (but not temporally) to the other end of the continuum. Now we are on earth looking upward, past the figure of Christ to the brightly illuminated heaven from which the Father's glory is descending on the Son. We can almost see the Father of *Paradise Lost* III pointing downward through the opening in the sky. The angels who hovered around the Heavenly Council with harps and "blest voices uttering joy" now encircle the baptism of Jesus in attitudes of prayer and adoration, their somber reverence in contrast to their celebratory postures in heaven, the two together expressing "the glory and the shame" of the Incarnation. Milton makes no specific reference to angels at the baptism, except Satan's speculation that the purpose of the baptism is for Christ to receive "the testimony of Heaven" (*PR* I, 78).[17] And in heaven the Father tells Gabriel, "this day by proof thou shalt behold, / Thou and all Angels conversant on Earth / With man or men's affairs, how I begin / To verify that solemn message," (I, 130–33) that message delivered to Mary which refers back to the Heavenly Council. To this news, the hosts of heaven, responding with admiration and awe, "into Hymns / Burst forth, and in Celestial measures mov'd, / Circling the Throne and Singing" (I, 169–72). This celebration, however, is in heaven with the Father, not on earth with Christ; but if Petrina is representing the Incarnation in its eternal, timeless significance, then those angels of *Paradise Lost* III may indeed be celebrating the event in *Paradise Regained* I—the temporal beginnings of Redemption—as well as the event in heaven. It is all part of the same act, the same eternal moment of Redemption, and the angels' presence in both illustrations emphasizes the spiritual interrelatedness of the baptism and the Heavenly Council.

Heaven and earth, in *Paradise Regained* I, are joined by the beam of light descending through the opening in the sky and shining upon the figure of Christ, picturing the moment after his baptism that "the heavens were opened unto him" (Matt. iii, 16). The light denotes heaven and heavenly illumination, and it may also embody John the Baptist's warning to the crowds that "he that cometh after me is mightier than I, whose shoes I am not worthy to bear: he shall baptize you with the Holy Ghost, and with fire" (Matt. iii, 11). Whether or not fire is implied in these brilliant beams, the "far-beaming blaze of Majesty," the Holy Ghost is certainly present in the form of the dove descending to Christ's head, also illustrating St. Matthew's observation of "the Spirit of God descending like a dove, and lighting upon him" (Matt. iii, 16). The Epic Voice paraphrases Matthew's: "Heaven open'd, and in likeness of a Dove / the Spirit descended, while the Father's voice / from Heav'n pronounc'd him his beloved Son" (PR I 30–33). Petrina's dove denotes this heavenly sign of approval and may also refer back to the invocation to Paradise Lost, Book I, where Milton calls on the birdlike Spirit for illumination and instruction. The spirit that was present at the foundations of the world now comes as a dove to guide Jesus to self-knowledge in the wilderness.

This educating role of the spirit-dove is further implied by Petrina with the open book descending from heaven on the beams of light. The book functions on several metaphorical levels. It may represent the voice of God. The Epic Voice echoes the gospel narrative, proclaiming that, "in likeness of a Dove / The Spirit descended, while the Father's voice / From Heav'n pronounc'd him his beloved Son" (PR I, 30–32). Later, Christ himself reflects on his baptism experience: "The Spirit descended on me like a Dove; / And last the sum of all, my Father's voice, / Audibly heard from Heav'n pronounc'd me his" (I, 282–84). The book also points up St. John's representation of Christ as the Word: "In the beginning was the Word, and the Word was with God, and the Word was God" (John i, 1), Petrina's book or "Word" (perhaps even the Bible as the word of God) hovers midway between Christ and heaven, thus providing another connection between Christ, the Father, and the preincarnate Son—between Paradise Lost III and Paradise Regained I.

Associated with the dove and the ensuing journey of Christ in the wilderness of self-examination, Petrina's open book may imply also the opening of knowledge and understanding. Setting out into the wilderness, Christ reflects on his past, noting his precocity: "above my years, / The Law of God I read, and found it sweet" (PR I, 206–07); and he remembers his later search through the Law and prophets for understanding of the Messiah: "and soon found of whom they spake / I am" (I, 262–63). Now, following his baptism, he is led "Into this Wilderness, to what intent, / I learn not yet; perhaps I need not know; / For what concerns my knowledge God reveals (I, 291–93). Petrina's book, open halfway through, is suggestive of Christ's search for knowledge of self and of purpose, to be completed in the wilderness *exercise:* "For what concerns my knowledge God reveals."

The group of onlookers in Petrina's *Paradise Regained* I supports the impression that Petrina is presenting the whole story of Redemption. Petrina's careful reading of both the biblical and Miltonic texts leads us to assume that it may be possible to identify the members of that group. Milton implies that Andrew and Simon were present. Quoting St. John, Merritt Y. Hughes comments that, "At the time of the baptism of Christ, Andrew and Simon Peter were with him and 'saw where he dwelt, and abode with him that day' (John i, 39)."[18] Nothing in Petrina's illustration, however, either confirms or discourages that assumption. We may, similarly, speculate on other persons. The kneeling woman, for instance, has the appearance of the *stabat mater,* and we might wonder if this is Mary, in a stance that prefigures her anguish at the foot of the cross. But the evangelists make no mention of her presence at the baptism, and in *Paradise Regained,* Mary reflects that her son is now "Full grown to Man, acknowledg'd, as I hear, / By John the Baptist" (II, 83–84). Her information about the baptism appears to be secondhand. Likewise, the sage elderly man near the center of the group and the old woman at his side evoke memories of Simeon and Anna. Indeed, Mary mentions Simeon in her reflections on the Baptism (II, 87); but Petrina would not likely have them in mind since Luke describes them as of great old age at the time of the Temple encounter (Luke ii, 25–38), and the baptism is thirty years later.

I am inclined, therefore, to view Petrina's observers as representative of those people we find in the gospels who responded to Christ's ministry. Petrina includes man and woman, child and parent, the wise and the simple, the elderly. Especially evocative of Christ's ministry are the figures on the right, the young man leading the old man who is either lame, infirm, or blind; and the man at the back who appears to have a patch over one eye. These are the many who "came unto him, having with them those that were lame, blind, dumb, maimed, and many others, and cast them down at Jesus' feet: and he healed them" (Matt. xv, 30); and they represent the future range of Christ's redemptive mission.

Christ, of course, is the central focus of the illustration, and he is in a striking pose, standing as he is with his back to the viewer. But also significant is his posture. Petrina illustrates the moment immediately following his baptism when he receives the dramatic approval of heaven, indeed, the "pleasure" of the Father. It is a moment of affirmation and glorification and blessing that prefigures his later experience on the Mount of Transfiguration. But she does not represent Christ at this moment with his head raised to receive the spirit and voice of God, as William Blake portrays him in his illustration of the baptism (1816–1818), or in the traditional prayerlike position, such as in *The Baptism of Christ* by Joachim Patenier (c. 1480–1524), where Christ stands with hands placed together and head slightly bowed. Petrina portrays him in a state of sorrow or even grief. Hers is a poignant image, intensified by our not being able to see Christ's face, only his hunched shoulders and bowed head. He is intensely human here, and vulnerable. It is an image that anticipates the suffering that follows when "the spirit driveth him into the wilderness" (Mark i, 12). It is the posture of Christ before his Roman torturers, ready for the scourge, and of one accepting death by crucifixion. It is an image that visualizes St. Paul's words in Romans vi, 3: "Know ye not, that so many of us as were baptized into Jesus Christ were baptized into his death? Therefore we are buried with him by baptism into death." Petrina's portrait thus evokes the important connection between baptism and death. Both Christ's baptism and his temptation in the wilderness (two nights, three days) are types of his passion (two nights and part of three days in the grave).

Barbara Lewalski and others have argued convincingly that the central drama of *Paradise Regained* arises from Christ's kenosis, the emptying of his divine understanding and power in the Incarnation.[19] Being fully human (as well as fully God), Christ undergoes a genuine test in the wilderness, involving a growing awareness of his own role and destiny. The question at issue for him, as Jon S. Lawry points out, is not "whether or not Jesus is the Son, for even Satan concedes that title, but of what it means that he is to 'save' himself and mankind";[20] indeed, "What does it mean to be the Word?"[21] I believe this drama is represented by Petrina in a visual commentary that is initially evoked by the provocative stance of Christ with his back to the viewer in *Paradise Regained* I. Nowhere else in her portraits of the Son or Christ in the illustrations to *Paradise Lost* and *Paradise Regained* is his face hidden; and so far as I can discover, such a stance is unique among visual representations of the baptism. Masolino's painting of the baptism (1435), for example, is typical in presenting Christ standing in the river fully facing the viewer, his hands raised in a natural manner. Similarly, the panel by Andrea del Verrocchio and Leonardo da Vinci (1470) places Christ, ankle deep in water, facing us with hands together and head bowed in a position of prayer. Joachim Patenier (c. 1480–1524) portrays Christ facing the viewer with his hands together in prayerful position in front of his chest, as does Piero della Francesca (c. 1416–1492).

Why then does Petrina thus represent Jesus as *faceless?* We, the viewers, know who this man is without seeing his face. Heaven knows who he is, the Father sending down his approval to his Son through the sequence of light, word, and dove that descends upon him. The surrounding angels too recognize him. But according to Milton, Satan can't identify him with certainty. And Milton suggests that Jesus himself at this time is not certain of who he is and what he is to do. Thus Petrina appropriately portrays Christ *faceless* at this moment, recognizing that a central subject of *Paradise Regained* is Jesus' (and Satan's) exploration and discovery of identity.

Petrina's placing of Jesus with his back to us has the additional effect of distancing us as observers from the event. We have the poorest view of anyone present. Displaced to a position inferior to that of the spectators, who see Jesus' face and are visually engaged with him and his baptism, we as viewers have a sense of eavesdropping; we are looking at a spectacular incident from the outside, unable to get the whole picture; we view the baptism as nonparticipants, we view it—and this is significant—as Satan views Christ's baptism and then reveals his uncertainty about Jesus' identity when he exhorts his midair council: "Who this is we must learn." (*PR* I, 93).

THE ILLUSTRATION FOR BOOK II:
THE BANQUET TEMPTATION

Point of view plays a crucial part in interpreting Petrina's illustration of the banquet in Book II (fig. 2) as well. In the most decorative of the four illustrations, Petrina represents the banquet as one would expect to find it on a richly woven tapestry, strikingly medieval in its characteristic vertical flatness. Some of the figures, however, are more classical than medieval in appearance, creating the air not only of a medieval Garden of Paradise but also of a "Garden of Adonis," appropriate to Milton's description:

> And at a stately sideboard by the wine
> That fragrant smell diffus'd, in order stood
> Tall stripling youths rich clad, of fairer hue
> Than *Ganymede* or *Hylas;* distant more
> Under the Trees now tripp'd, now solemn stood
> Nymphs of *Diana*'s train, and *Naiades*
> With fruits and flowers from *Amalthea*'s horn.   (*PR* II, 350–56)

These ideal figures—tossing petals, carrying cornucopias or jugs of wine, playing musical instruments—wind down toward the table in processionlike order and solemnity, creating a highly pleasing visual symmetry.

As we examine Petrina's banquet scene, we cannot help being struck by her deviation from Milton's description of the banquet table, considering her typically close reading of the text so evident in the other illustrations. According to Milton, the table was

> richly spread, in regal mode,
> With dishes pil'd, and meats of noblest sort
> And savor, Beasts of chase, or Fowl of game,
> In pastry built, or from the spit, or boil'd,
> Grisamber steam'd; all Fish from Sea or Shore,
> Freshet, or purling Brook, of shell or fin,
> And exquisitest name, for which was drain'd
> *Pontus* and *Lucrine* Bay, and *Afric* Coast.   (II, 340–47)

In spite of such lavish detail from Milton, Petrina presents us with merely a jug of wine and bowl of fruit. Petrina's choice at this point is especially curious since it appears to deflect the central significance of this first temptation. Jesus, in his physical deprivation, is being tempted with delectable food; indeed, Milton emphasizes the potency for evil of this lavish spread by comparing it ironically to the "crude Apple that diverted Eve," suggesting the greater severity of this test. In this sense, then, Petrina has radically diminished the power of the test by providing merely wine and a few apples. But point of view again provides illumination. The viewer stands with Jesus and Satan at the focal point of the production, the forward musicians playing directly to us, the young servants at the head of the procession clearly waiting on us. We recall that Petrina follows Milton in representing the baptism from the perspective of Satan. If Petrina is following Milton's narrative here also, then in this illustration we are seeing the banquet from the perspective of Christ, who "lifting up his eyes beheld / In ample space under the broadest shade / A Table richly spread." (II, 337–40).

If we view this scene as through Christ's eyes, it becomes clear that Petrina is representing a moment not only of Christ's victory over temptation, but of a step forward in his process of self-discovery. Petrina may be showing us what Christ himself sees in his "temperance invincible"; he sees not Satan's sumptuous dinner, which cloaks the sin of self-sufficiency, but a bowl full of fruit, a type of "the crude apple that diverted Eve." Christ, the second Adam, is not diverted by Satan's deception and sees food for what it is, through the eyes of the temperate. The lack of depth in

Petrina's tapestrylike picture reminds us of Jackson Cope's observation about Milton's portrayal of the temptations: "As there is no depth to the spatial dimension which is the symbolic framework of the temptations, so there is no depth to the sensual matter of the temptations or to the physical guises of tempter and tempted."[22] Christ "sees through" Satan's illusions and we see with him.

Furthermore, Petrina is once again compressing time, viewing "all things at one view" as through a telescope, as Marjorie Nicolson describes the effect of *Paradise Regained*.[23] Thus Christ, with new self-recognition, sees beyond the pleasures of this earthly banquet to the "Celestial food divine," which is—and will be—his as the victorious Son. For Christ, present in this temptation are all temptations, extending backward to Adam and the "forbidden fruit"—and to the protevangelium—and forward to the final apocalyptic banquet in the presence of the tree of life, which Petrina pictures in *Paradise Regained* IV (fig. 4).

This telescoping is brought into sharper focus when we view the wilderness banquet next to Petrina's depiction of Eden in her design for *Paradise Lost* IV (fig. 7). The similarity is striking. Both pictures present densely detailed, mosaiclike landscapes, teeming with lush, natural beauty and fecundity. And Eden, like Satan's "pleasant Grove," has about it not only the air of a densely textured medieval tapestry, but classical overtones of Ovidian myth. Martz suggests that Petrina's Eden in the illustration for *Paradise Lost* IV reflects Milton's "allusions to Ovidian myths in the pastoral scenes of *Paradise Lost* [which] combine to warn of the imminent change in paradise. . . . Ovid's persistent subversion of pastoral values serves as a warning that the threat of destructive power lurks everywhere in Milton's Eden."[24]

But the differences between Petrina's two gardens are nevertheless impressive. Absent at the wilderness banquet are the wild animals—the birds, monkeys, lion, and deer—that in Eden coexist peacefully with one another and with the solitary Adam and Eve. They are replaced in Satan's grove by domesticated animals—two tethered oxen serving as beasts of burden—and a throng of gaily attired young people. Contrasting with the primeval solitude of Eden, Satan's grove is a natural paradise that has been elaborately overlaid with artifice, with the highly stylized ornaments of civilization that make the landscape itself seem more tame and ordered than the flowery undergrowth of Eden "which not nice Art / . . . but Nature boon / Pour'd forth profuse" (*PL* IV, 241–43). The elaborately embroidered gowns, the musical instruments, the ornate urns, the highly stylized pageantry of the human figures and the oxen in ritualistic processional: all create a picture of sophisticated opulence.

The point that Petrina makes in these contrasts is a theological one that dovetails with the idea that Jesus sees Satan's banquet as merely a bowl of the old apples of temptation. For this is Satan's garden, a false paradise where, as in the Bower of Bliss, all is not as it seems, and it is for Christ to see through its deceptions. Thus just as Milton wishes us to connect Christ's wilderness temptation with Adam's, Petrina likewise establishes visually the theological interconnectedness of the two locales. They are, typologically, the selfsame place, altered by the Fall, but existing simultaneously in redemptive history, as Christ becomes Adam and reenacts the Edenic test. And the consequence of Christ's discernment and temperance is, as Milton says in the Nativity ode, that "Time will run back, and fetch the age of gold . . . And Hell itself will pass away" (135, 139).

Petrina places these gardens in a still larger context, again compressing time and connecting visually and theologically the pleasant grove and Eden with the "flow'ry valley" at the top of *Paradise Regained* IV (fig. 4), where Christ ascends after the temptation on the temple pinnacle. The "flow'ry valley" contains in Petrina's depiction elements of both Eden and the pleasant grove. Angels replace the youths of figure 2, but the large tree at their left closely resembles one similarly located in the "celestial valley" in figure 4. Petrina also draws from the wilderness banquet the festive atmosphere of music and celebration. From Eden she borrows and transmogrifies her water lilies, which now appear— slightly altered but highly reminiscent—as the flowers on the trees. Thus in Petrina's vision these three gardens, separated by the gulfs of temporal history, exist in eternity as the same place, the locus of Christ's redemptive act, reminding us also, perhaps, of the fourth garden, at Gethsemane.

The Illustration for Book III:
The Temptation to Power

We turn now to the design for *Paradise Regained* III, Christ's temptation to power (fig. 3), especially to world power and glory, to the political kingdom that his disciples and crowds of followers will mistakenly urge upon him. It is represented by Petrina in an energetic and highly detailed scene. The focal point is an elaborate, zigguratlike structure representing David's royal throne. The pavilion at the top contains the accoutrements of kingship—the throne, crown and scepter, ermine—but the throne is empty, waiting for Christ to step up to what Satan offers as his rightful place of conquest and power and restoration of Israel:

> Choose which thou wilt, by conquest or by league.
> By him thou shalt regain, without him not,
> That which alone can truly reinstall thee
> In *David*'s royal seat, his true Successor.   (*PR* III, 370–73)

Christ stands beside Satan in the upper left, on "a Mountain high" (252), overlooking David's throne:

> He look't and saw what numbers numberless
> The City gates outpour'd, light armed Troops
> In coats of Mail and military pride;
> In Mail thir horses clad, yet fleet and strong,
> Prancing their riders bore, the flower and choice
> Of many Provinces from bound to bound.   (310–15)

Petrina deviates here from typical renditions in paintings of the confrontation between Christ and Satan, which usually foreground Satan and make him the dramatic center of the design.[25] But Petrina keeps Satan in the background, a tiny figure in the corner who is rather more difficult to make out than the figure of Christ, who is tiny also but much more distinct.

Petrina takes this approach in the other three illustrations as well, where Satan—a central figure in *Paradise Regained*—is either merely an unseen presence, as in Books I and II, or the ignominious batlike creature falling at the bottom of Book IV, his size in striking contrast to that of the falling Satan in Duccio's famous painting *Temptation of Christ* (1308–1311), or Blake's illustration for *Paradise Regained* (1816–1818), in which the falling demon retains heroic dimensions.[26] Similarly, Petrina chooses not to accentuate or romanticize Satan in her illustrations to *Paradise Lost*. In her depiction of Satan's confrontation with Sin and Death in Book II, for example, she relegates Satan to the bottom of the design under the feet of Sin, showing only his tiny, startled face, barely visible. The effect of diminishing Satan is to augment Christ and to highlight him as the central presence in both sets of designs, especially the *Paradise Regained* illustrations.

Petrina's technique is not without precedent, however. Her depiction of the throne and battle is reminiscent of the city of Jerusalem in plate XVII of *The Nuremburg Chronicle* (1493). At the center in the *Chronicle* engraving is a domed temple with circular steps, much like the central throne in Petrina's design. In addition, the *Chronicle*'s plate LXIII of the destruction of Jerusalem contains a domed temple that is being consumed by flames, and at the upper left corner is a cone-shaped hill with two small figures surveying the city. One of the two figures has a satanic appearance: he has horns, and his left arm is outstretched, as in *Paradise Regained* III.

Petrina fills the lower third of the illustration with the "fleet and strong" horses and "armed Troops in coats of Mail and military pride" in hot pursuit of retreating invaders. So carefully she reads Milton's narrative that she includes the arrows Milton describes in a memorable onomatopoeic phrase:

> He saw them in thir forms of battle rang'd,
> How quick they wheel'd, and flying behind them *shot*
> *Sharp sleet of arrowy showers* against the face
> Of their pursuers, and overcame by flight;
>
> (III 322–25, italics mine)

Petrina's spirited warriors remind us of Paolo Uccello's *Battle of San Romano* (1445) in the Uffizi Gallery, with its upraised spears and pikes, carrousel-like horses rearing, all in a vigorous circular motion. A fallen horse lies at the forefront in Uccello's as in Petrina's picture. Like Uccello's, Petrina's seems a stylized representation rather than a real battle. It is a romanticized vision.

It is also a medieval vision. Roland Mushat Frye points out that "From the Middle Ages on, the visual arts had accustomed people to imagining the kingdoms offered to Christ as figuratively represented by fortified cities."[27] It is true that most of the components of the scene are appropriately biblical in appearance. The throne has an oriental flavor, as one might expect of the ancient throne of David and Solomon, and the battling soldiers have a first century Roman appearance. The pillars are classical. But Petrina has subtly medievalized this first-century scene by using the spatial treatment distinctive of Gothic paintings, the mixing of scales and proportions within the same view that is so distinctly medieval. The design of the throne, for example, is that of a major structure, but the horsemen below are disproportionately large in comparison. Similarly, the hill on which Christ and Satan stand gazing appears distant, relating visually to the even more distant cathedrals in the background. But the figures on the hill are much too large, proportionately, for the size of the hill or for their distance from the observer. The city gate below them appears more distant than they, even though it is in front.

The design is complicated further by the presence of a third artistic motif. One hardly need remember that these illustrations were produced in the 1930's to recognize the art deco quality of the throne—the round stairs, curving lines, and decorative quality reminiscent of some of the art, furnishings, and architecture of the period. Describing some of the features of art deco, William Fleming mentions the spired Chrysler Building built in New York in 1930, as well as the many theaters designed as "imaginary recreations of King Solomon's temple, Babylonian towers, Moslem mosques with Minarets, and Mayan jungle pyramids."[28]

Petrina's approach is remarkably expressive visually, and her mixing of classical, medieval, and modern elements in the same scene serves an interpretive, as well as an artistic, purpose. The hermeneutic element will be especially evident in the *Paradise Regained* IV illustration, where she places Christ's test on the pinnacle in Byzantine Christendom. But here too she is making a theological point. For Petrina, Christ's victory over the temptation to personal power and glory is a triumph of the church and part of the total act of Redemption, stretching, as it were, from first-century Palestine to twentieth-century New York. It is an act that transcends time, indeed, subsumes all of temporal history, blurring distinctions between historical periods.

This second test that Christ must endure is the temptation to power, the temptation to act on his own to bring about God's kingdom—and his victory over it is revealed both in his rejection of Satan's offer and in his subsequent trust in Providence on the temple pinnacle. Petrina's illustration captures the traditional excitement, glory, and artificiality of chivalric heroism, the dazzle of battle and kingly power, but it is a glamorized representation of heroism that Christ rejects and redefines in the redemptive heroism of sacrificial servanthood:

> Much ostentation vain of fleshly arm
> And fragile arms, much instrument of war
> Long in preparing, soon to nothing brought,
> Before mine eyes thou hast set.
>   . . . .
>   to mee worth naught.
>   (III, 387–90, 393)

In thus rejecting Satan's offer, Christ is further discovering his own values and destiny: "My time I told thee (and that time for thee / were better farthest off) is not yet come," (396–97).

Petrina again uses point of view to represent Christ's growing, prophetic self-knowledge. We see the no-longer-faceless Christ from afar, standing with Satan on the hill overlooking the city and throne. We are not seeing things from Christ's angle, however, as we were in *Paradise Regained* II, but are in fact seeing Satan's vision as Christ interprets it, the central clue being another incongruity in Petrina's design. David's throne is being consumed by flames. Milton's description of the city and battle makes no reference to its destruction in fire or flames, nor does Satan's discussion of David's throne. One might explain Petrina's flames as indebted to visual traditions rather than to Milton. But it may be that she is attending to Christ's response to Satan's temptation where he challenges Satan's hypocritical display of zeal for Israel:

> But whence to thee this zeal? Where was it then
> For *Israel*, or for *David*, or this Throne,
> When thou stood'st up his Tempter to the pride
> Of numb'ring *Israel*, which cost the lives
> Of threescore and ten thousand *Israelites*
> By three days' Pestilence? Such was thy zeal
> To *Israel* then, the same that now to me.   (III, 407–13)

Zeal is often "fiery," a word well-metaphorized by fire or flames, a crucial prophetic term in this context. Christ, in rejecting Satan's false zeal is indirectly affirming God's—and his own—true zeal that will bring about redemption and ultimate restoration of David's kingdom:

> My time I told thee (and that time for thee
> Were better farthest off) is not yet come;
> When that comes think not thou to find me slack
> On my part aught endeavoring.   (396–99)

This ominous warning may evoke the memory, in Christ's and possibly Satan's mind at this point, of the Son's fiery zeal in heaven when he "forth rush'd with whirl-wind sound / The Chariot of Paternal Deity" against the rebellious angels, and

> Drove them before him Thunder-struck, pursu'd
> With terrors and with furies to the bounds
> And Crystal wall of Heav'n, which op'ning wide,
> Roll'd inward, and a spacious Gap disclos'd
> Into the wasteful Deep; the monstrous sight
> Struck them with horror backward, but far worse
> Urg'd them behind; headlong themselves they threw
> Down from the verge of Heav'n, Eternal wrath
> Burn'd after them to the bottomless pit.   (*PL* VI, 858–66)

Moreover, early in Christ's ministry, according to St. John, not long after the wilderness temptation, Christ finds the temple being exploited by the moneychangers, and, making a "scourge of small cords," he drives them out of the temple in righteous fury. John says that his disciples, viewing that incident, "remembered that it was written, The zeal of thine house hath eaten me up," quoting Psalm lxix 9 (John ii, 17). Christ then prophesies about his own sacrificial death and resurrection: "Destroy this temple, and in three days I will raise it up" (John ii, 19).

Petrina's representation of David's throne engulfed in flames may enact God's zeal which will destroy the old earthly kingdom as it brings about the true, spiritual kingdom prophesied by Isaiah: "Of the increase of his government and peace there shall be no end, upon the throne of David, and upon his kingdom, to order it, and to establish it with judgment and with justice from henceforth even for ever. The zeal of the Lord of hosts will perform this" (Isaiah ix, 7). Petrina's image of David's throne being burned up, with battle raging around, invites comparison with her illustration of the Son driving his foes into destruction in *Paradise Lost* VI (fig. 8), and the flames surrounding the sword in *Paradise Lost* XII (fig. 9). Flames surround his chariot as they do the temple, and the energy of battle similarly charges both pictures. The "zeal of the Lord of hosts" that blasted the rebels from heaven and banished Adam and Eve from Paradise is the zeal that will soon destroy Satan and bring about the reestablishment of God's kingdom.

But in trying to tempt Christ by offering him an earthly, military kingdom, Satan misunderstands God's purpose of establishing a spiritual kingdom. David's throne is to be something other than Satan sees it. Georgia Christopher points out that "Milton reforms, or recasts, the aggressive warrior-Christ of his first epic into a character more like Abdiel, one who withstands and triumphs over interrogation, verbal attack, and misrepresentation of scriptural truth."[29] Thus it may be that Christ's increasingly clear eyes foresee that the throne that Satan is offering is burning up, is being destroyed to be rebuilt by the action that Christ will perform through his sacrificial death. Or perhaps what Petrina had in mind was simply a prophetic vision of the coming destruction of Jerusalem in A.D. 70, as seen in *The Nuremburg Chronicle* or other visual analogs.

THE ILLUSTRATION FOR BOOK IV:
THE PINNACLE AND CHRIST'S VICTORY

Here Petrina pictures the triumphal moment after Jesus has responded to Satan's challenge of the pinnacle: "There stand, if thou wilt stand . . . If not to stand, / Cast thyself down" (IV, 551, 554–55):

> To whom thus Jesus. Also it is written,
> Tempt not the Lord thy God; he said and stood.
> But Satan smitten with amazement fell.   (IV, 560–62)

Elucidating "Cast thyself down," John Carey mentions that in Luke iv, 9–11, "Satan intends Christ to choose; the temptation is to presumption":

In Milton it is clear that Satan thinks Christ has no choice: he expects him to fall, and is amazed when he stands (562, 571). 'Cast thyself down' is therefore sarcastic: Christ's fall as Satan sees it, will settle the problem of his identity: if he is not merely perfect man, but something more, angels will save him: if he is merely perfect man, he will die.[30]

Petrina's illustration is thus a visual representation of *Paradise Regained* IV, 560–95, and, typically, Petrina has done a close reading of the text. Present are such textual details as Christ "upbore" from the temple pinnacle "As on a floating couch through the blithe Air" (584–85), borne aloft by "Angels on full sail of wing" (583), carrying him to what we perceive in the background to be "a flow'ry valley" where the angels will "set him down / On a green bank, and set before him spread, / A table of Celestial Food, Divine, / Ambrosial, Fruits fetcht from the tree of life" (586–89). And at the lower left corner Petrina portrays Satan:

> So struck with dread and anguish fell the Fiend,
> And to his crew, that sat consulting, brought
> Joyless triumphals of his hop't success,
> Ruin, and desperation, and dismay,
> Who durst so proudly tempt the Son of God.
> So Satan fell.   (576–81)

He is a batlike figure here. This illustration has images in common with Andrea da Firenze's fresco cycle (c. 1366–1368), *Triumph of the Church* located in the Spanish Chapel of Santa Maria Novella in Florence, one of three great churches in Florence most likely to be seen by visitors to Florence. In Andrea's cycle, Christ is seated at the top of the scene, surrounded by saints and angels, in a posture and wearing loose raiment reminiscent of Petrina's illustration of Christ on the floating couch. Below and to the left of Christ's right foot is a birdlike demon figure who is sitting disconsolately—rather than falling as in Petrina's design. And below Christ and to his right is a cluster of domes. The middle section of the fresco portrays life in the world outside the church, and the rural landscape is filled with people engaged in lighthearted frivolity, dancing and playing instruments—a scene that brings to mind Petrina's depiction of the wilderness banquet (Fig. 2). Present are monks administering sacraments and directing people to the gates of heaven above the cathedral domes. The fresco proclaims the plenitude and inclusiveness of Christ's kingdom. And Petrina's four illustrations likewise present a cross section of life that includes the secular and spiritual, with Christ present everywhere. As in the painting by Andrea da Firenze, the triumph of Petrina's

Christ in figure 4—indeed, in each of the illustrations—is also a "triumph of the Church."

Although lines 576–81 of *Paradise Regained* help to provide the narrative detail for Petrina's fourth illustration, I believe it is the passage that follows—IV, 596–611— that provides the theology and interpretive entrance:

> True Image of the Father, whether thron'd
> In the bosom of bliss, and light of light
> Conceiving, or remote from Heaven, enshrin'd
> In fleshly Tabernacle, and human form,
> Wand'ring the Wilderness, whatever place,
> Habit, or state, or motion, still expressing
> The Son of God, with Godlike force endu'd
> Against th Attempter of thy Father's Throne,
> And Thief of Paradise; him long of old
> Thou didst debel, and down from Heav'n cast
> With all his Army; now thou hast aveng'd
> Supplanted *Adam*, and by vanquishing
> Temptation, hast regain'd lost Paradise,
> And frustrated the conquest fraudulent:
> He never more henceforth will dare set foot
> in Paradise to tempt; his snares are broke.

The focal point of the illustration is, of course, the figure of Christ in the upper left, now a glorified figure whose face has much in common with the heavenly glory of the Father in *Paradise Lost* III. In Petrina's image he is indeed both: "True Image of the Father . . . enshrin'd / In fleshly Tabernacle, and human form" (*PR* IV, 596–99). Raised aloft from the temple pinnacle, he is midway between heaven and earth, fully God and fully man in his Incarnation.

Petrina's presentation of the pinnacle experience contains, typologically, not only Christ's victory over temptation, but also the passion and resurrection: "Now thou hast aveng'd / Supplanted Adam, and by vanquishing / Temptation, hast regain'd lost Paradise" (IV, 606–608). The swift upward motion achieved with the graceful art deco curves of the angels and the raised (almost flying) arms of Christ, suggests ascension in multiple meanings. Christ is raised off the pinnacle, suggesting, typologically, his resurrection from the tomb and, in addition, his assumption into heaven. The contrast of light and dark enhance this effect. The angelic entourage is divided into the lower angels in darkness below the upper angels in dazzling light suggesting earth and sky, a resurrection image. Christ's raised hands may suggest the posture of crucifixion, as well as swift upward motion. And the heavenly garden in the background, with its tree of life, hints of the Apocalypse, the new Eden described by St. John in his vision:

And he shewed me a pure river of water of life, clear as crystal, proceeding out of the throne of God and of the Lamb. In the midst of the street of it, and on either side of the river, was there the tree of life, which bare twelve manner of fruits, and yielded her fruit every month: and the leaves of the tree were for the healing of the nations. (Rev. xxii, 1–2)

This illustration for *Paradise Regained* IV, in company with *Paradise Lost* III and *Paradise Regained* I, completes a triptych in which Petrina presents the whole gospel, the *evangel* of Christ. This is made plainer by her representation of the structures that Milton refers to in his description of Jerusalem and its temple:

> fair *Jerusalem*,
> The holy City, lifted high her Towers,
> And higher yet the glorious Temple rear'd
> Her pile, far off appearing like a Mount
> Of Alabaster, top't with golden Spires. (IV, 544–48)

The scene of the baptism in Petrina's illustration for Book I has the traditional flavor of first-century Palestine. In contrast, Petrina's structures in the illustration for Book IV have the distinct flavor not of old Jerusalem but of late medieval Christendom, appearing as fourteenth-century Byzantine cathedrals.

The anachronistic quality of these structures is heightened by the presence of crosses on nearly every pinnacle. A version of the Greek cross—the "Cross Trefflee" or "Cross Clechee"—stands atop the central temple pinnacle. The domes to its lower left hold variations on the Greek cross, the cross and X monogram (i.e., the Greek cross superimposed on the Chi, the first letter of the Greek word for Christ). The spire at far left appears to contain the traditional Latin cross. Petrina is perhaps representing the temple rescue in its broader implications, these various crosses prefiguring both the passion and the *evangel*—the extension of Christ's kingdom beyond the Jews to the Gentile nations. The juxtaposing of Christ's wilderness victory, with its suggestions of passion and resurrection, with emblems of medieval Christianity reinforces the conception begun in *Paradise Lost* III of the Incarnation and Redemption of humankind represented visually as an act narrated temporally, but with each temporal moment containing suggestions of the entire action—simultaneously looking forward and backward in redemptive history.

Lloyd F. Dickson has called attention to the variation Petrina introduces in the decorative scroll that carries the number of each book of
Paradise Lost, adapting each scroll to the subject matter of the portrayal.[31]
In the illustrations for *Paradise Regained,* Petrina makes similar adaptations: we see the stark simplicity of the scroll that marks the baptism, the
baroque ornateness—bordering on decadence—of the banquet temptation scroll, the arrow-pierced ribbon beneath a fallen warrior in the illustration of the temptation to power, and most impressive of all, an unfurl-
ing documentary scroll in Book IV that might well record all of redemptive history.

The image of Satan beneath the scroll in Book IV returns us to the
Paradise Lost illustrations. Referring to "the Thief of Paradise,"

> him long of old
> Thou didst debel, and down from Heav'n cast
> With all his Army; now thou hast aveng'd
> Supplanted Adam, and by vanquishing
> Temptation, hast regain'd lost Paradise,
> And frustrated the conquest fraudulent:
> He never more henceforth will dare set foot
> In Paradise to tempt; his snares are broke.   (IV, 604–611).

These lines, in which Milton is summarizing redemptive history, are represented by Petrina in *Paradise Lost* I (Satan's vanquishing "long of old") and
Paradise Regained IV ("vanquishing Temptation"). Leonard Mustazza has
observed that "Satan is knocked down, literally and figuratively, in the
poem, but we must also notice that the Satan of *Paradise Regained* also
looks backward in a variety of subtle and apparent ways to the Satan of
Paradise Lost."[32] Indeed, placed side by side, Petrina's *Paradise Lost* I (fig.
5) and the lower left section of *Paradise Regained* IV (fig. 4) seem almost
part of the same sequence. In *Paradise Lost* I, Satan is falling ignominiously
downward, out of control, toward the flames of hell and the strewn bodies of
his fallen cohorts. *Paradise Regained* IV appears visually—as it is in fact
theologically—as a continuation of that moment. Satan, whose angel wings
of *Paradise Lost* I have now transformed to bat or dragon wings of *Paradise
Regained* IV, seems almost to be completing an inverted somersault on his
way to the abyss. The flames in *Paradise Regained* IV are reaching up to
receive him, hinting of his final damnation when he will be chained in the
lake of fire, "never more henceforth will dare set foot in Paradise to tempt":
again an apocalyptic glimpse into redemptive history, signifying events far
ahead in time from the temple pinnacle incident.

Jon S. Lawry has noted the presence of such upward and downward motions in *Paradise Regained:* "An unobtrusive vertical pattern insists that in each unwilled physical ascent in the poem (from Jordan to the plateau, to the mount, to the Temple) the Son regains or reaffirms his exaltation to the saving 'blissful seat' of reunion with God, and that by contrast each willful ascent by Satan leads him to his own renewed fall."[33] So too, Petrina's theological progression sees Christ moving upward from the death of baptism to self-knowledge and heavenly glory, with Satan continuing his fall to damnation. Petrina thus presents the Son as "author and finisher of our faith" in the Incarnation, much as Milton conceives it in the Nativity ode.

As Christ is borne upward from the pinnacle here in Petrina's final illustration, there appear in the background the flowers and trees of his heavenly destination. Milton describes the celestial feast yet to come— the restorative food that Christ is offered by the angels after he has been brought on his floating couch to a "flow'ry valley":

> A table of Celestial Food, Divine,
> Ambrosial, Fruits fetcht from the tree of life,
> And from the fount of life Ambrosial drink,
> That soon refresh'd him wearied, and repair'd
> What hunger, if aught hunger had impair'd,
> Or thirst. (*PR* IV, 588–92)

As I noted earlier, the celestial valley of *Paradise Regained* IV is connected visually and theologically to the "pleasant Grove" of Satan's banquet in Book II and the Eden of *Paradise Lost* IV.

Petrina's representation of Christ's progressive illumination is completed and epitomized in her illustration for *Paradise Regained* IV. In this closing illustration, Christ's face appears serene and bathed in light, suggesting his awareness and acceptance of his destiny. He is glorified, and he regains somewhat the appearance of his heavenly state as the Son, just as Christ is later transfigured on the mountain: "And his raiment became shining, exceeding white as snow; so as no fuller on earth can white them" (Mark IX, 3). Satan's recognition of Christ as the Son, in contrast, sends him tumbling down into flames.

This final image of Christ in a blaze of glory with a battered Satan falling below him—at once creature and Creator, "far-beaming blaze of Majesty" and "darksome House of mortal Clay"—is the image that best stands for Carlotta Petrina's conception of Milton's vision. When we place side by side her illustrations for the two epics we discover that the Christocentric vision of the *Paradise Lost* illustrations is not merely carried over to *Paradise Regained*, but that Christ is the integrating motif that binds them together visually and thematically and engages them with Scripture. In her final image, Petrina pictures Christ as at once the suffering servant of *Paradise Regained* I and the *Christus Victor* of *Paradise Lost* VI, a conception that Walter MacKellar articulates succinctly in his discussion of *Paradise Regained:* "From the experience of trial Christ gains a fuller and fuller revelation of his own nature and mission, which becomes complete on the pinnacle of the temple, where at last by merit he proves himself to be the heroic Son of God."[34]

This focus on the ascendancy of Christ grows out of Petrina's manner of reading the two epics, a way of reading analogous to Milton's own approach to the Old and New Testaments. As Mary Ann Radzinowicz observes:

[*Paradise Regained*] is a particularly good place to see what reading the Bible meant to Milton, since it engages with Jesus at the moment when by his own reading of Scripture he understands his messiahship and holds to it throughout Satan's temptations. At that moment, the New Testament interpets the Old, changing, for Milton, the way the Hebrew Bible should thereafter be understood . . . He read its two Testaments thematically as forming one body of saving truth, consistent but gradually becoming clearer to the understanding.[35]

Similarly, the intricate visual interconnectedness that we have observed in Petrina's designs communicates her view of the interrelatedness of the two epics and the essential unity of their message of Redemption. The progressive but singular unfolding of "saving truth" is certainly what Petrina presents in her sixteen illustrations. She reads the Bible and Milton's epics for their narrative themes, and she finds that all the narratives converge on the image of Christ as Redeemer-King.

This astutely perceptive thematic focus is the source of the unique utterance Petrina gives to Milton's vision. The special value of her art is its facility for compressing dynamic historical narratives to convey their static, underlying, redemptive significance. Her images offer a sense of simultaneity and immediacy to the vision that Milton, in his verbal art, builds up incrementally in elaborately arranged narratives. Her images possess that quality of Scripture that Radzinowicz describes as "an abstract serenity conveying the moral equipoise of purposes long maturing" (pp. 221–22). Wendy Furman perceives this quality in the illustrations of Blake and Mary Groom as well as Petrina. She suggests that "Like Revelation itself, and like Michael's message to Adam and Eve, they portray all of history in their designs, revealing the *synchronisme* in which *chronos* and *kairos* meet."[36]

In addition, Petrina's visual images bear the marks of her own age:

"Anything an artist does is of its own era as well," she remarked. The intensely personal nature of her vision is evident in the art deco and surrealistic aspects of the designs, and, more importantly, in the ominous suggestions of war and destruction that appear with startling fierceness in some of the illustrations. We are reminded that during part of the time she was drawing these illustrations, Petrina resided in Italy, Mussolini was ascending in power, and the world was on the brink of war. But for Petrina, warfare is not only a worldwide event but a personal spiritual reality. Furman notes that Petrina, "however assailed by modern doubt, takes a stance as prophetic as Blake's: apocalypse her glass, she looks through it, albeit darkly, to a final, eschatological redemption."[37] Thus the fearful image of the warfaring Christ in *Paradise Lost* VI is transformed and redeemed in the glorified face of Christ in *Paradise Regained* IV, the victor of spiritual battle, who exemplifies true Christian heroism:

> to obey is best,
> And love with fear the only God, to walk
> As in his presence, ever to observe
> His providence, and on him sole depend,
> Merciful over all his works, with good
> Still overcoming evil, and by small
> Accomplishing great things, by things deem'd weak
> Subverting worldly strong, and worldly wise
> By simply meek; that suffering for Truth's sake
> Is fortitude to highest victory.   (*PL* XII, 561–70)[38]

Carlotta Petrina's illustrations offer both an important rearticulation of Milton's vision—"making strange" his theological arguments—and an intense personalization of that vision by a talented artist who is skilled, sensitive, informed, and sympathetic. Contributing to her vision are her life-long thematic reading of the Bible and Milton, her appreciation for medieval and Renaissance art, and her abiding interest in her subject.

The vogue for elegantly printed and illustrated literary classics died out after World War II. In the following decades, Carlotta Petrina's work includes lithographs, drawings, pastels and, most of all, oil paintings, mainly on canvas but also in recent years on plywood and plexiglass. Her subject matter varies: In her early years there were Italian landscapes, Provençal peasants, Venetian peasants, Portico di S. Apostoli in Venice, spring in Venice, architectural drawings and paintings, scenes from Brittany, scenes from Capri—"many from memory and much from fantasy." In subsequent decades, her oil paintings have moved from the semisurrealistic to the allegorical. Most of them include the figures of human or mythic beings. Her interest in the narrative of our first parents continues in the late eighties and early nineties of the twentieth century, which are also the eighties and nineties of her own life span. Her recent work includes many sketches of Christ and five large oil paintings of Adam and Eve.

University of Texas, El Paso

NOTES

All illustrations are by Carlotta Petrina and are reprinted with permission of the Limited Editions Club. Photographs of the illustrations were provided by the Williams Andrews Clark Memorial Library.

1. I am indebted to Wendy Furman, Eunice Howe, and Virginia Tufte for generously sharing information from interviews with Carlotta Petrina to be included in articles and a biography they are writing. I appreciate also information provided by Margaret Noble Mikula. The publication of Petrina's Milton illustrations antedated by a year the publication of those by Mary Groom (1902–1958). Groom, an English wood engraver, apparently the only other woman to illustrate Milton, illustrated only *Paradise Lost*, making twenty-nine engravings, five of which she showed in an exhibition in London in 1935. Her work appears in the edition published by the Golden Cockerel Press in 1937. Furman, Howe, and Tufte have articles in press about Groom's illustrations and are also writing a Groom biography.

2. In 1992 Petrina saw for the first time the following published comments about her illustrations: Louis Martz, *Poet of Exile: A Study of Milton's Poetry* (New Haven, 1980), pp. 229–31. Wendy Furman, "With Dreadful Faces Throng'd and Fiery Arms: Apocalyptic 'Synchronisme' in Three Illustrations of *Paradise Lost*," *Coranto* XXV (1990), 20–33. Michael Lieb, " 'The Chariot of Paternal Deitie': Some Visual Renderings," in *Milton's Legacy in the Arts*, ed. Albert C. Labriola and Edward Sichi, Jr. (University Park, Pa., 1988), pp. 21–58. Lloyd F. Dickson, "Against the Wiles of the Devil: Carlotta Petrina's Christocentric Illustrations of *Paradise Lost*, " in *Milton Studies* XXV, ed. James D. Simmonds (Pittsburgh, 1989), pp. 161–90.

3. Dickson, "Against the Wiles of the Devil," p. 161.

4. The illustrations from both epics reproduced here are photographs made by the William Andrews Clark Memorial Library, University of California, Los Angeles, from the copy in their collection.

5. Among galleries where Petrina's work has been exhibited are these: In France, the Salon des Artistes Français, Salon Nationale des Beaux Arts, and Salon d'Autumne; in Rome, La Finestra; in the United States, at the Architecture League, Pennsylvania Academy, Print Club of Philadelphia, Cleveland Museum, and the Chicago Art Institute. Her work is in the permanent collections of the New York Public Library, the Brooklyn Museum, and others, as well as in private collections.

6. Martz, *Poet of Exile*, p. 231.

7. Dickson, "Against the Wiles of the Devil," p. 161.

8. Lieb, " 'The Chariot of Paternal Deitie,' " p. 50.

9. Ibid., pp. 50–51.

10. Ibid, p. 52.

11. Furman, "Apocalyptic 'Synchronisme' in Three Illustrations of *Paradise Lost*," p. 29.

12. Ibid., p. 29.

13. Unpublished telephone interview with Virginia Tufte, 8 April 1992.

14. Ashraf H. A. Rushdy, "Of *Paradise Regained:* The Interpretation of Career," in *Milton Studies* XXIV, ed. James D. Simmonds (Pittsburgh, 1989), p. 255.

15. James M. Pearce, "The Theology of Representation: The Meta-Argument of *Paradise Regained*," in *Milton Studies* XXIV, ed. James D. Simmonds (Pittsburgh, 1989), pp. 287–88.

16. Lieb, " 'The Chariot of Paternal Deitie,' " p. 50.

17. *John Milton: Complete Poems and Major Prose*, ed. Merritt Y. Hughes (New York, 1957). All quotations from Milton's poetry are from this edition.

18. Ibid., note, p. 494.

19. Barbara Lewalski, *Milton's Brief Epic: The Genre, Meaning, and Art of Paradise Regained* (Providence, 1966).

20. Jon S. Lawry, *The Shadow of Heaven: Matter and Stance in Milton's Poetry* (Ithaca, 1968), p. 302.

21. Ibid., p. 303.

22. Jackson Cope, *The Metaphoric Structure of "Paradise Lost"* (Baltimore, 1962), p. 64.

23. Marjorie Nicolson, "Milton and the Telescope," *ELH* II (1935), 81.

24. Martz, *Poet of Exile*, p. 220.

25. For a sampling of biblical depictions of Christ and Satan, see Roland Mushat Frye, *Milton's Imagery and the Visual Arts: Iconographic Tradition in the Epic Poems* (Princeton, 1978), plates 231–36.

26. The Duccio panel is in the Frick Collection, New York. Blake's twelve illustrations for *Paradise Regained* (1816–1825) are in the Fitzwilliam Museum at Cambridge, England.

27. Frye, *Milton's Imagery and the Visual Arts*, p. 323.

28. William Fleming, *Arts and Ideas*, 7th ed. (New York, 1986), p. 448.

29. Georgia Christopher, *Milton and the Science of the Saints* (Princeton, 1982), p. 205.

30. John Carey, ed., *Paradise Regained* in *The Poems of John Milton* (London, 1968), p. 1162.

31. Dickson, "Against the Wiles of the Devil," p. 164.

32. Leonard Mustazza, *"Such Prompt Eloquence": Language as Agency and Character in Milton's Epics* (Lewisburg, 1988), p. 152.

33. Lawry, *The Shadow of Heaven* pp. 302–03.

34. Walter MacKellar, *A Variorum Commentary on the Poems of John Milton* (New York, 1975), vol. iv, p. 22.

35. Mary Ann Radzinowicz, "How Milton Read the Bible: The Case of *Paradise Regained*," in *The Cambridge Companion to Milton*, ed. Dennis Danielson (Cambridge, 1989), p. 207.

36. Furman, "Apocalyptic 'Synchronisme' in Three Illustrations of *Paradise Lost*," 25.

37 Ibid., p. 29.

38. MacKellar suggests that *Paradise Regained* amplifies these lines from *Paradise Lost:* "These principles are the two themes announced in the opening lines of *Paradise Regained;* and as the poem advances we see Christ perfectly translating them into action" (*Variorium*, vol. iv, p. 22).